A CRITICAL FRIENDSHIP

A CRITICAL FRIENDSHIP

DONALD JUSTICE AND RICHARD STERN, 1946–1961

EDITED BY *Elizabeth Murphy* | University of Nebraska Press

FOREWORD BY *William Logan* | LINCOLN AND LONDON

© 2013 by the Board of Regents of the
University of Nebraska. All rights reserved.
Manufactured in the United States of America

Library of Congress
Cataloging-in-Publication Data
A critical friendship: Donald Justice and
Richard Stern, 1946-1961 / edited by Elizabeth
Murphy; foreword by William Logan.
pages cm   Summary: "A selection of letters
from the first fifteen years of a sixty-year
friendship between American poet Donald
Justice and American novelist Richard
Stern"—Provided by publisher. Includes
bibliographical references and index.
ISBN 978-0-8032-4504-4 (hardback: alk. paper)
1. Justice, Donald, 1925-2004—
Correspondence. 2. Poets, American—20th
century—Correspondence. 3. Stern, Richard,
1928-2013—Correspondence. 4. Novelists,
American—20th century—Correspondence.
I. Murphy, Elizabeth, 1983- II. Justice,
Donald, 1925-2004. Correspondence.
Selections. III. Stern, Richard, 1928-2013.
Correspondence. Selections.
PS3519.U825Z48 2013
811'.52—dc23   2013024668

Set in Lyon by Laura Wellington.
Designed by Nathan Putens.

This book is for Gary, my friend in letters and in life.

CONTENTS

FOREWORD | *A Literary Friendship*

William Logan

Literary friendships are based on a terrible longing, the longing to be understood. Every close friendship is a love affair—or, between writers, really four love affairs: between the writers themselves, between each writer and the work of the other, and at last between the two bodies of work. Such bonds may be formed through communion of interest, mutual admiration, desire for flattery, hope of reward, or the need for an acutely critical eye—just the odd combination of vices and virtues any friendship requires for what psychologists call "fit." Devotion may also prove a powerful goad to ambition, if the writer doesn't feel worthy of the friendship. Such a desire was perhaps in part responsible for the depth and reach of *Moby-Dick*, which Melville dedicated to Hawthorne.

If writers want an audience in general, they want readers in specific; and for most writers a single sympathetic and passionate reader will do—if he's a fellow writer. Such closeness of spirit gives the writer someone to write to, as well as for. It might be argued that writers write for themselves, but those who have enjoyed intense friendship know that to have a perfect audience of one—the one who does not live in the mirror—is very different. There ought also to be some *mésalliance* between friends, some telling disparity in age or social class, wealth or reputation, some longing on both sides toward an opposite. George Sand and Gustave Flaubert found in their incompatible politics and the gap in their ages precisely what became the strengths of friendship. (I'm aware of only three sets of identical twins with literary careers. It would be instructive to know if they possess the bond described here. I would hazard that they do not, and perhaps cannot.)

Coleridge and Wordsworth, Byron and Shelley, Emerson and Thoreau, Twain and Howells, Wharton and James, Eliot and Pound, Sartre and Camus, Bishop and Lowell, Larkin and Amis—literature is littered with literary friendships, often more interesting for their asymmetries and disproportions. Emily Dickinson pined for a fellow spirit and came closest to finding one in the somewhat unsuitable Thomas Higginson. Lewis Carroll discovered such a spirit, for a time, in Alice. Perhaps this friendship is one of the strangest—it does not belong simply to that category of worship and bullying that forms the relation between artist and muse. (A muse must be aloof and unreachable—and she is not obliged to give anything back.) Before the breach between Carroll and Alice's family, which prefigured what would have been almost inevitable once she was grown, Alice was more than a muse to him. It was the intensity and intelligence of her pleasure that drove the young deacon to his peculiar fraught ingenuity. None of the other little girls who became his friends had that effect—and afterward there were no books as brilliant as the two written for Alice.

Like love affairs, such *liaisons dangereuses* are quickly contracted and all too easily broken. Literary friendship is rarer than romantic love and comes with its own peculiar liabilities. (It hardly need be said that romance and literary friendship almost never coexist.) Such friendships rarely occur more than once in a life, and when there has been a fatal rupture the loss is often felt permanently. Friendships founder on rivalry, jealousy, mutual incomprehension, petty slights, trivial misunderstandings—such bonds are even more fragile than love's. Fitzgerald was devastated when Hemingway betrayed him—he needed the younger man's approval, the one thing Hemingway could never give. The young and overbearing Melville never understood how he had scared off the shy, prissy Hawthorne. Scholars who want to eroticize literary friendship apparently have no friends—or have been reading too much Freud.

Donald Justice and Richard Stern were unusually fortunate in enjoying a lifelong friendship ending only with Justice's death in 2004. They met in 1944 in the library of the University of North Carolina (now the University of North Carolina at Chapel Hill), where Justice came upon a young man reading an anthology of modern poetry. "Good stuff," he remarked. There the acquaintance began, though Stern, then only sixteen, admits that he had only recently acquired a taste for poetry. Such chance encounters give friendship the sense of inevitability usually reserved for romance. (Byron wrote that "Friendship is Love without his wings," which says something about Byron but much more about friendship.)

This edition of the Justice and Stern letters reminds us how fluid a young writer's art may be. The art that exists before craft may be plastic, unformed in substance even when driven by the deepest ambition. Though Justice was already leaning toward poetry and Stern toward prose, a range of possibilities seemed latent in the imaginative act. Justice tried stories (eventually writing some prize-winning ones) and fruitlessly attacked a novel, while Stern struggled to compose poems; but their imaginative command, and later achievement, lay close to their early inclinations. (Perhaps this division secured their friendship.) This record of the first fifteen years of their friendship shows the unsteady progress of their art—the false starts, the good ideas gone bad, and occasionally the bad idea forced to be good. The letters take us from raw apprenticeship to the publication of their first books, Justice's *The Summer Anniversaries* and Stern's *Golk*.

It is rare for a literary friendship to leave such a full account—during the friendship's formative stages, writers usually live within hailing distance. Except for a brief period in the fifties when Justice and Stern were both graduate students in Iowa City, their letters had to supply what they lost to geography. (The letters are one reason to be grateful for the high long-distance phone rates of the day.) Their friendship is uncommon for having begun so early, before either had much hope of success. It is also unusual for having weathered the upheavals of maturity, since the argument with style can become a quarrel with friends, and success can be just as debilitating to *amitié* as failure. Perhaps distance worked to their advantage—the sole occasion they tried to collaborate, while staying two weeks together one summer in Connecticut, was a disaster. The house had a porch, and the porch a single comfy chair. The pair agreed to take turns in the chair while they drafted a play. One morning they argued over the chair, and the partnership was over.

If at times the great works of an author can seem an elegy for lost friendship, a wish to prove that the bond should never have been broken, it is perhaps more common for a writer's work never again to reach the heights achieved during such a friendship. To find one person who has an intuitive and complete understanding of your work makes a writer feel that the game is not so hopeless after all.

ACKNOWLEDGMENTS

I am extremely grateful to Richard Stern, Jean Justice, and the Donald Justice estate, without whose support this book would not have been possible. Thank you also to the patient and knowledgeable staff at the Regenstein Library at the University of Chicago and at the University of Delaware Special Collections Library. And for her guidance through the permissions process, thank you also to Deborah Garrison.

In the process of editing these letters, I was fortunate to have gained two great teachers. They shared their time and knowledge with me generously and without obligation. Their confidence in me was vital to this project. Thank you to William Logan, for entrusting me with the task of editing Donald Justice's letters. He advised me always with patience and good humor, and for this I am deeply grateful. Thank you also to Bonnie Costello, for her early encouragement and unending support.

Finally, for this book about friendship, I thank my friends.

INTRODUCTION

In 1944 the nineteen-year-old Donald Justice (1925–2004) headed north to New York City from his home in Florida, where he was completing his BA at the University of Miami. His plans to move to the city following graduation fit the ambitions of a young man whose interests ranged from writing poetry to composing music. During a stopover at the University of North Carolina, Justice made a visit to the campus library, where he was pleased to recognize a book in the hands of the young Richard Stern (1928–2013), Louis Untermeyer's *Modern British and American Poetry*. "Good stuff," Justice remarked, peering over Stern's shoulder. "Like it?"

Stern, then sixteen years old and a freshman studying English literature, had picked up the anthology only an hour earlier. Before that, he said, he knew nothing of the poets gathered there. In a memoir, Stern acknowledged the lucky coincidence of being introduced to the modern poets in Untermeyer's anthology and to Justice himself almost simultaneously.[1] Stern recalled how impressed he was by Justice's worldliness—"He was from Miami," he would joke years later. After exchanging addresses, Justice continued north. Throughout the following year, the two kept in touch, and in 1946 Justice returned to Chapel Hill to begin his graduate work.

The time the two men spent together as students at Chapel Hill solidified an acquaintance that had been at first, of necessity, epistolary. There they formed lasting friendships with Edgar Bowers (1924–2000) and Paul Ramsey (1924–94)—poets who feature prominently in their correspondence—as well as the fiction writer Jean Catherine Ross (1924–), whom Justice met in a Chaucer class. Not long after, he married her.

Outside of their time in Chapel Hill and the two years they later spent together at the Writers' Workshop at the University of Iowa, Justice and Stern wrote to each other. The handwritten and typed letters, postcards, and—much later—e-mails that form their correspondence, which lasted sixty years, ended only with Justice's death in August 2004. These letters document the growth of two literary figures whose writing spans an extended period in American literature.

The first extant letter was written by Justice shortly before he began work toward his MA at Chapel Hill, where Stern was in his last year of undergraduate study. *A Critical Friendship* begins there and concludes in 1961, one year after the publication of both writers' first books. The correspondence reveals the extent to which the friendship provided an outlet for their early drafts. In Justice's case, these include the poems eventually published in his 1951 chapbook, *The Old Bachelor and Other Poems*, and in *The Summer Anniversaries*, as well as versions of many that remain unpublished. In his own letters, Stern worked over the ideas that became his early stories and his first novel, *Golk*.

This early period of their correspondence conveys what both writers valued most in their friendship, their delight in the give and take of criticism. During these years, Stern sent Justice many stories and poems for his reactions. As Stern recalls, "No criticism, however harsh, was out of bounds."[2] Justice agreed, in turn sending poems, novels, plays, and music to Stern.

Though Stern's primary interest was fiction and Justice's poetry, each wrote seriously in the other genre. Those who know Justice primarily as a poet might be surprised to learn that, before entering the Writers' Workshop, he contemplated writing a novel for his dissertation. Stern wrote and published poetry throughout their correspondence and in an early letter discussed plans for a volume of it.[3] Their ambitions seemed to stifle any hint of unhealthy competition. To the contrary, the friendship inspired each to experiment. "How *do* you write a novel?" Justice enquired in a letter dated February 29, 1948.

Stern received a needed boost from Justice's interest in his verse. "Don introduced me to the rigors of composition. . . . Any half-decent turn of phrase or meter fired the generosity. When I finally wrote one fair line, 'The sun makes shadows of us all,' the generosity was like a confirmation."[4] The effect was mutual. Justice looked to Stern for advice on whatever story he was plotting. In a letter dated October 8, 1956, the poet confided, "You are my barometer, my sensitive instrument, which tells me I am fair & warmer or cool & cloudy. So?"

What I hope to convey in the selection of their letters is a friendship for which writing and the sharing of ideas formed the foundation but did not set the limits. The substance of their generosity ranged from praise to chiding analysis, as well as pointed banter. In a letter dated March 3, 1946, Justice wrote, "The two poems you sent me I will be honest about. I did not like them. Although nobody else could have written them, they were not original." Though still a young poet, Justice demonstrated a keen sense of his literary standards, as when he proposed just "what is really wrong with the poems":

> They show lack of organization, no feeling for form (though as I remember one was cast into a rough sort of sonnet wasn't it?, there was still no *form* there), uncontrolled meter, now and then an obvious rhyme, and quite often a banal or borrowed image; furthermore, no suggestion of a complete world-picture was there, no moral structure behind or beneath the surface of the poems which would serve to give them meaning and life. . . . They seemed hurried and probably were, though I have the faith that you must on some things spend a great deal of time.

It is a rare friendship that offers honest criticism without causing trouble. Justice's critical remarks, if rigorous, were offered in the spirit of good-natured dialogue. Though seemingly harsh, his response was couched in an otherwise genial, even self-deprecating letter about his own efforts in poetry, a recently failed relationship, and somewhat extravagant plans for a trip to New York. He also asked Stern to send more poems.

With regard to the sometimes sharp banter between them, it would be tempting to think Stern the more vulnerable party, since he was younger and a less practiced poet. However, his willingness to accept criticism demonstrated qualities not commonly attributable to young writers, and his replies matched Justice's in confidence. In response to a draft of Justice's unpublished poem "Perhaps the Morning," Stern wrote,

> You are preoccupied also with the inter-rhymes—flesh, thresh, fresh etc.—which may look good, but do not sound good (to me, at any rate). Some of your lines lack mutual support. For instance 'We like two idiots grow innocent together'—What addition to our image does the coupling of idiots [make] to the growing of innocence? An idiot grows innocent yes—but are two discretely significant? If so, they are not to the average poetry reader.[5]

In closing, he added, "Excuse the frank criticisms, Don. I want the same." Stern's criticism was both intelligent and resourceful, offering Justice more than a willing ear. In much the same way that Stern felt only his friend could "do justice" to a particular piece of prose or verse, Justice recognized in Stern a unique set of literary standards—what the poet valued as "stern sense." Justice did not merely excuse his friend's suggestions, he put them to good use, as a study of subsequent drafts reveals.

Taken together, these letters invite witness to the construction, conscious or unconscious, of two literary lives. Much here articulates how they created themselves as writers, not least in their determination to keep writing. Their moments of self-consciousness perhaps best demonstrate their attempts at self-invention. For Justice, these often sprang from an acknowledgment of his literary influences. As he wrote, with regard to a particularly convoluted plot-outline, "If you begin to suspect that what I tell you of it sounds not unlike Faulkner, I'm afraid you're right. The style has turned out to be, all unwillfully on my part, what the reviewers (if any) will call (if clever) an outright imitation, which is not quite true."[6]

Here and elsewhere, Justice anticipated the major criticism he encountered throughout his career. Such criticism did not govern the course of his writing. He continued experimenting with imitative forms, and, with practice, honed the craft that many later praised as a distinctive feature of his poetry.

The selected letters also present fascinating character studies of the two writers. In the same letter where Justice struggles with his revision of a sestina, he rues his failure to bet on a horse at Hialeah, reports Jean's and his latest attempt to "win puzzles" in the *Miami Daily News*, and considers volunteering his services at a local production of Lillian Hellman's *Another Part of the Forest*, which he felt could be improved.[7] Many of Justice's friends and former students have published accounts of his competitive spirit, some attributing it to his approach to craft.[8] His penchant for games and sport is often expressed in letters to Stern, who was many times his friendly rival.

While this period saw Justice working meticulously to master traditional forms, Stern was often experimenting, producing work in a range of genres.[9] Early on, Stern's letters expressed his dedication to fiction and poetry, and later his interest in writing for stage, film, and television. Despite his first impression of Justice, Stern was by far the more worldly. An eager traveler, his letters arrived from points across Europe—where he taught for a time at College Jules Ferry in France and Heidelberg University in Germany—and throughout the Middle East, where he made an extended side trip. While Justice's stories and poems focused largely on southern themes, Stern's spanned the globe.[10]

Two decades before Justice and Stern met in Chapel Hill, and about twenty miles north at Vanderbilt, a small contingent of undergraduates produced a magazine called the *Fugitive*. The young poets and critics in this group, soon known as the Fugitives, included the young John Crowe Ransom, Robert Penn Warren, Allen Tate, and Cleanth Brooks, all eventually major figures in the American literary scene.[11] The *Fugitive* and its editors promoted a new approach to the writing and study of literature, longing for a return to tradition in a poetry that focused on form and technique.[12] Their interests extended beyond poetry and into criticism. Like their poems, the work of the Fugitives and of the later, overlapping group called the Agrarians expressed a desire to return to the social and religious traditions of the Old South (including an agrarian way of life) while rebelling against the romanticism that often defined the region's literature.

The influence of the Fugitives extended beyond the South and helped lay the groundwork for what became the dominant approach to American literature in the mid-twentieth century. New Criticism emphasized methods of close reading, regarding works of literature, and in particular poetry, as aesthetic objects distinct from their historical, political, and biographical contexts.[13] Although the Fugitives had largely disbanded by 1946, the pre-eminence of New Criticism thereafter is evidence of their legacy. Writing programs, which began as experiments at schools like Kenyon College and the University of Iowa, found their place not only within the academy but within critical circles as well. Notably, critics like Tate, Ransom, Brooks, and Warren, as well as William Empson, Kenneth Burke, Yvor Winters, and I. A. Richards, influenced this shift by fostering the development of younger writers.

Though Justice had grown up in the South and Stern in the North, the literary tenor of Chapel Hill, their meeting ground, was crucial to the direction of their careers. In the 1940s Chapel Hill was steeped in the southern literary tradition revived by the Fugitives and preserved in the values and methods taught by the New Critics. While at Chapel Hill, Justice sent drafts of his poems to the Fugitive poet George Marion O'Donnell and focused his master's thesis, "The Fugitive-Agrarian Myth," on the poets of this group.[14] As the letters reveal, his stories and poems during this period and even much later resonate with the language and themes of Fugitives like Ransom and Tate.

Readers familiar with this moment in American letters will hear the influence of the New Critics in the early writing of Justice and Stern as well as in their letters to one another.[15] The echoes can be subtle, as in their criticism of Shakespeare's sonnets.[16] At times, the discussion of these influences is the occasion of their exchange. In a letter of April 14, 1949, Justice wrote, "Nobody dislikes 'scientism' more than I think I do; still, faith's hard nowadays, and I don't see why we can't write poems about its difficulty"—a statement that speaks as much to Justice's struggles with New Critical ideas as to his acceptance of them.[17]

Justice and Stern followed closely the work of the New Critics in journals like *Sewanee Review, Kenyon Review, Accent,* and *Partisan Review.* In 1947, after receiving a copy of *In Defense of Reason* from Stern as a wedding gift, Justice worked up a special interest in Yvor Winters. The following year he traveled to Stanford in hopes of studying under the influential poet and critic. However, he was soon somewhat disenchanted with Winters—and with the bureaucracy that made it difficult for him to pursue his studies.[18] Justice returned to Miami without his PhD. What he had gained, however, was a vivid comprehension of meter—a celebrated feature of his poetry—and a rueful picture of his idol.

A good deal has been written about Justice's literary influences. What some have praised in his poems as a "deep engagement" with literature and a modern resourcefulness with traditional forms and styles, others have dismissed as an overt dependence on Baudelaire, Rimbaud, Yeats, Auden, Ransom, and Stevens.[19] One of the most fascinating aspects of Justice's letters is his open acknowledgment of his influences, sometimes embracing them, at other times seeking distance. Early in his correspondence with Stern, Justice frets about sounding too much like Yeats (in poetry) and Faulkner (in prose). When he wasn't worrying about such things, he was building a strong case for certain forms of imitation. As even his earliest drafts demonstrate, Justice was a devoted student of the writers he admired, and he learned well from them.

Much less has been written about Stern's influences, though his letters are often revealing. As a young writer, Stern read the criticism of Burke and Empson with great interest and even attempted their critical and poetic styles. If Justice's idol in prose was Faulkner, Stern's seems to have been James and, later, Beckett. Unlike Justice, Stern was often critical of Winters. "Winters is Winters because nobody takes his poetry seriously, which means his major premise, that the finest poets are the finest appraisers of life, undermines even his criticism." Still, he added, "I think I'll retract this, too."[20]

Another influence in both writers' lives, as well as an occasional participant in their correspondence, was Jean Ross Justice. From the time they met, the Justices spent little time apart, and Jean played an important role in the friendship of the two men. Before the birth of the Justices' son Nathaniel in 1961, Jean was busy as a writer. Her husband's letters to Stern discuss the plots of her stories while boasting of her success. In his replies, Stern addresses

Jean directly, joining in gossip and inside jokes, asking her advice on stories, and congratulating her when her own work was published.

Reading Justice's letters, one receives the impression that Jean often sat nearby as he wrote, chiming in. Justice occasionally pointed out how she poked fun at his letters as he wrote them. "Jean's been reading the first page of this letter and making snide comments, objecting to every word I say about her, and adding that I can't use the word 'bloomers' in a letter."[21] Often her remarks were placed in the margins or in postscripts.

A collection of the entire correspondence would fill several volumes, while a selection covering all sixty years would not fairly represent any one period in their friendship. The later letters, while at times better written, lack the energy—if also the naïveté—that marked their earlier exchanges.

The letters here represent a single period of their correspondence, telling a story rarely shared, that of two writers inventing themselves. It could easily be said that these years represent their most fervent as writers, though both remained largely unknown before 1960. That year Justice celebrated the publication of his collection *The Summer Anniversaries* and Stern of his novel *Golk*. *A Critical Friendship* ends with their reactions to the reviews.

The largest gap in the correspondence, from the fall of 1952 to the summer of 1954, marks the two years they spent together as graduate students at the Writers' Workshop, a time both writers referred to fondly. Before and after, these friends often planned to live near each other or ideally to teach at the same school. The professional decisions they faced always presented the question of the distance that would come between them, the likelihood of visits, and even the kind of transportation required. As their families grew, they continued to see each other as much as possible, spending holidays and summer vacations together.

In 1955 Stern took a job at the University of Chicago, a position first offered to Justice, who turned it down because of the reservations he and Jean felt about city life. There Stern became a distinguished member of the university's faculty, retiring in 2002 as Regenstein Professor Emeritus. Justice spent two periods of his career teaching at the Writers' Workshop but he was also a professor for shorter terms at Syracuse University; the University of

California, Irvine; the University of Virginia; and elsewhere, before moving to the University of Florida in 1982.

The miles between them inspired frequent letter writing—at times weekly, and usually at least monthly. Shortly after Stern accepted his job at Chicago and Justice his at Hamline, the latter wrote, "I counted up the distance on a road map the other day—as I remember, it's just under 400 miles from Columbia, Mo. Not too far for [a] week-end now and then, I hope."[22] The invitations to Miami, Paris, New York, Chapel Hill, and Chicago—wherever one or the other was living—seem never-ending. "I would like to get down to Miami more than anything," wrote Stern in response to one, "but I'm pretty sure I won't."[23] In 1992 Justice retired to Iowa City—about four hours' drive from Stern.

My guiding premise in this selection has been to establish a chronology of both writers' early work—beginning with their meeting and culminating with the publication of their first books—and to highlight the influence of their friendship on their literary careers. In many instances, a letter has been left out because its content repeats that of another included or because it discusses the less remarkable details of their daily lives. The absent letters cover many of the same topics and themes and include further drafts by both writers. Viewed together, the published and unpublished letters reveal each writer's development in greater detail. In the current selection, I have tried—as Justice described his method of selecting poems for his first collection—to "keep only the cream."[24]

Brief contextualizing statements accompany some of the letters and are intended to punctuate lengthier gaps in their exchanges. Cross-references are also provided in the notes to help readers navigate the published letters as well as to guide them to those omitted letters whose contents might be relevant. There is only one letter here whose contents have not been reproduced in full—in one of his letters from Harvard, Stern enclosed two student poems by T. S. Eliot, first published in the *Harvard Advocate*.[25] These have been cited but not reprinted.

In order not to disrupt the flow of the correspondence, editorial alterations and standardizations have been kept to a minimum. Missing articles have been added in brackets. Misspellings and errors of punctuation have been silently corrected. In the early letters, for example, both writers often misplaced or omitted apostrophes. Later on—in Stern's case, just after his completion of his PhD at Iowa—these infelicities vanish. However, I have retained what appear to be intentional misspellings. Both authors derived a great deal of pleasure from their typographical errors and from the puns that these errors occasionally created. Mistakes judged to be of this sort are left uncorrected here.

Biographical notes, including birth and death dates, have been provided for all individuals relevant to the American literary scene, as well as for persons whose appearance in the letters might be further clarified by such a note. In all cases, I have tried to keep notes brief, focused on the lives and work of Justice and Stern. T. S. Eliot therefore receives a substantial biographical note because of his importance to them as well as his significance to the New Critical work of the period; Bette Davis is described simply as an "American film actress." When biographical information was unavailable, and for more obscure acquaintances of the authors, a note reads simply "unidentified." Where vital statistics have been omitted, it is because they could not be found.

The poems included in these letters, though an exciting and distinctive element of the correspondence, are not annotated for their allusions. The emphasis here has been on the letters, though such annotations may be an important task for future critics.

For salutations, addresses, and postscripts, some standardization was necessary, if only to guide the reader from one letter to the next without confusion. Addresses written or typed on the original letter, as well as those in letterhead, are set in upper- and lowercase. All postscripts have been placed at end of the letter, though in the originals they are at times written in the margins. All other marginalia or insertions have been placed within the text where indicated by the letter writer.

Though not displayed with consistency in the original letters, all titles of books, plays, and films have been set in italics. Titles of poems, articles, essays, and stories are set off with quotation marks. The symbol for "and" has been standardized as an ampersand. Justice occasionally used ampersands in his handwritten letters, Stern at times what might be called a plus symbol.

While Stern's mode of abbreviation is an element of the physiognomy of the letters, its standardization as an ampersand here seems the least distracting choice.

Using contextual evidence from the letters, I have placed undated and unmarked letters within this sequence as accurately as possible. The approximate date and the probable place of composition have been enclosed in brackets. Following the close of each letter, the source or the depository where the original letter can be found has been noted, including the box and folder number when applicable. All letters marked "private" were provided by Jean Justice. Letters are also marked "MS" or "TS," indicating manuscript or typescript, respectively.

A CRITICAL FRIENDSHIP

THE LETTERS

CORRESPONDENCE OF 1946 TO 1947

Feb 5, 1946 | 1829 NW 46 St | Miami

Dear Dick—

My apology will have to be poems. I have done nearly fifty in the last two months, which is prolific for me. Many by now are destroyed because they were valueless, but some remain, doing their best to stand the test of time. Also stories, and my book (which I had to abandon because it soon seemed to contain too much bad and immature writing.)[1] That worries me not, however, for there are acres of time. There were a few other more mundane reasons for not writing letters to you. I was arrested, thrown out of where I lived, spent (almost literally) nights in the snow, got sick, and returned to the climate that birthed me.[2] Principally, to recuperate my fortunes I hope, so that I will be able to return to New York in the spring. After that California, Mexico, Paris, Ultima Thule. Yes?

Here are some poems.

Perhaps the morning

Its own kindnesses

Can never reproduce

But once, out of the night

Where we with leaves

Had left our excrement,

It raised up antlers of its scent,

Smelling us like birddogs out,

And smoking us from holes

Where we were burrowed in our mirrors,

Till, our plumage terrorized,

Like two wild birds we flew

Toward one another's sex,

And laid the eggs of sleep

Thus in our waking

More than ever in our sleep

Another.

Every moving groove of flesh dovetailing,
Threshing, flailing granaries fresh of love
Under the autumn of a falling weather,
We like two idiots grow innocent together,
Etc.

(The rest of this poem is not polished enough to show you.)
A new idiom?

Never go
Nobody so
But you
And after me
Has been before
You'll know
I go
And went
But never go
Nor want
But when
You say so
Or no[3]

In the same idiom.

Go back
If you can
To all that
Before now
Came
And seemed
Went

And another.

Through you
I do
And through me
You be
Too
It's true
Though you see no
And say so
You are yes
You are

Modified version.

What heat I give
And have
Only reflectioned from
The piece of glass
Where you've come
To shine
Though I confess
Long look to find
What used to be
The splinter of my self
Kindled there

And slightly different, not quite polished.

Poe and Virginia

The creature that between them slept
Was more than cats, and what warmed her
Hardly the fur, or even his hot words
That tumbled like hurt black birds
From lips she never kissed, or missed.

And though he hid the secret in a bottle,
That multiplied his enemies like children,
And curled the coil of her virginity
Into a snake to strike at him.
Thus she, in waterfalling drops of blood,
Surrendered daily inches of her life,
While he bled only hemorrhage of poems
From the consumption of his own original sin.

Excerpts.

From D. H. Lawrence (unpolished)

Even in Mexico he could not find
That colliery he had lost somewhere behind,
From which he still might mine the heat
That beat like wings to urge him on to flight. Etc.

Under the sun, that, afternoons,
Caressed him like a wife
He had grown weary with, Etc.

From Father and Son (unfinished and unpolished)

Am I that thing that melts the snow,
Makes it turn color run away and go,
Where no one not a fool may follow?

Those kissing words work wonders here,
Within the maze where worries wander,
Dolorous and dazed;
Warn me away to where
My world will never wounded be.

Thus beneath the rain's warm tent,
Convinced of guilt,

Lost in eclectic excrement,
How possibly can I remain content,
My thing impaled against
The sad blue fence of disappointment?

And on and on through the night.

I was sorry you missed me in New York. But I will not be such a fool next time, and make better plans for seeing you. I am sorry to have robbed posterity by losing your letter to me; but therefore I cannot remember exactly what you said, nor what your poems said, so am rendered innocent of comment.

At any rate, let me know what you are doing. I will expect a letter soon.

Don Justice

Stern Papers, Regenstein Library, 38:4; TS.

Richard G. Stern | 27 Steele Dorm. | Chapel Hill, N.C.
February 7, 1946

Dear Don,

It was good to hear from you. You seem to supply the action of our drama, while we here are merely a background. However we have our aches also, if they are a little less basic than yours.

To your Poetry:

You are writing euphoniously (except your attraction to "excrement" and your new idiom which seems pointless, showyily[4] empty and empty of good show)—your images flow very rapidly bearing your thought, instead of the usual—thought bearing them. Sometimes they are contradictory such as "Raised up antlers of its scent / smelling us like birddogs out, and smoking us from holes"—this is awkward. It blurs our impression while you are obviously trying to heighten with the many-angled quickness of the metaphors.

I don't exactly get the point of "Perhaps the morning" but it is rather nice anyway.

You are preoccupied also with the inter-rhymes—flesh, thresh, fresh etc.—which may look good, but do not sound good (to me, at any rate). Some of your lines lack mutual support. For instance "We like two idiots grow innocent together"—What addition to our image does the coupling of idiots [make] to the growing of innocence? An idiot grows innocent yes—but are two discretely significant? If so, they are not to the average poetry reader.

The "D. H. Lawrence" fragment is swell. Your images are held together and their intensity brings like feeling to the reader.—Don't make it too long and it will succeed.

"Poe and Virginia" should be, and isn't, cohesive. Many nice phrases "—hurt black birds."

Your poetry sounds on the whole slightly more polished. But I'd try writing something, say like ballads, to get a line continuum serving your images. Read Spender,[5] a poet whom you resemble but are now much inferior to.

Excuse the frank criticisms, Don. I want the same, but more I want you to be——supply the dashes.

Since I wrote the first part of the letter I have seen Virginia.[6] She is apparently fed up and at that bewildering "falling out of love" stage. Poor Virginia (not intended as a pun for "Poe & V")![7]

Now let me indulge—these are not good but are *new*—and slightly better.

You cannot write: heat and twisted junctions
Do not make for perfect journeys cross the continent of things.
So if Excuse decides that cramped compunctions
Are the cause, remember Daedalus' wings
Brought safety, so be not afraid
To scorn the solar Triumph that passion's fit
For greater strength than yours. Some strayed
Starlet breaking rudely from predicted orbit
Perhaps, but not you. You were built
For softer things. The alpine snows
Will wait tho Hannibal lost. They won't wilt
If you decline seduction. Soft you now, doze

The sunswept day. A fresh chance
Breathes again tomorrow. Oh, life's romance.

From "An Eliot Apostate"

You are not Messiah, nor were you meant to be
An angel, suckling at the rim
The sweeter caressed air.
But mongrel martyr are you
Nuzzling the broken carpals with your broken caution.

Why, oh why did you dissolve
Into the river's fond paternity,
When with one more breath and one more lunge
You might have found the sea,
Messiah to Messiah to Messiah
Rivulet, delight the countryside.

Das ist alles.
Be good.
Dick

Private MS.

March 3, 1946 | 1829 N.W. 46th St | Miami

Dear Dick,

Don't feel like writing a long explanatory and dull letter just now. I answered your letter once before but never mailed it. In that letter I got involved in justifying my tortuous images so that it ran on for thirteen pages before I tired. A similar error in taste I will now try to avoid.

Since here (in Miami) I've written two fine short stories, several poems; and revised some ancient and recent stuff; but so little of it ever seems to get to the final, satisfying state. This is a terrifying existence, never being able to say just what you mean, and even when you come close to it having your best friends say "It has all been a mistake," or "I don't quite see what you mean," and all along you know they are wrong, dead wrong. But there is nothing to do about it. Do you remember, I think we talked about communication not being the purpose of art? I still believe this, though it is difficult and heart-breaking at times to work under this belief.

The two poems you sent me I will be honest about. I did not like them. Although nobody else could have written them, they were not original. You are trying to be Elizabethan, modern, and Stern all at the same time. You should really be more stern about it. I realize this is bad criticism, not cut-ting to the heart of any matter, really nothing but a minor witticism, which is what too many critics of the *New Yorker* school repeat all their lives. What is really wrong with the poems is that they show lack of organization, no feel-ing for form (though as I remember one was cast into a rough sort of sonnet wasn't it?, there was still no *form* there), uncontrolled meter, now and then an obvious rhyme, and quite often a banal or borrowed image; furthermore, no suggestion of a complete world-picture was there, no moral structure behind or beneath the surface of the poems which would serve to give them meaning and life. Of course I am a fool if I expect to find such in only two poems. Nevertheless, it is true that I would like to. Some good things in them, principally in a few phrases, such as the "continent of things." But this entire paragraph is really rather superfluous because you must have known before you sent them how I would react, or at least what was really wrong and what really right about them. They seemed hurried and probably were, though I have the faith that you must on some things spend a great deal of time. At any rate, send me some more of your work and at least let me look at it. If you'd rather, I can keep my mouth closed about it.

You were of course right about Virginia's being "fed up" with it. I cannot blame her. When I've got it straightened out with myself I intend to write her a beautiful little letter. She had a kind of courage and perception of beauty, and a desire to do good and right, but not enough of something either to believe or to give up what she believed good for what I believed. It is no great tragedy. And I do not mean this to sound ironic.

I and a friend have earned enough to fly back to New York when the snows go. It will be sometime in April. They say there it is lovely then. That is what I want and need—a lovely place, a lovely time. And lovely people perhaps around me. We expect to have an apartment with records and books and pictures and people and warmth and whatever else good things there are necessary, and I will send you my address. Because I would like you to visit me when you can.

It seems I cannot get started on the same novel again or on another nobler one. The other, as I think I wrote you, turned out to be nothing but corny and immature. A great disappointment to me.

The poems I have written seem to mount up slowly; soon they may grow into a book. This is what I hope, though I tell myself it does not really matter. I may try to start getting things published soon. I have not heard, by the way, anything from New Directions for a long time, so as yet do not know my final fate there.

Write me again with news of yourself, and put in some poems.

Don

Stern Papers, Regenstein Library, 33:1, TS.

In the fall of 1946 Justice returned to the University of North Carolina, where Stern was in his last year of undergraduate study. Following graduation, Stern moved to New York City. Justice remained in Chapel Hill until August 1947, when he completed his master's degree in English literature.

Richard G. Stern | 239 Central Park West | New York 24, N.Y.[8]

Monday night [September 1947]

Dear Jean & Don,

I hope the hurricanes haven't touched you—at the most new styles of architecture, a little metaphor[9]—your marriage notice arrived today and its solidarity persuades that you'll survive much more than that.[10]

A little news. The Paramount business is off for six months or so.[11] I'm job-hunting—daily I feel the little silk strands criss-crossing on my neck and will soon find myself hanged by the neck till rich ($100 a week in 31 years or so). This is about the worst thing I can think of but I find it inevitable especially since I'm very much in love and want to marry Jo as soon as possible.[12] Perhaps in five years I can go back and teach—after I've seen things & etcetered. As for writing, it is my moral responsibility and need. I will try at any rate.

New York is quite horrible. I am very lonely—my boyhood friends have unthinkingly made their abortive compromise with L—FE,[13] the streets are filled with ugly people, phallic symbols and signs of weakness, signs of woe.[14]

I will probably get a job in publishing or magazine work, at the worst advertising or a salesman—in the former at least the company is more congenial.

I've thought of hundreds of plots, formerly my chief difficulty (I think). Here are a couple I'm trying to work on.

1) Boy home from prep school wakes up to see a girl (of 12 or so) across the apartment house court peeking in his window. Without looking at her he strips and does exercise. I'm not sure about the dénouement.
2) Old man nearly goes crazy when two kids pretending park bench is a train refuse to let him sit down till he gives them a ticket.

Of course these mean little as yet.

No poems except "Notes for an Audenesque" which I woke up to one night (blue pajamas).[15] Here it is anyhow.

Towers rot
Youngish men stiffen in strides
Mice scream definitely in corners

Imprecision surely in decay of cloud
Forgetting of narratives
Universal suspicion of murder

In earlier months
Stretching for orderly arrangement
In competition with unknown strength
We found riot and derangement.
Peace in quarrels
Solution in yawns, in yellow glasses

Spring used every primary color
Left us itself
Yes—some slept on the grass
Took two weeks in the mountains
Resumed the painting of a tree in Connecticut or Maine—
But we, given dried tubes, old brushes, canvases wet with failure
Cluttered our individual country angers
To pack & leave for the more general madness.

—(Haven't made a poem of it as yet—might try)

Went down to the Gotham Book Shop to subscribe to *Sewanee Review* (a link with my past & future (?)) & found a Fugitive display. Think they have Tate & Warren's poems etc.[16] Will get them for you if you want me to. Tate works for Henry Holt—thought I'd write but despite our mutual acquaintances he might think me rude—I will hunt illegally & anonymous a while longer.

What's Edgar's address?[17]

Please send poems, personal news, literary gossip and any inspirational matter you can spare—I'm destitute.

Dick

Private MS.

October 26, 1947 | 1825 N.W. 46th Street | Miami

Dear Dick,

I'm terribly sorry not to have replied to your nice, dramatic letter sooner. Jean and I have been thinking about you a lot lately, about Edgar too, and even about Chapel Hill. But, believe me, we have really been living in what Jean calls a mad whirl ever since I started teaching, which was the first of the month.[18] I have my just complaints about arrangements here; I won't bore you with the details, but with the generality—they overwork their teachers here. I haven't had one minute to write, hardly even a minute to read (though I did finish Mrs. Wharton's *Age of Innocence*).[19] Jean has to work too; so she got a job in the university library. Because of some fool rule about not hiring faculty wives in the same department, she couldn't get on teaching English, though they needed a teacher. By the time she finishes cooking (she's still having a few problems with that), and she or I finishes the dishes, it's usually nearly eight o'clock. Then I have to prepare my lectures, or grade papers. We have to retire then—because the alarm is set for six. So when do we have time to be ourselves?

Miami, by the way, seems lonely too to us. For my friends—or most of them—have in one way or another grown alien as could have been—and was—expected.

I can't tell you how much of a boon that Winters book has been to me.[20] Among other things, I am reading parts of it to my sophomore classes. (I have two of these, and three freshman courses; the sophomores study World Lit, and the freshman Composition. We're reading, in sophomore, the *Odyssey* this week.) They are a little baffled. For instance, I read them the description of the Romantic theory of literature and human nature in his preface and asked them if he seemed favorable or unfavorable to it—favorable, the majority replied.[21]

I haven't made friends very well among the faculty. For one thing, I got into an argument with Big Shot No. 2—he was all for relativism in taste, and I for absolutism (since my conversion). We got pretty mad at each other. I do have two friends about my age who are also English instructors, one of whom used to go to school here with me, and the other of whom wrote his master's thesis at Columbia on James Joyce's Epiphanies (ha!).[22] But they're not friends in the sense you and Edgar have been.

I talked the idea of starting the literary review over with some of the faculty. They seemed favorable; they thought we might be able to get the money from the university for it. But I'm far from certain that I would want to get tangled up here in any sort of compromise, for I (and Jean, too, I think) want to clear out of here as soon as my contract is up. I certainly intend to apply at Stanford, not only for one of those writing fellowships, but for a teaching assistanceship, in case I don't win one of the free ones.

Which brings us around to Edgar. I haven't heard from him since he got to Stanford, though I did have a couple of notes from the West Coast. I am really dying to hear the story. His address is P.O. Box 525, Stanford U., Palo Alto, Calif.

Have you got Paul's address?[23] I seem to have lost it, and would like to write him.

I got a poem started—pretty well, I thought—on the honeymoon. But since then, I've only been lucky enough to add two lines, and those before I started teaching. I'm looking for the clouds to clear up soon. If not, I'm going to start neglecting my job. I won't enclose the lines, but hope I can show you a finished version soon.

What about Jo? Where is she? And when do you think it would be possible for you all to get married? Be sure to let us know. And send her our regards, or something like that. If she's in Orlando now, and plans to come to Miami for anything, tell her to come by to see us, please.

Thanks for offering to get the Fugitive poetry, but Jean and I have placed an order for about two dozen books with a local bookstore that handles the longhair trade around here, and their poetry is included. We've already got *Personae*[24] and *Go Down Moses*[25] and several other things to bolster our bookshelves.

We've both been a little sick with colds the past week, and aren't quite recovered yet. But, you know, the old trouper must on with the show. So I haven't missed a day's work.

I *am* afraid this has been terribly dull, but once I can get out of this fog I think things will grow livelier.

Best of luck in your job-hunting.

Jean sends her love of course.

And *do* write very soon, Dick.

Don

Once the blessed routine starts rolling smoothly, so do we (I hope).

Monday—By the way, Edgar's letter came back in the mails today. That Stanford address is apparently wrong. You could try Box 311, Decatur, Georgia, from which I suppose it would be forwarded.

Stern Papers, Regenstein Library, 56:2; TS.

Monday [November 1947] | [Evansville IN]

Dear Don & Jean,

Have just read your letter and I won't tell you how much it meant hearing from you. If the return address is surprising to you it is still bewildering to me.

I am the asst. mgr. of a dept. store specializing in women's wear. I make $35 a wk. reduced by the Int. Rev. Bureau to $29. On this I live. I am in a room with some people called Metcalfe.

I believe I'll stay here awhile but I know for sure now that this isn't my alley—I am speaking more broadly than brassieres. —That is comforting at any rate. In case you're wondering how I got here—after two months of trying everything in N.Y. (the Paramount job is off till December or March) and even writing & getting a nice if formal answer from Allen Tate at Henry Holt, I was sort of floundering. A friend of my uncle's offered me this and I was out of N.Y. two weeks ago Thurs. night. At least I'm out of the city & alone or rather lonely. The work is ridiculous but it has funny moments. I am treated with inordinate respect by a staff of 50 women & 4 men & try to look extremely wise and certain. The work piles up at times especially Fri.

& Sat. nights (11 & 12 o'clock) so I flirt with the office girls & this concludes my social life.

Edgar wrote about a week after I wrote—enclosing a Lowellistic[26] poem, which I thought the best thing he's done—I wrote him to Box 525 and have heard nothing. Paul wrote at the same time & I answered to 205 Whitehead, but have not heard, but I'm sure this address is right.

I wrote a companion piece to "The sun—"[27] starting with "The moon makes monsters"[28] and have written two other poems which I'll write out—The first has been at *Kenyon Review* a month without answer. The second I started revising today.

> Walking in the sun we will side-step the cars,
> Obey the stop-lights, cushion with hands the itching sores
> Shot by formula round the street. We will think well,
> Softened by warmth, cognizant of universals,
>
> Though uncertain, as if our nerves lay, jerked out, on the floor
> (Aware in abstraction of infinite complication, sore
> And aware) while this other we, blood soaking skin-knit lore
> Feels somehow warmth and stone and movement in the sun.
>
> Some have felt differently. For example, Kafka
> Found the flawless groundwork bloomed
> Impossible bulbs, coughed up
>
> Monsters of unlikeliness, assumed
> Oversubtle, hidden guises, Trains delayed,
> False arrests made, love undermined.
>
> There the enzymes that dismayed
> The sugars of his life and laid
> Him youthful in the ground, amazed, decayed.

I have planned a novel around a short story I wrote about the fellow who studies himself in college—the story turned out seriously—I just can't start the novel. I still don't feel capable of decent work but it's pleasant trying—

Jo is in Orlando, upset & confused as usual. I don't know when we could afford to get married—apparently not for years but you can't tell. She's writing advertising copy for a radio station and is not terrifically happy.

I read during lunch hours (and home in the nights) & have read faster (my race with time) than I ever have in my life due to the pressure of business—I read *The Castle*[29] in 3¾ hr. periods—was overwhelmed with it. Am reading *The Magic Mountain*[30] now and am surprisingly impressed by it—my absolutism is also removed from presumptuousness I feel. At home I read quite a lot—Yeats, *The Duino Elegies*,[31] Fitzgerald (*Tender is the Night*[32] is in many ways better than *Gatsby*[33]), M. Twain, all sorts of things—*The Wings of the Dove*[34] (which was tough going).

It's awful that you don't have time to do what you want—your situation sounded idyllic & enviable—which reminds me—do you think they could use me down there—if I took an M.A. while teaching could I support myself? Still interested. How much are the Stanford writing fellowships—how many are handed out? It certainly would be fine with you two & Edgar. Is Peter's book out[35]—I go into bookshops asking for it & tell them to be sure to get it in—meeting him once I feel like a missionary to the Eskimos. On the plane I met a lady[36] who "talks" about books on Indiana, Ill. & Kentucky radio stations & to book clubs—I told her the name of it, my name, your names, Edgar's & Paul's—told her to watch out. She gave me her card, told me to attend her Evansville lecture, listen to her radio program &—said she would—all in the day's work.

What about you, Don—how do you write a novel—how can you "delay" the things that happen & the things you want to say—I guess you just have to write two or more novels & either halve the characters' names or just amalgamate (outside of *War & Peace*,[37] the writing of which—as I recall—would give one a pain in the arm)—there's much to it.

I hope you get to work, get rid of your colds & be happy. Write very soon.

Dick

If a child should stand tensed like a Greek before a trolley
Waiting for a catch, motionless in holy folly

We will leap to save, dam with blood a generation's grieving,
Snatch our nerves, tingling like a music box, leafing
Time to graft the whole earth's stillness. Like balloons,
If we flesh we sink. Yet we reach into the palefaced moon's
Smug grab-box, bloat with words the tides rise to,
And medals that must rip to raise you.

Listen, upon these minutes I say there are no walks
In the sun, no firmnesses scudding like rails through
    sleep, stalks
Growing up to Jack or Giant. Ten million stars
Dash to us with planets, moons and grocery stores.
We at bat, nine men in one, must face them all.
Each step we take is a cotillion ball!
Each breath's a quiver whose most subtle arrows
Quibble not at men or mills or sparrows![38]

(I called it "Quixote Knew" tho I don't like this title.)

Songs I've Been Taught

Learning the postures of love, its peculiar measures,
There is no need to stumble, innocent
Like Ali Baba at the cavern of pleasures.

When we were ignorant with infant wonderment,
Continually discovering the same, unaware of the sum
(Like Valéry's gold fish), even the past was renascent.

But sprung from the tunnel, we gaped deaf and dumb
Before the endless spotless tracks, the railroad palace
Where one could lounge and drink or thumb

The schedules of malice,
Laugh discreetly with grey-headed wisdom
About the explorations of the phallus.

In the train, the wheels' kingdom,
We lay, relaxed and taxed with sureness,
For only outside error could corrupt the boredom.

Our stomachs felt no qualms of nearness,
We were always <u>there</u> and laughed
At gauche intrusions of newness.

Private MS.

CORRESPONDENCE OF 1948

January 14, 1948 | [Evansville IN]

Dear Don & Jean,

Sorry I have been so lax—Bloomingdale's is a pretty mediocre correspondent.[1]

Have been relaxing with acedia but as of today things are tightening up. I had been planning to go to graduate school, in March to Carolina, in the summer to Columbia, in the fall to Harvard, but Monday I start working for Paramount—six or eight months of "training" (I guess learning how to run a projector & evade taxes) and then the Orient—China or Manila or Bombay. (Where is Empson—specifically?)[2] But before that, the East, so maybe I'll build in Cabib.

Also, I am helping the *Hudson Review*. (Heard about it?—I'll send you a prospectus) so far doing errands—Today I brought an article by D. S. Savage[3] on Hemingway to John Hall Wheelock[4] who seems to be the chief editor at Scribner's. It's a good article and this seems to be the adjective for the review. First issue has articles & poems by Lowell,[5] Stevens, Winters, Tate, Blackmur[6] et al.—I've only met two of the editors (Joseph Bennett, who is fairly nice and Fred Morgan, who is fine[7]—did you read his article on Williams in the Fall *Sewanee*?)[8] However, you probably know all this as Peter[9] is going to contribute. When I start reading manuscripts (next week, I guess) send up some poems—16 E 95th — N.Y.C. 'Twill be a pleasure! There is one other editor (William Arrowsmith,[10] whom I haven't met) & two female assistant editors[11] (ditto)—I am, number 6—so you see *Factotum*[12] is a likely title pour moi—gratis at that. It's good though, good work, good people—et goodium.

I was supposed to meet Ken & Burke Shipley for lunch today, but I missed them (Ken just called up & said he wasn't there anyway).[13] He's going to Columbia in Feb.

I saw Paul in Chapel Hill—he had your wedding present—*In Defense of Reason*—but I had mentioned that you were reading your own copy, so he gave it to me for Christmas—so thanks—I really ought to give him something he can give you. Chapel Hill was cold & rainy, very lovely and sort of eviscerated. Perhaps it was me.

I imagine you did some writing on your vacation. Where did you go & what did you do? How about Stanford?

I miss you all and wish I'd stayed—corruption is motion.

How many people do you know that'll subscribe to the *Hudson*? I don't know but 5 or 6.

I've come to the unhappy conclusion that I have read absolutely nothing and don't know anything outside of a fog of an eighteenth of Eng. lit and a wisp of philosophy. The only book I've read recently is *The Red & the Black*[14] and that just made me realize I've never read *La Chartreuse*,[15] Balzac, most of Flaubert, *Mlle de Maupin*,[16] *La Princese de Clèves*[17] and that I was ignorant of any other titles appropriate to this list. It would have been so much easier to have material for years and years.

How did the debate turn out or was it called off at the last moment due to lack of a hall or influenza?

Oh yes, I've read Freud (the Master would look askance at this lapsus memoriae)—a truly lovely person (in many ways) (and at this addendum) (and this).[18]

With Jo at the radio station (did I write you I wrote copy for another radio station & started to announce) I nearly forgot her but now that I'm in N.Y. I miss her. I believe I'll marry her before I go to the 'East' but much may happen, it, j'espère qu'il arrivera.[19]

I haven't written anything—still I'm afraid my "talent" was a thymus condition.

Volpone[20] is pretty funny—do they show foreign pictures down there? *Shoe Shine*[21] is pretty pink—I'd like to see *Verdoux*[22] again—thinking back it's lost most of its perfection, or is that my life welling up!

Do you see your house in that shot of Miami in *Life*[23]—if you do, point it out please. I looked for 10 minutes—*Life* cheated us again, je crois.

Well, excuse the writing & the letter being worse than usual.

Best to your folks and much love,

Dick

I gave Ken your address on request.

Private MS.

February 29 [1948] | Miami

Dear Dick,

Paul writes that he sent some things off to Stanford. I wasn't so lucky. I got the novel "outlined" in a very rough fashion and one of the middle chapters outlined in what I thought was very great detail indeed until I started writing it out.[24] How *do* you write a novel? I had planned it to be a flashback from Time A (the temporal setting of the main story) to Time B—but what it turned out to be was a flashback, first from Time A to Time B, then within that to Time C, and then to Time D (and one or two flashes within that to Time E);—so that after a couple of thousand words I felt as if I were trying to prove something to Faulkner. And there was my outline staring me in my face with only Time A (which had in the meantime been revised completely out of the written chapter) and Time B planned for. Instead of writing about Jamie Strowd's year at college on a football scholarship, I found that I was writing about how Ezra, his grandfather, had first come to Tooker (their town)—and I hadn't even guessed that Ezra existed prior to the actual writing. It turns out that I've got a very long chapter, from which I find I can extract one complete short story (Ezra's), or else use the whole chapter as a novelette complete in itself, or do both—or is this fair? Now, as Dante says of Satan, think how great in size the whole must be if each part corresponds.[25] And all I thought when I conceived the whole book is that it might be a long novelette if I stretched it. What excites me most is that it fits, it's not just padding and story-telling for its own sake (which of course I don't frown on by reflex). If you begin to suspect that what I tell you of it sounds not unlike Faulkner, I'm afraid you're right. The style has turned out to be, all unwillfully on my part, what the reviewers (if any) will call (if clever) an outright imitation, which is not quite true. But I have borrowed a trick or two from the master. One trick, certainly, which helps in shifting time (and seems to me good in itself) is the *timelessness* of so much of his writing that gives him free play to speak of the past and the future at once; and another is his care to designate what a thing is *not* before he says what it is. What I did manage to get written before the deadline was just not polished or shapely enough to dispatch, even if there had been enough of it, which there wasn't. And besides, how could I have been presumptuous enough to send them an outline of the whole thing when I had

just witnessed what happens to outlines. Not, mind you, that I am objecting
to outlines in themselves—but I do think that if Sinclair Lewis actually does
construct models of the houses and cities he plans to write about in a book it
is simply because he has a repressed urge to be an architect or city-planner
that he perhaps, after all, shouldn't have repressed. (Or is my humor, as usual,
too heavy-handed; I wrote this letter in longhand several days ago—not my
usual practice—and now typing it, that joke sounds pretty stinko.) So now at
any rate Paul and I have established for all time our characters: he's the kind
who gets things off in time, and I'm the other kind. I hope he gets one of the
fellowships; I think he's got at least a chance, don't you? I liked about a couple
of the dozen or so poems he sent copies of recently.

While in that burst of activity that's now recessed, I skimmed some of
those old "textbooks" on how to write fiction, short-stories, etc., just to
be sure I hadn't missed anything when I first looked [at] them years ago; I
hadn't. They were just as lousy as anybody could have told me. Not so Percy
Lubbock's book.[26] It started off rather despairingly, but by the time he gets
to *Madame Bovary*,[27] Thackeray, Balzac and James, the book seemed to me
a pure delight, much superior to anything on fiction I'd ever seen; he may
not always be perfectly right, but he's never *wrong*. Also in preparation (the
novice taking vows) I very carefully read *The Great Gatsby* again, it being
the shortest decent book I knew, in order to watch the structure and mark
the margins, etc.; incidentally, I made, I think, enough minor discoveries to
justify a paper, if I ever get the time. Right now I'm reading Edith Wharton
on the writing of fiction[28] (doesn't seem like much) and looking around for
James' prefaces.

I read *Père Goriot*—after your letter—and was embarrassed by its clum-
siness until the final two and a half pages (Eugene at Goriot's funeral,
remember?), at which point I was completely overawed, transported, subdued, and forgave the whole book at once.[29] But Balzac has nothing to teach
me at this stage—by that I mean nothing that I could learn, so I won't be reading *Eugenie Grandet* right away.[30] Instead I think I'll try *The Ambassadors*,[31]
if I can find a copy. Pocket Books just issued *The Wild Palms* (the love story
half of it anyway),[32] which seemed to me more like an ordinary novel than
the other Faulkner I've read, whatever that means; the scene at the mine in

Utah particularly impressed me, though I liked the rest (except for the girl's corniness and artiness) tremendously too. Have you tried it yet?

From Claiborne of your *Review* I got a three-line note—something about showing considerable talent in my "verse" (sic), and sending more, but their not being able to fit them into their publishing schedule. I'm afraid I didn't take it as kindly as I hope it was meant. But don't get me wrong—I appreciate what you did greatly.

From Chapel Hill I at last received via mail my diploma. I had all along had a secret fear that they had somehow discovered a faked footnote or two and was already preparing my ironic smile.

Jean still works on her story now and then. It is just on the edge of being finished, but seems a goal that ever recedes the nearer she comes. I'm about to go back to my Easter poem from last year—another receding goal.[33] (The novel can wait till summer, for I feel it requires a sort of sustained drive rather than a Blitzkrieg.)

I've applied for Kenyon's summer school, but may be too late or unwanted even if on time. Have you thought about going?

We still plan to go to Greensboro in a couple of weeks, not exactly for the Arts Forum, but to see Jean's folks, and perhaps to catch a fleeting glimpse of Ransom as he strides blithely past us on his way downtown.[34] The English department here may not let me off, but we're going anyway. That is, if we can ditch our old Buick onto some sucker (it's on its last legs), and find another in running condition before the twelfth of the month. Maybe you could come down too?[35]

I have, as a sort of final gesture, applied to Stanford for a teaching fellowship, or assistanceship, or whatever they have—sort of thrown myself on the mercy of the court. I've had my records sent out, and asked Cotten[36] for a letter of recommendation (but no reply from him—of course I didn't ask him to write *me*, just *them*), and asked Russell[37] too (oh that I had made friends with Craig,[38] who is the kind of big shot who could really swing it), and plan to get a couple of letters from here. They've already promised me a "leave of absence." Jones, the head of the department out there, wrote me a nice letter, though it was hinted therein that a host of applicants was swarming at the gates. Have you abandoned all thoughts of going West (too)?[39]

Write us soon and tell us what you're doing—in detail. Just this morning (meaning the day I originally wrote this thing) I received a letter postmarked "Canal Zone" and the only person I could think who might be there was you—it turned out, though, to be a student of mine who'd been shipwrecked during vacation. In other words, we have very little idea what you're doing or are going to do. Why we've postponed this letter so long is that I've been busy doing some hackwork for the department—a bibliography of contemporary criticism; I made it a descriptive one, and got my reward by calling half of them Marxists in my comments, and damning the rest (except for the you-know-who's) with some would-be wisecracks (which seemed easy at the time). The result is that the library is ordering *all* of the books (about $600 worth), like the nouveau riche purchasing, say, *all* the impressionists.

You're not leaving New York before summer are you?

Sincerely,

Don

P.S. John Ford has certainly made some lousy movies (in addition to the good ones). We'll skip *The Fugitive*,[40] but *How Green Was My Valley*[41] was one big cliché (we saw a revival), and *Tobacco Road*[42] (another revival) was one of the worst movies in all ways that we ever saw part of. *Grapes of Wrath*[43] was better than any of these (another revival) except for the unbearable propagandic ending. We liked *Treasure*,[44] Huston's movie, except for about 4 arty shots and speeches. And you?

P.S.— Has Bob Vaughn[45] gotten in touch with you? I hope you didn't mind my giving him your address. I asked him to *phone* you. We here haven't heard from him since he went back to New York.

Stern Papers, Regenstein Library, 33:1; TS.

March 20, 1948 | 1825 N.W. 46th St. | [Miami]

Dear Dick,

We missed you at Arts Forum greatly. B.A.[46] got a day off and came down; so did Paul, though we had to drive him back the same night for exams. I suppose Paul must have written you by now of what all happened; it wasn't much, and yet Jean and I had our morales boosted tremendously (especially Jean, I think, at seeing her folks). Jarrell was of course there;[47] and Ransom; and Lowell; and that Kafka imitator, Isaac Rosenfeld[48] who kept running on about how the short story was a dead form and needed "new forms, new meanings" at which Peter inwardly smouldered (don't relay this), and Rosenfeld even had the temerity to mention Kafka in public, which I thought was sort of letting the cat out of the bag. Maybe Paul didn't mention our memorable croquet game (with Randall's set in the backyard of his and Peter's duplex); Peter thrashed us badly, but both Paul and I managed to beat Cal,[49] who played the game of a madman. Cal said he was working on a long poem; and I inferred from his remarks that he soon might try his hand at verse play. We all shook Ransom's hand and he struck me just about like Tate seems to have struck you: chivalrous, still Southern, not quite as ancient-looking as I had expected. Jean thought he looked like a Methodist minister.

Peter and Eleanor have bought an old farm near Norwood; the farmhouse was built just after the Revolution by one of Eleanor and Jean's forbears. It needs remodeling of course. But it's a wonderful place. We drove by and inspected it; cold and empty, but charming and so old that they used wooden pegs in place of nails. Peter and Eleanor have invited us to spend the summer with them there; we're to help with the remodeling and the garden. Naturally we're excited about it.

I'm glad you and Bob are getting on. I hope he's not still taking the Village seriously (I don't mean to sound high-hat, of course, but one can court destruction only so long). Tell him when you see him next that Norma Troetschel[50] went with us to Greensboro and seemed to have a wonderful time. And tell him that I went by his house the other day and borrowed his French and Italian pocket dictionaries. And tell him too that I wish he'd write us; and Norma would like to hear from him too.

Edgar sent two poems about the Catholic Bavarians, which I thought were wonderful.[51] Have you seen them? He's coming back to Georgia this week until next fall, and he expects to go to Kenyon. I guess I wrote you that we've abandoned that prospect for lack of funds.

I'm working on my "Easter in Venice" poem.[52] Jean is still putting the finishing touches on her story, but even I can see the end in sight now. We ought to be able to get a lot done this summer.

Larry Donovan[53] quit *Flotsam*; so, since I and the others don't get along, I'm afraid I couldn't do anything for your poem, much as I'd like to. By the way, I still think your "Poco Commedia" is the best thing you've done; I don't guess you do; but I liked (and like) it a lot.

We haven't heard anything from Stanford yet, but I think the odds (the gods too, I hope) are in our favor.

You will be in New York this summer, won't you? For Jean and I plan to stop by there a few days and would not like to miss you.

Don

Stern Papers, Regenstein Library, 56:2; TS.

Holy Saturday in Venice

Now that the lilies are all out and in bloom,
Writes mother. Do the innocents still climb
Toward their purgation in the choir loft?
When my soprano cracked I coughed and coughed.
And mother wept. Those tears were acid as lime
Juice on my linen vest. I've heard the boom
Of cannon can convulse the soggy dead,
Jerking them upwards; so these memories
Are resurrected, borne on the flood they say
Time is. It must have been those bronze giants' way

Of hammering the darkness to its knees
On their great bell that roused me. Or what she said.

Or both. This room is ice. I listen for
The blades of gondolas or ghosts of blades.
One's will is brass that smoked at her lips' touch;
Hers were the strings that danced one. "Such and such,"
I say, "is done. The dead are dead." Night fades.
One wrestles with one's mother on the floor.

Their dead are planted in St. Michael's bog.
Friday I watched those black boats slithering past
Our chipped and staring palaces in route
That each day sink toward hell another foot.
The sun set with its usual splash at last,
Breaking its heart on the lagoon. First fog,

Now rain and rain and rain. Outside, the square
Is almost empty. Where is the sun? Things
Will never be the same. I see the doves
Blackening the eyes of St. Mark's with their loves.
Now all at once, led by the lion with wings,
They rise, they rise together, flailing the air,

Spokes of one mighty fan that turns and turns
Upon its pivot, driving the winds before:
Thereby the Grand Canal's all frozen. I
Cry for the skinny youngster sliding by.
The ice is thin. His mother is a whore.
It cracks. He falls into the pit and burns.

The bell is shaking me. Who understands
One's flesh and blood? <u>all pink, I will be blunt—</u>
<u>The whites are mostly gone since you left home.</u>

She dreams behind the blinds that I will come
Crashing through the orchard toward her, home from the hunt,
The hare slaughtered, blood steaming on my hands.

> Don Justice
>
> TO R. G. STERN
>
> 239 CENTRAL PARK WEST
>
> NEW YORK, N.Y.

> Stern Papers, Regenstein Library, 33:1; TS.

Friday [April 1948] | [New York]

Dear Don and Jean,

I really missed the Arts Forum and more so now that the descriptions are in. Thank you so much for your telegram—it started a lengthy if unsuccessful debate. If I'd known I was going to be drafted I'd of course have come but I do have a job and I didn't feel like ruining Paramount's hopes for a sensational year by leaving on a Wednesday. Anyway I'm glad you all enjoyed it so much.

I have been in the process of writing you to come to New York for two weeks. My folks are going to California from July 1 to the middle of August. The house is yours and letters are in the mail to Edgar and Paul. It would be fine if we could congregate even in the Nawth.[54]

Your Easter poem excited me to composition, which I enclosed.[55] I will send your poem off as soon as I can. Though there is much in it that I like, and though what may be called the strategy is unimpeachable I have the feeling that there is a great body of reference material, which I personally know little about. I refer to the cannon business, even the lime juice which is a pretty specific sort of thing (is it a religious or Floridian or Venetian reference) because I don't like it. I especially like the enjambments, the slight modifications by typography are really most effective. I don't like I will be blunt[56] in the mother's letter, nor do I like home from the hunt. Otherwise the last stanza is wonderful as is the paraphrase of Baudelaire. I do like the beginning, and though more praise is unnecessary I don't know of a precedent. The tightening of the poem is superb. "Hers were the strings that danced one" is not worth it. The wrestling with mother is appropriately horrible of course. You omitted the "clacking" line, which I liked. Thanks for the poem—one could not ask for much more. I hope you will excuse the imitation, which I had planned to a certain point—when I had to attend a screening of *Waterfront at Midnight*.[57] It is very different from what little I've done and though one reading sounds absurd to me, others sound fairly exciting. There should be no spaces in the stanzas (rather between).

I am completely reconciled to Tate—he read his own poems, made a few cutting remarks about Brooks and Warren, especially Brooks, said sweet things about Eliot's character and is wonderful.

Please pray that they will not draft me, even though it will do no good. Can you ignore brutal stupidity when it's got you by the throat—exactly how I feel. I am outraged, I'll become a Marxist, shoot Truman or maybe just snicker.[58] I'm very excited about it—two years!

The Great Gatsby is being talked about as Fitzgerald's classic novel but I don't think much will be done about it. I guess Ladd will be alright and Betty Field almost looks the part and the rest are not too good except for Nicholas Joy as the man in the house who wears sneakers and plays the piano—they've changed the gangster's name to Myron Lupus naturally—pretty clever though & funny.[59]

Bob spends most of his time planning thefts from the bookshop but he doesn't or isn't able to carry them out. The man who owns it is called H so you can imagine what it all sounds like. Bob knows Rosenfeld. Found him recently reading Wilhelm Reich[60] in Central Park.

I found Warren's introduction to Peter's book rather offensive—I haven't had time to read more of the stories yet—"Allegiance" is not too good I think.[61]

Adolf Zukor the second works in my office—I'm in publicity now trying to get "the grave's a fine and private place" etc.[62] into an ad—he has said 11 words in one week. The other people are French, Italian, German and Jewish so it is fairly funny.

But oh I do miss the south. I can't pass Faulkner without a groan. I guess Kenyon is out of my line too—I can't make any plans now. If getting married would keep me out of the draft I would seriously consider it.

Fine about Stanford. Winters will soon be having a change of heart or maybe an expansion. Or have you?

Again, you are expected in NY and incidentally if I'm not there you will still use the apartment.

Dick

Private MS.

April 3, 1948 | Miami

Dear Dick,

Nothing I could possibly say about what Edgar calls the mad world would be anything but corny. I simply refuse to accept inwardly (where I hope it counts) any of the responsibility for Their doings. Jean and I are even thinking, rather foolishly and haphazardly I suppose, of a farm somewhere with bomb cellars. We wish you as much luck as we wish ourselves.

Thanks so much for what you thought of my poem. And for your own version, which Jean and I have been puzzling over. I am sure of my admiration for the line, "The clam is its own dark and its own calm," or however it goes, as well as for a couple of other effects. But for one thing I felt embarrassed by not knowing how I was supposed to take it—serious, half-serious, or otherwise. It seemed so easy when you did it, as most of your poems seem; would that I had been given your facility as well as your felicity of phrase. (I don't mean to be praising this poem specifically; if I could be sure that it was completely serious I'd say I didn't like it. If it was just an occasional poem for fun I'd say I thought it charming.)

And thanks even more for your invitation. We certainly mean to take advantage of it, at least for a week. Edgar writes that he may be going to Kenyon, which means he couldn't get to New York till about the eighth of

August, in which case we'd plan to be there then too. But all this planning must wait on time and circumstance to be straightened out. If it is going to be possible for us to invite friends of our own to Peter and Eleanor's while we sponge on them (too) this summer, you must by all means drop down for a while. We'll let you know how this situation stands as soon as we find out ourselves.

The head of the department here, who had written me a letter of recommendation, got a letter from Stanford that I interpreted as rather favorable. But we probably won't hear definitely for maybe a month yet. In the meantime we are holding our breaths.

I suppose I told you that we've abandoned the idea of going to Kenyon. I've rationalized by telling myself that perhaps not for a long time again will we have the opportunity of working uninterruptedly and in such pleasant surroundings for so many months as we will have this summer. For I have been absolved from the responsibility of working this summer; and we have just about enough money to coast through from the first of June till we get to Stanford or else are boomeranged back here next fall. We are going through the motions required by our jobs at present in a sort of half-sleep, not really expecting to awake till June. I rather expect Jean to start counting the days any day now; if she doesn't soon, I will. Only two months, etc.

The English department has promised me, if I do come back next fall, a course in "Current Poetry." It's the prize of a crop of new, similar courses—"Current Essay," "Current Drama," etc.—which the department is wisely throwing as a sort of bone to the young instructors hungry for something besides freshman English. My course seems to be the plum. Not that I am being seduced into returning. But, whether my luck fails me at Stanford or not, the university is planning to publish a baby anthology of poems written within the last eight or ten years; it is to have good paper, board covers, and the pages are to be inserted in loose-leaf fashion so that at any time new poems can be put in or old ones taken out; it will have about eighty pages, seventy of poems, ten of notes;—the gimmick, as I suppose you've guessed, is that I am to be the compiler. So if you've any suggestions please tell me. What about Empson's poems other than the anthology pieces? He's impossible to procure.[63] And what do you like of MacNeice,[64] if anything? And what of R. P. Blackmur,[65] if anything (I doubt it)? And so on.

I will try to write again very soon.

Don

P.S. If I can work it in (and if time hasn't withered it in either your or my mind), I think I'd like to try including your "Poco Commedia" in the anthology. Would you mind sending me a copy?

Stern Papers, Regenstein Library, 33:1; T S.

[May 1948] | [New York NY]

Dear Don and Jean,

Hudson Review returned "Holy Sat."[66] and "Poco Commedia" regretfully, but decisively. They were almost offensively effusive—"immense pleasure," "deeply regret" "please send us more of your work" etc. Your poem was unquestionably superior to all the poems in their first issue including that clumsy Stevens piece and I immodestly think mine was better than some of it.[67]

Vaughn showed Tate your poems and he liked them very much.

He also recalled Jean and the Ross family (rather like the Brontës, he said—I mean they're all talented he added etc.).[68] He directed his last class entirely at Vaughn and myself and that further endeared him to me—he seems to be the nicest person.

I'll be in New York this summer and I definitely anticipate and insist on your spending a minimum of two weeks here—how about coming up the middle of July and staying till the eleventh of August or something.

Harvard accepted me for Sept. so if it'll defer me from the draft and this job won't, I'll go.

It's wonderful about Stanford—there's a definite possibility that you'll have a remarkably good time.

I've let Vaughn in on my plans to make a scenario out of *Tender Is the Night*—maybe something will come of it in the summer.

Tate said it took him two years to write *The Fathers*[69] (which, in case I haven't told you I recently read with enormous delight and profit) with a lay-off of four months. He didn't write a scenario and unexpected things happened as he wrote. He used a blue pen—except on odd Wednesdays.

Include John Peale Bishop's "Perspectives and Precipices"[70] in your anthology won't you—it's in the Williams Treasury[71]—Tate says it's based on a Chirico picture. Do you think it's as fine as I do?

Saw *The Alchemist*[72] burlesqued out of its seams the other night but it was still wonderful.

Am reading the *Confessions of Zeno*, which is pretty funny.[73]

Received a salesman alert from Paul and have asked the Gotham Book Mart to store ten or twenty-five copies.[74] Lowell, Tate, Marianne Moore and Louise Bogan are going to read their poems at a New School festival next week so I will put on my palms and attend.[75] I anticipate meeting Auden there—why, I don't know. He is a professor of religion at Barnard.[76]

My ten-thousand-word novelization of *Sealed Verdict*[77] was sent back for drastic revisions, in which task I have immersed myself. I may make a verse play of it.

Vaughn was fired from the book shop and since he and Nancy have parted company he was thinking of leaving NY, but someone gave him an apartment on 180th Street and since he is undoubtedly desirous of returning to Nancy he is staying. He is a very nice fellow, though his opinions are almost completely devoid of stern sense.

Today I hope to have a fairly easy day—see two pictures, *The Adventures of Casanova*[78] and *Shoeshine* for the second time.

I had thought of going to Kenyon this summer, but the best I could do would be to audit a week there.

The Lady from Shanghai[79] hasn't arrived in the city as yet—maybe they'll ban it because Orson Welles gave Chaplin the idea for *Monsieur Verdoux*.

I saw Jackson once and I never heard of Weidman's sister—we're on different floors.[80] I suppose I told you John Peale Bishop worked here from 1924 to 1925.[81]

It's getting enormously tiresome, but I can't afford school and no one seems inclined to afford it for me.

There is absolutely no news—I'm sure I've told you that I've seen Burke and Ken at Columbia.[82]

Write soon.

Dick

Private MS.

After their visit with Stern in New York, the Justices headed to Norwood, North Carolina, where they spent the summer with the Taylors, Peter and Eleanor Ross.

August 1, 1948 | Norwood [NC]

Dear Dick,

I hope you'll pardon me if I'm a little tardy in informing you that we have been writing letters to everybody but you about what a fine host you make, etc. . . . But I'm afraid I'm not the best bread-and-butter letter-writer there is, so from here on you'll have to take the will for the deed. We did enjoy our visit enormously—naturally—and want you to know it.

It's Sunday night, and raining. (It's been nice and cool save for a couple of days since we returned.) Peter and Eleanor are downstairs surrounded by odds and ends of furniture, china, silver, glass, pictures, books and clothing, packing for their departure which is scheduled for Tuesday. They want to arrive in Bloomington a good while in advance of the expected arrival of Matthew Hillsman Taylor, III. It goes without saying that we'll be awfully sorry to see them go. James Ross[83] has agreed to keep the place up for them during the winter, and he'll be moving in as they are moving out; he's likely to have a terrible time of it this winter with no heat but from what wood he can cut from the woods and consume in the fireplaces downstairs. We'll be moving the same day too—back to the Rosses, where we'll more than likely settle down for the duration of the summer. (I already have a mental picture of myself walking the nearly four miles of dusty—or worse, muddy—country road into town to register for the draft next month. And of course we'll have to walk in for supplies or drive the wagon, though thank God we won't need many, what with the garden, chickens, cows, etc.)

I suppose you have by now inferred that we have managed at last to unload the car. It was impossible to sell it in or around Norwood; they all said they couldn't use a "big car"; it seems all the farmers want is "A-models." (Can you hear the bitter tone creep into my voice?) And Albemarle, county seat of Stanley County, about 10,000 population, was just as bad; none of the four used car lots there would take it. The dealers had all so impressed me with the "bigness" of the Buick that once I let out a Freudian slip and called it "the bus" by mistake. So in growing frenzy we betook ourselves the fifty miles to Charlotte, our last hope. (That was after having put an ad in the bi-weekly county newspaper with absolutely no results.) There we drove around in the sun yesterday from one car-lot to another, about a dozen all told, and most would make us no offer at all, or something as miserly as "two hundred," delivered out of the side of the mouth and with eyes averted; finally we hit what turned out to be the right one and at the right moment. This one was the only one who seemed to be doing any business at all; he told us proudly that they had sold thirteen cars just this last week. He was young, introduced himself as "Fred C."—no, not Dobbs—"Dibby." And made us the best offer of the day, which we were rather glad, under the circumstances, to take. Three hundred! A great blow, of course, but we may be able to eke it out to California. We can send the twenty-five we owe you on now if you need it, and will of course be glad to; but I think you can understand if we tell you that it would be a little easier on us if you could wait till we were settled in Palo Alto. But, by all means tell us the truth as to whether the postponement would be any hardship on you. Your "investment" at any rate is a good one, let me assure you.

A letter from Paul was waiting when we returned; and we have received another already. Out here in the country with so little mail as we get, his loyalty is much appreciated. I sent him a short article on Peter's stories, which I had re-worked a good deal, but which was still disappointing; it only makes one or two points, good ones I think, but it leaves a lot unsaid and says what it does in too flippant a way. And I sent him another revision of my poem, which I might as well type out for you right here.

> Though books say nothing can save
> Love from an early grave
> And love from the wear and tear,
> What flesh and blood was ours for love's repair
> We freely gave.

> This way and that we have
> Eased love into the grave
> And covered all with dirt
> And laid the spirit too, through that witch's heart
> Knocking the stave.

I've tried working on an old Christmas monologue, with no results whatever. And I thought of a stray line today—"When migrant hooters track the varnished sky." And I wrote twenty-five pages of a story, then decided it ought to be a play instead, a three-acter at that. So that will consume the next few weeks. It's about a huge Southern family, the father of which is about to get married for the fourth time, to a girl a third his age; the conflict is between him and his eldest son, a rather stodgy fellow; it's a little closer to comedy than to anything else, I suppose. Something might come of it.[84]

Jean has finished her story and sent it off to *Mademoiselle*. I think it turned out awfully well.

I finally wrote a letter that had to be pretty delicate to Edgar; no reply as yet. I trust Paul has informed you of Edgar's latest depredation.[85] I can't understand what's got into him.

And before I forget it, many thanks for getting that information from the library for me. I finally got that piece of work off to the fellow at Miami, a great relief.

Write us soon. A letter in the country is worth two in the city, especially to ones marooned as we will be for the next six weeks.

Don

Stern Papers, Regenstein Library, 56:2; TS.

Paramount International Films, Inc. | 1501 Broadway New York 18. N.Y.

Wednesday August 12, 1948

Dear Don and Jean,

What a lovely packet. You have heroined me into a habit with one shot, Jean. But why Don's letter should shrink in proportion I do not know.

I liked the poem[86]—it's a brief jewel on the outside of that enormous Faulknerian pattern I'm sure you are evolving.[87] I think *Harper's* would print it.

The intellectual magazines are certainly getting a play from you all-lll. But apparently *Mademoiselle* is as bad as she sounds.

Gerry Shavelson[88] is back from Kenyon, worshipping Empson, who has a straggly, Chinese beard, two children and a wife in Peking, a sense of humor, a social conscience and a return passport, John Crowe who is lovable, disliking Tate "as a man," faintly admiring Bentley,[89] and full of ecstasy.

Wanda Hendrix and I did not have each other's pleasure, despite the ambassadorial services of my cousin-on-the-coast. She got engaged to Audie the night before.[90] I was humiliated and crushed. Yesterday at noon, Gwyned and Charley got engaged, an event which I celebrated in the following:[91]

Prothalamium

These noons are filling up the graphs of passion;
One plots a hundred stories to a line.
Each typical's become a glass of fashion,
Watches the highway wither to one lane.
From St. Charles to Charles St. one cannot linger.
All roamers know that "Vita brevis, amor longa."

What numbers clamor in what calculation
To join their figures in the famous sum,
Yet never calculate the maculation
Unwashable by either lux or hymn?
Freedom is a strength, but bonds are stronger.
The errant find that "Vita brevis, amor longa."

We who stew ourselves in the vast bowls,
Screaming the quarterwits into their pattern,
Are moving desperately for those same goals,
All of us the same from stem to stern.
We're all stocked up in someone's dirty corner,
Collecting dust like "Vita brevis, amor longa."

We all grope in the dark; few come to light,
With or without the Ariadne line.
Theseus was a hero in a fight,
But learned no litigation lay in loin.
These facts are open to the probing finger.
Then one accepts the "Vita brevis, amor longa."

This longest journey's plotted out in metal,
Straight as the sun—which warms us hand in hand.
As we lie in Pullmans or decline in hotels,
The sea seems nearer, like us, engaged to sand.
Now we think the end of that long hunger.
We eat our words, "Oh vita brevis, amor longa."

Time has passed and taken the magic from the poem.

I saw *Him*[92] at the Provincetown Playhouse. It was very funny, very well done and occasionally exciting.

I wrote a delicate letter to Edgar, but no answer has arrived as yet.

Nothing exciting has happened before or since your visit.

Will you be in Chapel Hill after Labor Day? I mean North Carolina. If not, I'll try and get down in a week or two and tell you the exact day, a few days before.

I bought a *German Grammar*, but it looks terribly difficult.

My parents arrived Monday and could not get in the house for two hours. The lock had jammed. Apparently the local lares and penates were revolting after their breath of our southern cousins.

Have seen only the *Sainted Sisters*[93] since the last volume.

The Blue Angel[94] is at the museum next week.

Your literary activities sound really exciting. Norwood as white and responsive as a strait-jacket.

Did Peter disapprove of my recommending his stories to Jackson?[95] Perhaps his agent has exclusive rights or something.

I simply can't write another word. The next letter should be less jumpy. Do write soon.

Dick

Private TS.

In the fall of 1948, the Justices moved to Palo Alto, California, where Justice began work toward his PhD at Stanford. Around the same time, Stern left New York for Cambridge, Massachusetts, where he earned his master's in English literature at Harvard.

Norwood [SC] | August 24, 1948

Dear Dick,

Why not recommend *Boston Adventure*[96] to Jackson before you leave? As a movie it would have almost everything for somebody like Bette Davis[97] (yes, I know she's Warners', isn't she?): a wonderful child's part, two terrifically emotional roles for ingenues, a marvellous character part for an old woman, an ending that could be twisted either way, and even a little romance. I expect a small percentage if Paramount films it.

It might not be any worse to get married than to go to Harvard, and a much more certain way of side-stepping the draft. Perhaps the best way of all is to become a conscientious objector. There are any number of girls, though, who ought to be willing. I think it would be best if you could marry a starlet: maybe then you could get a job in Hollywood (and get me one too). I'm not un-serious.

We finally heard from Edgar, a pretty nice letter, but he simply skirts delicate issues; I invited him to stop by Chapel Hill on his way to San Francisco (my mean streak, I guess), which he undoubtedly will not do.

We finally walked into Norwood yesterday, got on the bus for Albemarle, and saw *Berlin Express*,[98] which was the worst in a long time. Today we have been recovering from sun-stroke, for the weather has taken a turn for the worst (which means it will be harder to get anything done).

We have decided we will, after all, be able to come to Chapel Hill when you do, and stay one night if we can find a cheap place. Be sure and let us know some time in advance when you expect to arrive; yes, I know you said the 8th, but the letter we finally had yesterday from Paul led me to doubt that he plans to be there then.

The big news of the week is that *Poetry* magazine has taken a poem of mine.[99] And just when I had decided that you had to know Somebody. It's the one you call my "iddy-biddy" poem, the one with the witch. They pay 50¢ a line, that is, $5. And—this will kill you—they not only want my autobiography, but my picture (you know they've been printing contributors' pictures lately). We're thinking of sending them the one (did you see it?) of me in cowboy chaps and neckerchief, beating the buffalo I am perched on with a ten-gallon hat (it's in the same series with the ones of Jean in the embrace of a bear). Of course I understand that to boast of this acceptance is to my shame, considering what foul shape *Poetry* magazine is in, but then, it's not one of my better poems (I keep telling myself).

Did I tell you that Jean is again dabbling with her thesis?[100] And thinking of beginning a third story.

There's no other news. And besides, it's awfully hot.

Write soon. We're looking forward to seeing you soon in Chapel Hill.

Don

P.S. — They say the poem won't come out for 4 months at least. Jesus!

(This is the first part of a two-part poem on which I spent most of last week; I hope to finish it this week.)

This first cool day in weeks, here sucking grapes
From my own arbor, I have rocked away
My time, half in the dark from mother's drapes,
That sift the sunlight till I cannot see
My turn-of-century
Sleek thoroughbreds rear on the wall; a cricket scrapes

His legs together out-of-doors: no sound
But this, and the hulls popping in my mouth.
"This land was goodly that the good Lord found
And gave to the best people of the South,
Withholding storm and drouth
Till He could plant His chosen in His chosen ground . . . "

So I have heard my mother's brother preach
One Sunday after another, while I slept.
Only the hounds were mine from youth, to teach
And shoot when they turned feeble; I'd have kept
A hundred dogs, except
For mother and her kin, whose hearts were hard to reach.

I shoveled my last bitch into her hole
A week ago, where my browned meadows slope
To meet the creek, and left a kitchen bowl
For flowers. Watching all week the buzzards mope
And worry my last hope,
I wondered: How will my remains support a soul?

That precious seed was rotten from the start:
The roots struck shallow, and the tree will groan
And double like a knife to kiss the dirt
In Zion's churchyard, bowed down by the stone

Fruit it brought forth. Alone

Now, and my boots rest on their natural flint heart.

Stern Papers, Regenstein Library, 56:2; TS.

Paramount International Films, Inc. |

1501 Broadway New York 18, N.Y.

Monday August 30, 1948

Dear Don and Jean,

Paul will be up here from the second till the day after Labor Day I presume, whence I further presume, we will wander to Chapel Hill to meet you. Is that right? We ought to get there Tuesday morning, but I guess Paul knows the details.

I like a great deal of your poem. The most effective stanza, or rather, as Lowell says, the purplest passage, the last stanza, is I find slightly confused with reference to the last line of the penultimate stanza.[101] Hulls popping and all your precise verbs are wonderful. The development is fine, though perhaps the preacher and the hounds should have stanzaic separation. I still feel a little fillering, but what am I to feel? I omitted to say the burial of the bitch with your characteristic if *general* (too?) detail is lovely.

Boston Adventure stands recommended.

As you undoubtedly have heard New Yorkers have been untied by that supreme Thomist, the HEAT. Paramount even got out early a couple of days which enabled me to see *M*, a lot of which I thought fascinating. Peter Lorre is very good.[102] As in *Der Blaue Engel* (just practicing) a cuckoo clock is fairly prominent—what did Dr. Kracauer have to say about that?[103]

Congratulations on *Poetry* and congratulations to *Poetry* and poetry.

Let's plan something spectacular for Chapel Hill. You plan.

I'm sure this job with Paramount will have been the easiest of my career.

I've interviewed six starlets, seven DuPonts and the daughter of the head of the draft board and I'm still going to Harvard.

I have written Edgar off my conscience.

We see Bob Hope and Jane Russell in the air-conditioned *Paleface*[104] this après midi.

I forget, since I juggle three weekly letters, whether I wrote you that Selznick is filming *Tender Is the Night* without my permission,[105] but with a letter from me outlining the difficulties he must overcome with the transubstantiation, that I have already overcome—gratis. He is casting some famous Italian in it, probably as Barban. Dark skin, you know. Let's hope Louis Jordan doesn't play Dick Diver—I suppose it'll be Gregory Peck.

I have written two elaborate stanzas, which I will add to and recite I hope at our reunion, which incidentally I hope will last more than the few hours you planned on.

I saw twenty-one of my relatives around the pool yesterday, but I guess everybody in Norwood is related to you.

Tell me about the stories, Jean, and send me five pages of your journal, and tell me about your thesis because perhaps I'll do some work on Faulkner. Please?

I guess you know Auden is writing an opera with Stravinsky[106]—I think that *Time* came out while you were in the world.

I met Kay Francis Friday night. She is in *The Last of Mrs. Chaney*[107] a buhright[108] comedy of the drawing room. A friend of mine mangled one of the roles, and for this I was permitted into the interesting recesses of the theater where the bweezy Miss Francis stopped taking sleeping pills long enough to check her name off my score card. My friend was so absolutely lousy that I was in the hair-shirt state of absolutely not being able to congratulate her or even to tell her she was lousy.

Will see you next week.[109] Sustain thyselves on this epistolary affection.

Dick

Private MS.

October 15, 1948 | 3790 La Selva Drive | Palo Alto, Calif.

Dear Dick,

You must reconcile yourself to a dull letter. The weather is just not cold enough for inspiration or even labor: in the morning you can blow smoke but by noon you're sorry, nor will there be snow except about a half an inch in the mountains where Edgar lives in luxury (the third highest paid poet in the country, or thereabouts), nor is there even fog down here in the valley.

We are thinking of buying an old model-A if we can find one not painted red like Edgar's Stanford jacket. Edgar, by the way is transformed: he loves football games (he says), wears this jacket, hob-nobs with everybody (who treat him as a fellowshipper with awe), is Winters' pet, and is applying for a Rhodes scholarship. He is completely in his element and talks about buying a house and settling down here. And the model-A will be for us not only convenient (we have, like the other local commuters, to ride Greyhound busses; everybody out here loathes Greyhound, by the way) but decorous, for none of the students ride in anything but Hispano-Suizas and Cadillac limousines (one of which was advertised in the *Stanford Daily* last week, adding that it could be used as a bus).

We are still in our room, and if you have a hanger to sleep on, we have a double hanger. The lavatory in the public bathroom, according to inked instructions, must be mopped out with the paper towels furnished for that purpose, a laborious process which will make us late to work any day now.

But you know what chronic gripers we are anyway. We were probably spoiled by having a place, however small, to ourselves last year and a commodious convertible, and a position not wholly without respect on the faculty. (Here "part-time acting instructors" don't even have library privileges, though we do get called "Mr.," just as any student would be. The students, by the way, are bright.)

And I'm taking Old English.

There is a brighter side. We're invited to tea at the Joneses[110] (Eng. dept. chairman) tomorrow afternoon. Of course that's not the brighter side. But I did get a raise. Jones, by the way, in my interview with him counseled "plain living and high thinking, my boy,"[111] when I told him that I just had to have two courses to teach. And they say he lives in a palace.

But, as I say, we're the snarling bourgeoisie.

And I am permitted to "sit in" Winters' Poetry-Writing class. Which is full of nincompoops and long-haired hatchet-faced young men. None of whom can write. Or haven't yet. Edgar and Trimpi[112] (who had something in the *Hudson*, remember?) also sit in. And except for them I am the bright star, with such little things as the one I enclose. He has been very nice to me. And that is, I suppose, the sum of the brighter side. His first assignment was a string of descriptive couplets.[113] I chose Scuppernong, which had such brilliant lines as:

Sleeping among the roots, catfish and chub
Are seldom stirred by any wriggling grub,
Nor by the dragonflies that skim all day
Along the surface, dipping for small prey.

Yet they were the best in the class. So will it be worth it "after all"?[114]

The Taylors' baby has arrived, a 7½ lb. girl named Katherine Baird.

Winters, by the way, says of Tate that "God gave that man a great gift. If he'd only listened to me . . . " In his dissertation, Appendix III is entitled *Two More Major Poets: Allen Tate and Howard Baker*.[115]

Here is the poem of mine he read to class yesterday. He doesn't like the ellipses in the second stanza, nor the possibility of the pun on "rest" in the last, even after I referred him to G. Herbert; and he thought it sounded better on first reading than after several. That was just about the sum of his criticism, though he defended it ably against the attacks of several Romantics in class (one girl said she thought you were *supposed* to *love* the good.)[116]

Love not the good.
The lightest touch
Of flesh and blood
Discolors much,

Discolors it
Beyond removing,

Darkly unfit
For farther loving.

Nor love the rest
Denied us here.
No love is best.
Come not too near.

So that is what we pilgrimaged for.[117]

Of course Jean says she is going to have to write you a letter to give you the full picture. If she doesn't in time to put in with this, use your imagination.[118] We aren't really unsatisfied, not really.

And be sure to write us a long letter about the Stanford of the East.[119]

Don

Stern Papers, Regenstein Library, 56:2; TS.

December 10, 1948 | Rt. 1, Box 467-A | Mt. View, Calif.

Dear Dick,

Your letter as always was cheering. Harvard sounds bleak and stately and I would gladly exchange places. Although for some reason in the last few days I have again been thinking that if I and maybe Jean too could take two of the fellowships and if we could find a cheap lovely little house and various other things, we might even stay next year. Which is rather like saying we'll see you in the East next year.

Jean and I both insist that you send us a copy of your novelette.[120] If you don't have a spare, you must lend us the official copy for a week or so; we'll send it back in good shape. Why hell Dick, you didn't even say what it was about or include a sample of the style or tell us the title. Rush news immediately. I think I'll write one about some medieval plague or other and if I can persuade Jean to write one too, why we'll publish our *Trois Contes* in a neat little volume.[121]

Today was the last of the quarter. That—I have just decided—is the aforesaid unknown reason for the slight elevation of my spirits. I've been grading research papers this week; a very interesting one on Black Widows, a mildly Gibbonese[122] one on the Easter Island statues, one on the Battle of Chancellorsville, and altogether too many on Reclamation Projects and Gas Turbines. I have decided that henceforth I will assign research topics, on subjects I want to write about—such as Medieval Plagues, the Topography of the Coast of North Carolina, the Ku Klux Klan, Gunshot Wounds, the Undertaking Profession, etc. Now, though, all papers are graded, all grades ready to turn in, and only the Old English final (4 hrs. here) to look forward to. (Strangely enough I'm not worried, having made an A on the last test with only a few hours' study.) Near the end of the quarter I sort of gave up teaching and started making my students read Dr. Johnson,[123] the middle part of *Moby Dick*,[124] and Macaulay[125] as models; result—one fine sentence from a talented New York neurotic girl—"Anxious to dispatch his victim, the executioner laid several frenzied strokes upon that neck; each time the body moved in reply—testimony that it yet lived."

Edgar has already flown back to Atlanta for his Rhodes interview.

Winters, by the way, announced to his class today in what he called a "sermon," that I was the best student in it (that doesn't include Edgar of course), though none of my poems were yet "achieved."

Further, you may be pleased to know that your remarks, together with the ones in a recent letter from Paul, perfectly comprised the total of Winters' criticism of my Stevensish poem, plus a little Stern and Ramsey for good measure.[126] I was not altogether convinced by Winters; but I am by the amazing confluence of minds. The poem, if I ever think about it again, must be drastically done over.

Winters has lately been trying to interest the class in translating from the French, especially Heredia,[127] whom he says is simple. His advice in translating is to pick out the best lines in French, try to translate them as literally as possible, and then work out the other connective lines. Heredia's line "La nuit monte trop vite et ton espoir est vain," Winters rendered on the spur of the moment as "Night mounts too fast and thy hope is vain," the meter of which (as iambic pentameter, which he of course says should be used for the French alexandrine) we hastened to point out was faulty—a rare opportunity for us.

Minor triumphs, I know, but such is Stanford.

I have decided to go back to my novel. The same story as always, you know, the incest and revenge one. Though I have worked out more ironies, ambiguities, subtleties, symbols, and complexities of characters. And a more straightforward presentation. It goes very slow, but I am counting on the long holidays. (How long did 75 pages take you?) For one thing, I think I have solved some of the problems by making the narrator more intelligent. I think, like Jean, I will begin to keep a journal (especially since I caught her in the act of buying me one for Christmas). In it I can jot down all sorts of first sentences for chapters (beginnings always seem easy for me, but I can seldom or never get beyond the first paragraph); samples: "Grooversville is named after some of my dead kin, on mother's side"; "That summer I slept without a sheet, in the raw. The feather bed sank beneath me, the pillow got damp against my neck. There was mother's Jessamine under the window, and the smell of it thick as nigger perfume. My Grandfather Strowd built our house of green timbers and, if I drowsed, the creaking of those old timbers was enough to rouse me, or the refrigerator suddenly shutting off. Then I would listen, etc." (Such is the first chapter beginning); or "I looked out the window and saw my brother Will turn in at the gate. It was twilight, when the light seems to come welling up all around you, coming from nowhere, etc."; and several others at random. If you've got any suggestions about the story (if you remember it), or any tricks you learned in 75 pages, or any advice at all, please send it. I need it. By the way, the narrator works in town as the undertaker's assistant. I'm thinking of calling it *The Animated Dead*. But what do you think?

I understand from Paul that *Factotum* no. 2 is on the stands. Is your article in it?[128] Mr. W's comment on " ":[129] "They seem like an intelligent bunch." Don't blame me. I didn't show it to him.

Did you see Peter's story in the *New Yorker*?[130] It was one originally published in *Hika* years ago,[131] when he was an undergraduate. Funny thing, it sounded like a *New Yorker* story, not very good Peter. And also his story in *Harper's Bazaar*?[132] That's from his novelette.

I suppose we told you the Taylors' infant arrived. Christened Katherine Baird.

By the way, in case nobody's told you this either—Memorial Auditorium on the Stanford Campus, which has rainbow-colored panels of holy stories where the gargoyles ought to be on the outside, is dedicated in big letters "To God and Leland Stanford, Jr."

We've in the last few days just missed out on a couple of fine living places, so maybe luck's turning. We're trying to get out of our lease too; some student of mine's going to take it over. But we still so far are riding in the jeep; it's the rainy season, and at dawn when we set out the open back of the jeep is like a bucket, partly filled with the night's drippings. Horrible.

Jean's story is now at *Atlantic Monthly Firsts*. She calls it "The Correspondence World." A couple of people here—fellow instructors—whom we let read it thought she did not make her points clearly enough; Lord, isn't subtlety to be prized? I am very pleased with the story myself.

I'm reading *Middlemarch* these days, though nearly bogging down in the second volume.[133] It's a lot better than I'd expected though.

Afraid this has been a rambling and circumstantial report on trivia. But please reply notwithstanding.

And Merry Christmas from both of us

Don & Jean

Stern Papers, Regenstein Library, 32:13; TS.

December 27, 1948 | 1015 Forest Avenue | Palo Alto, Calif.

Dear Dick,

Your handwriting is getting as mysterious as Edgar's used to be, but the parts I could make out were as interesting as always.

Yes, we've moved. Ten minutes to town, half a block to the bus. Sub-let the old place. No more jeep rides. This is three large rooms, counting the bath, in the attic of a colossal old house (old for California), which the landlord says were always rooms but don't look it unless they were the servant's. Nevertheless, it's a grand place—slanting ceilings (we bump our heads) that make it look like a Greenwich Village arty apartment, but we hope to dispel some of that atmosphere with cheery fox-hunting prints (the red coats to match the rug and sofa). We are quite taken away with the whole place. Out the kitchen window (which is level with the floor of course) there's a view through some fantastic California tree of the house next door which is even older than this one and marvellously grotesque, baroque, and what have you, with picture windows actually tinted and dainty fluff curtains hanging in them that look like bloomers, also turrets, towers, flagpoles, knobs, mottoes, domes, and good luck charms. Quite a relief from these California ranch style flat houses made of redwood. Jean says it's the kind of house she wants us to buy. We'll give you one of the towers whenever you come to visit us.

This long vacation we sleep late in the mornings, go to bed late at night. The only thing I could ask for is some whiskey, which we don't have any of, and a few visitors, which we are expecting (though Jean doesn't want any of either). Trying to get Jean to work at writing is a full time job. You know she has written four stories in her life (three before we were married or met), and keeps going back to them to rework them; one that I thought she had given up for dead she took out today, read over, got me to read again, and dropped a hint that she was thinking of retouching it. She's even got me doing it. In the process of moving I came across half of a story I started this summer,[134] and having decided already to give up the novel again (more about this later—you must be tired of hearing about it, though, like Artie Shaw and his wives),[135] and further, wanting to have something to show Katherine Anne Porter to get admission into her class[136]—well, in short, I went to work on it. Maybe you've heard the story before, but you can't stop me if you have. The oldest son of a man in his sixties returns home to be present at the wedding of his father and his fourth wife, a young one, daughter of wife number 3 by a former marriage; this oldest son, Whitsun, is straight-laced, a salesman, lives in Cincinnati at a widow's boarding house with his brother Hen, who is feeble-minded and whom he takes care of; there are seven other children, all lusty and loose as is the father himself; Whitsun tries to stop the wedding, but the Old Man tells him the girl is pregnant, so Whitsun gets the girl alone and proposes to her himself (he's forty); she turns him down preferring the Old Man, who's pretty well-fixed, but that's not the main reason; then even Brother Hen, the moron, turns against Whitsun and decides to stay behind with his father and the others; and Whitsun goes back to his boarding-house up North, nearly convinced that all his previous standards are wrong. It'll be maybe fifty pages long; I have a rough draft of it down to the proposal scene, and ten pages polished. When I finish it, I'm going to start on one about a tongue-tied, dumb colored boy who lives with a very old colored man who's maybe his father, and when the old man dies, the boy is so dumb he does not realize the man is dead for days, and continues to sleep in the same cot with him. Rather Faulknerian, I know.

About the novel—reading George Eliot and Tolstoy I decided that a novel ought to be about a lot of people, about probably a whole community or family group at least, and cover some years and a good many more changes, and not have such a tight story as the one I conceived. My plot was more one for a novelette. (Why didn't you or somebody tell me before?) Besides, it got too tough for me to handle, absolutely impossible to convey all the things I saw in it in my clumsy open-handed style (I can't "weave" things in with imagery or "subterraneously"). I put this badly, but you'll know what I mean. And instead of doing things with words in fiction, I've decided you ought to do it with details, bits of action, behavior, illustrations, even Dickensian tags, and symbolic character description (Rough sample from Irving: Ichabod Crane looked like a crane, long, thin, etc.). James, for instance, in the *Turn of the Screw*[137] (a convenient but not too good illustration) instead of using words to say that the governess is sex crazy, as our popular novelists would do, has her see the children playing with a stick which fits into some sort of round hole; I'm afraid this is a terrible example of what I mean, it sounds so Freudian and Wm. York Tindallish,[138] and even Wilson comments on it.[139] But say, for instance, instead of Tolstoy just saying it in words, or thinking up imagery for it, he convinces you that Pierre wants to do good for man, but doesn't quite know how, by showing him joining the Freemasons.

I'm afraid that paragraph sounds like one of my lectures, completely disjointed.

I read *Nightwood* a long time ago in New York.[140] I started it in the midst of a narcotic fog—truly—due to my condition, for isn't it clumsy exposition and as slow as any Victorian beginning? I don't remember whether I finished it in a fog or not, but I didn't like it. Perhaps because the people didn't seem human, they didn't seem to do anything, and I was beginning to get tired of the same kind of people who were in my current circle and the same kind of attitude it seems to me the author herself, by sharing, becomes the dupe of. Anyway, what the hell happens in the last chapter (I begin to sound Rotarian), but I never did figure it out? Jean has a little story about this book which Eleanor she thinks it was told her: someone asked in the Gotham Book Mt. for a copy, and the witch in there replied something like, "Aren't you a little behind the times?" I know you won't mind my saying all this about it, and on your say-so, I'm going to look the book up again, even if it did make me sick at heart when I first read it. Peter, by the way, once had lunch with Djuna (same publisher or agent or something) in one of those sidewalk café places near Washington Square, and all he remembers of it is that she had the biggest hat he'd ever seen.

I guess I told you that Peter also had a story in *Harper's Bazaar*, not quite as disappointing as the one in the *New Yorker*, which I guess I told you also originally came out in *Hika* when he was a student there.[141]

Jean's been reading the first page of this letter and making snide comments, objecting to every word I say about her, and adding that I can't use the word "bloomers" in a letter.

By the way, I ordered a copy of one of Empson's books of poetry all the way from England, which I was going to give to you—ordered it way last spring but it never arrived.[142]

It's funny that you should translate Heredia. I can't remember whether I mentioned to you last time that Winters thinks he's the easiest and best to translate. I may try "Le Chevrier."[143] I can't tell whether yours is good as a translation, but it seems OK (at least) as a poem, though I don't particularly like "rich dark deep," and I've never understood how you could get away with such metrical liberties.

Even if Guerard is mean (and I can't imagine his having that much nerve) you must send us the novelette. I've never appeared in fiction before, and even if I'm uglier in it than you say, it would be quite flattering. I'm sure to think the whole thing's wonderful, if for no better reason than that (I hope I recognize me), and I'm sure there'll be a lot of better reasons. (I want to put Paul in a story sometime myself; he sent us a Christmas card with something on it about Christ; is he really going to become a rector? I'd put you into something, as a return favor—or slap—only I don't understand you. Maybe I don't understand Paul either, but at least I think I do, and that's what counts.) The title of your novelette sounds fine; the quotation apt and witty; your broad Harvard education will at least provide you something (meaning quotations) though I hope not a jargon to compare with that of every Columbia student I've ever met (excepting Ken, and nothing could spoil him, not even turning Red,[144] which all at once reminds me how mean I was to him one night last summer, and makes me feel guilty, though of course I feel guilty about more than one night last summer in New York and if I've not said I was sorry before I might as well now while I'm thinking of it).

For weeks now I've not thought of one line of poetry, only prose, which every now and then comes in sort of sick bursts as lines of poetry used to, sometimes a whole paragraph at once, and I feel silly rushing to write it down, though I used to feel childishly exalted rushing to write the poetry down years ago. This is not to be interpreted as my farewell to poetry, by the way.

As Keats would say, that word farewell reminds me that I've run on long enough.[145]

Write soon. Jean promised to write you some day soon (maybe that will break the "inflexible alternation") and in the meantime sends her love.

What kind of job are you going to get?

We haven't made up our minds yet where we're going next—still thinking of N.Y. though.

Don

Winters likes Ellen Glasgow,[146] but I think she's boring, especially in conversation. It goes like this: "Then you *will* come to my birthday party Tuesday?" Maybe Jean is right about Winters after all, she thinks he's "crazy."

Stern Papers, Regenstein Library, 38:4; TS.

CORRESPONDENCE OF 1949 TO 1950

January 17, 1949 | 1015 Forest Ave. | Palo Alto, Calif.

Dear Dick,

Just got yours today. I thought the Eliot poem—brace yourself—was something you'd tossed off as a postscript, till I saw the date. I can't make heads or tails of the Empson;[1] like the little girl said, "It's something about the wheels."[2] But I am as ever very fond of "This last pain for the damned the fathers found," or however it goes.[3]

If you've got an extra of the novelette, send it on anyway. It can't be as horrible as you make the minus imply. Only don't blame me if I misread it—maybe my criticisms would be good too for that reason. Besides, I'm nuts about drafts—not only is that the only thing I seem able to write (I just finished one for the Faulknerian story), but I even had my students turn in their rough drafts for one assignment, and you'd be surprised at the improvements they either made or faked. And I'm sure yours isn't rough anyway, but silky. By the way, I nearly choked on a swig of coffee from laughing at [the] Mann-Porter idea in reverse (probably a misreading too)—be sure to call the French woman novelist Madame Femme and the translator something like Cooley.[4] It could probably be wonderful; get down to work tonight, right after writing a reply to this. To hell with graduate school. I'm not taking any courses this quarter, why should you? I have Tuesday, Thursday, Saturday, and of course Sunday, off—or maybe I told you this before—and should get something done, though I can't compete with your terrifying speed.

A campmate of yours named Dick Simmons was camped in my office this morning when I came back from the faculty john. Seems a nice boy. Mentioned Larry.[5] Said he and Winters didn't get along; an old story out here. I told him I was disgusted with Stanford and wanted to go to Harvard because you made it sound so intellectual, and he implied that you wanted to come to Stanford etc. By the way, if you really do, you'd probably stand a better chance with a novelette (stories, or a novel) than with poetry because Winters is so pig-headed. Don't get me wrong: I am very fond of both Winters and your poetry, but habits are habits. Do I sound too much like a complete Relativist? Of course you could always get a job teaching here with a Harvard M.A., which would knock their provincial eyes out. But wouldn't it be nicer if we could all—you and I and Paul, for example—get a teaching job at some little college like Auburn in the South for next year? I just had that bright idea and must write it to Paul. Then we could really start a movement, though you know that isn't exactly what I mean. But out here I feel that I am—to misquote—dying in Egypt, dying, for lack of fellows.[6] Which reminds me that Edgar visited us the other night for the first time, bringing along six cans of "Eastern" beer for moral support. And to return to my train of thought—we certainly don't intend to stay out here, even if they would give us fellowships. Jean likes it better than I do—as I'm sure I've told you before—but neither of us is very ecstatic. Even the weather, as you've doubtless read in the papers, has been disappointing.

As soon as I polish my story I'll send you a copy. Title: "A Hopeless Case." Told from the point of view of the doctor who owns house and land on which the old colored man and boy work. (I've grown fond of de Maupassantish titles lately.) For the time being I've abandoned the "Desire under the Elms" story—I've never read that play, Dick.[7] Thinking of another—did I mention this before?—about a bastard from New Orleans, like *Gatsby* with none of the advantages, who loves the Agrarian ideas, settles in a small Southern town as a high-school teacher, and organizes the kiddies in Confederate pageants and later into marching clubs. That to be called (like the dead novel) *The Animated Dead*. Oh yes, the Whitsun story's title is "The Older Generation." What would Freud have to say—or you, for that matter—about this obsession with titles?

Speaking of Freud reminds me it's bedtime. (Jean just got into her pink Christmas pajamas and picked up the first page of this letter from the table to read—she always makes fun of my letters—of course I don't blame her, but ...)

Jean just pointed out that I'd better hasten to reassure you that I refer to dreams. Have you had any good ones lately. Jean wants to know. Yes, we heard from B. A.,[8] but nothing ever happens in Salisbury. Tell us more of Ken, and any other news about old friends you know.

And write soon.

Don

P.S. And watch out for those New England landladies.

Stern Papers, Regenstein Library 38:3; TS.

Sunday [January 1949] | [Cambridge, MA]

Dear Don and Jean,

My exams are all over and I've had a week to do all sorts of things and have
not even gone down to Cape Cod, let alone write about Madame Femme and
Mr. Cooley (the latter I will use thank you, though I did not visualize it as a
comedy till your swig of coffee). So you see, I don't even get *drafts* done. I
had wanted to write an essay for the Bowdoin Prize[9]—three hundred dollars
and prestige, prestige—all about modern writing as reaction to the age of
exposure and all, but I've been reading Kenneth Burke's[10] *Attitudes toward
History*[11] and I've decided I'm not even bright enough for the Bowdoin Prize
(incidentally, the reason Harry Levin[12] is Chairman of Comparative Lit. with
a B.A.; other winners: Peter Viereck—I think that thing on Metapolitiks, or
-ics[13]—and je crois Howard Baker, or is it Nemerov—and it may be both).
At any rate Burke is good, but I think he overawes more than he stimulates
me—and I keep thinking of what Einstein, though he's only a physicist, says
about reading too much. I did want to rework the novel also—all I've done
is to cut out some of the pustules—so I could send it to you. Well, I have
another week, though I'll probably go to New York—it's a nice drive and
some graduate history student has a wife who has a car and a home in N.Y.

Thank you for hosting Dick Simmons.[14] When he was smaller and chub-
bier he was a "great tackle and a punishing fighter."[15] It is so nice to hear him
talk about Winters and Edwin Arlington R.[16]

Oh yes, I did start a birthday-graduation ode to Larry (he's 21) but I quit
after: "Drifting under as well as farther, each piece / Of us that turns to island
panders coherence / To dissolution." And sent him Auden's *Collected Poems*.[17]

The Reanimated Dead sounds fine.[18] I was toying with the agrarian as a
female, but decided against it. I'm anxious to see both stories.

Titlitis[19] is a form of pantheism.

I'm not completely reassured about the dreams—your pen scratched
writing Jean's name—and 'pink Christmas pajamas' isn't in the Index to the
Interpretation of the same.

Empson says man's life cycle added to a beast's—or Immortal's—life cycle
was disbelieved by Lucretius and Johnson, and Iago didn't believe mixed
marriages could make a go of it either.[20] So, like Ixion, who wanted to make

himself immortal by marrying Juno, we are punished by mortality (because we have no beliefs because of Johnson and Lucretius and Iago, I suppose), but science is "overcoming" all this—Alexis Carrel's chicken heart culture outlived him and Darwin could intermarry mortal with immortal trees.[21] Also, Du Bartas, Bruce Barton, and Jonathan Edwards.[22] So courage: wheels within wheels.[23]

The idea, or was it only a joke, about teaching in the South—not Auburn, please,—is all right with me. Seriously. You pick it.

I too am keeping a journal, but then I used to do push-ups one autumn—every third morning.

I am reading *Walden* and then I remembered the Faculty-Student Literary Society and you presided at our Thoreau meeting.[24]

I too am "dying in Egypt." Though half the undergraduates read Gide[25] on the trains.

I saw *Symphonie Pastorale* again and liked it better.[26] It gets painfully explicit towards the end and raises issues which you're not prepared to answer but I imagine that's Gide's fault. The father-son mix-up on all counts is intricately handled and only needed a more imaginative camera (what Burke would do to this adjective)[27] to work in every way.

Peter's play is also intricately worked out and I liked it enormously well. I felt the need for violence somehow, but I think that was after, not during the reading. He can get too pat with characters though can't he? Even though that's the way they line up factually as well as symbolically. Any writer who's not a mystic must counteract mass symbolic patterns—I think Burke might say, or Paul—at least till he's shown he's not really using them.

This sort of stuff sounds nonsensical on this machine.

Levin gave me A- as did Rollins[28] the man who said on my analysis of "They flee from me"[29] that I put too much of myself—"in the manner of the Tate-Brooks-Empson crowd"—into the poem and not enough Wyatt. The idea is to get as many A's as B's for the PhD invitation. (The man who issues these conducted the Chaucer course by reading every line of *Troilus* in class and tracing the linguistic families. People are waiting to see what he does with *The Canterbury Tales*. These anticipations are the meat and potatoes of the graduate student's life.)

But this *is* the school which solicited these lines from a recent Nobel Prize winner.[30] [...]

Of course it's unfair but one should submit these to Winters: "A Promising Poet: the young Eliot."

I may ask you to write endorsements of my character and scholarship. There are all sorts of things to apply to—Swedish fellowships and so on.

I hope that I'll have something interesting to say next time and maybe another poem of Eliot's or one of the early novels of Henry James. Write on arrival.

Dick

What do they pay instructors with M.A.s from Harvard? and could one exist without marrying another bread-winner?

Private TS.

February 15, 1949 | 1055 Forest | Palo Alto [CA]

Dear Dick,

Happy Valentine.

I have been reading Shakespeare's sonnets and find they are not very good.[31] That is, not more than a dozen are first-rate poetry, though you can save lines and passages almost anywhere. And yet even the middling ones show so much more energy and sense than anybody else save Milton and Sidney in the sonnet (or maybe Wyatt, whom I don't know) that there is nobody else to imitate but him. So I have been trying for two days and have six lines, whereas I feel he would have had six sonnets in the same time. Trying the sonnet I feel more than ever that we are unlucky nowadays: we lack so much: not only three or four grand hackneyed subjects to extemporize on, but an approved manner, an available form, the second person familiar, and inversion. My favorite passage of the moment is that "beauty like a dial hand etc."[32] and my favorite sonnet No. 87 "Farewell thou are too dear for my possessing" (which I think must have been written to a woman and misplaced by Thorpe because of the wonderful but common dirty joke in the first line).[33] Here are my first three lines:

> Are you grown old in love, and double bent,
> To try me first, rather than quit me straight?
> Charging to me all you premeditate   (Line no. 4)

I am going to try to finish it so as to have something to enter in the $500 contest, though nobody has a chance against Edgar (who has written a good poem called "The Stoic," about some European lady remembering Berlin and Venice etc.).[34] Tell me if you think my lines are too old-fashioned, too obvious, or whatever. Is the sonnet possible?

I am also trying to work out the beginning of the story of the Agrarian. I have a forty-chapter plan roughed out, and a few pages smoothed. Again, as with the sonnet, I feel the need of a master (Stanford, perhaps the hierarchy, perhaps just being a student again, one of the sheep, has as you see broken down my confidence, or is it that we're getting old?); so I take Tolstoy, especially *Anna*,[35] which I may have told you I just finished. Taking steps backward here too, you see, into the past and its manners. The third-person point of view, the omniscient eye; and trying a little to break the scenic down toward the pictorial with some exposition, forthright analysis of motives and so on; without forgetting all the possibilities (that I know of) of what you (and Peter) call "poetic organization."

Maybe I told you I finished the story about the Negroes;[36] if I told you that I must have told you too that it sounded too Faulknerian to let anybody see. Well, Edgar saw it anyway, and liked it better than I did. (He's begun his war novel, a page or two that sound like—you'd never guess—a slightly brainier and sweeter Hemingway.) So I am sending it (unless I get cold feet in the meantime) on to you, knowing that it is horribly overwritten and derivative.

Edgar thinks the scene with the wife is weak; also got offended by the "grave" business on the last page; and didn't understand that the story is also a criticism of the doctor. You don't have to send it back. (But in exchange, I do hope you will send us your novelette; it can't be as embarrassing as this story; and we promise to send it back.)

In my classes I am getting book reports. They think the *Age of Innocence* is a satire; *Gatsby* silly; and *War and Peace* dull. I am so bored with the classes that I can keep from yawning no more than the students can.

We went to a party of English graduate students Friday night at which someone said homosexuality was the original sin, and another kept telling me that if I were in France I'd be a Communist; it ended with everybody else singing risqué songs on nothing but beer, and the president of the graduate club rolling up his shirt sleeves and saying, "Fellows, I won't object if any of you want to stay around and help us clean up." (He is reported to have said when nominated for the office: "Gee, fellows, I don't think I really deserve it.")

Winters won't be here next quarter and I will miss him. He was in an automobile accident the other day and currently has a scab on his nose from it.

Haven't seen Dick Simmons since the day he dropped by my office. Why?

Egad (I meant to type Edgar—figure it out) has been more friendly of late; came by for spaghetti here the other night and brought a bottle of wine; talked so long that the landlady had to ask him to leave.

Speaking of typographical errors, Paul made the best I've ever seen in his last letter. Don't tell him I said so. Examples: "If I can revive my poem in time, etc."; "I feel goffed tonight"; and in the poem about Christmas, in a very serious place, something about Where the holly etc., he typed "Weee the holly" xxx! He promised to send me that *Factotum* but it hasn't arrived yet.

Have you seen the dissection of K. Burke in *Scrutiny*?[37] And don't you think we could write better papers than the one that won the prize last summer at Kenyon?[38]

Maybe you don't think so after reading this stupid letter ("dumb" as Paul would say), but I can't understand how Edgar and Yvor ever managed to do anything decent here when I can't. I enclose some verse I wrote early last fall as further proof (I don't show it to just anybody but I thought you might think it funny).

The Royal Forest of Wolmer (After Gilbert White)

("Natural Observations at Selbourne, 1805"—In *Five Kinds of Writing*, ed. by Th. Morrison, which we use here as a freshman reader in imitation of Harvard.)[39]

Ferns nowadays scarce hide the sand.
Yet Anne once stopped a progress here
To feed hundreds of tame red deer
Out of her royal hand.

Still old men of a frosty night
Warm over steaming pints of ale
Each his own hoary sporting tale:
How this one tracked the flight

Of swollen-bellied hinds to where
The calf was dropped, and pared its feet
Down to the quick, returning there
Next season for the flesh grown sweet;

How that one, watching in his field
For wandering deer, once by the moon
Halfway confounded, fired too soon,
Laming his neighbor where he kneeled.

Now every royal stag and hind
Being gone, no longer can provoke
Mischief among the common folk:
They leave a waste behind.

I am going to write to some schools this week for jobs. If you are serious—and if any place sounds good—I'll tell you.

Wasn't *Hamlet* awful;[40] or am I being snobbish?

That's enough.

Write soon.

Don

Stern Papers, Regenstein Library 56:2; TS.

[February 1949] | [Cambridge MA]

Dear Jean and Don,

A fine package. I hope that it will be the first of a long series. I am taking the liberty you suggested of returning the story desecrated with "semi-instinctive" criticism. I like the story, and like it enough to repeat what Pound told Eliot about writing couplets, "Don't, unless you are going to parody Pope."[41] I am not Pound, and you are a descendent of Eliot's, but I feel that I must continually make reference to a Faulkner framework and that makes me uneasy. I'm sorry if this is irrelevant criticism: the story has its own problems and mechanics etc. and so many virtues that I resent my feelings about it. Most of the criticism is on the paper, negligible and unsure, but as to the doctor "scene," I think it would be interesting and virtuoistic if you could write the "same" doctor-guilty story by writing from the Negro's side, not of course in the first person, for that would be a Benjy story.[42]

The sonnet lines are good but the same thing applies. The sonnet is finished, Robinson, Tate, Cummings, and Ransom are the last voices. Thus speaks Max Zarathustra. Not finished, but it has to cool off, though I don't know Rilke's. There is *too* much tradition in it, like the sonata. I've never thought this before, so I retract it.

In the same mail with your letters, was your thesis, which I requisitioned on Inter-Library loan. I am writing on Ransom for Perry Miller[43] and I thought I'd have the last word. Despite your assertions, the thesis is perfect and I shall probably steal much from it, especially bibliography, tho Stallman's is pretty complete. Incidentally, Jarrell's criticism of Ransom is one of the finest critical articles I've read, don't you think so?[44] What I probably will do is trace the Blake-Yeats-Ransom tradition and show how it modified as science kept winning. I want to write it in a week so I can hand it in for the Bowdoin prize. This won't do anything but get it out of the way. I talked to Richard Ellmann the other day. I'm sure he's not as charming as Kathleen Norris,[45] but one can see how he bowled over Mrs. Yeats, Eliot, Valéry,[46] et al. I'm not sure that he's too good, but he's possible.

Guerard's book on Bridges is dedicated to Arthur Yvor Winters and I see the reason for Guerard's hamletness (very small "h").[47]

Paul wrote "I'm sending you some jung" but changed it to a "k" on revision, or reviving.

I guess Dick Simmons thought he was paying a courtesy call and that was all you were allowed with the faculty.

Winters is Winters because nobody takes his poetry seriously, which means his major premise, that the finest poets are the finest appraisers of life, undermines even his criticism. I think I'll retract this too.

Somebody around here has Auden's *Collected Poems* corrected by Auden. Swarthmore boys say he acted (wonderfully) the bishop in the *Ascent of F-6*,[48] that he replies "You know Goddamn well I am" to "Are you Wystan Hugh—." Etc. You know his version of the narcissus myth? One, Narcissus as N., two, narcissus as a hydrocephalic idiot who gazes at his image mumbling "On me it looks good," and three, narcissus as you and I who regard the image and question it with "Haven't we seen each other somewhere before?"

Burke Shipley's father is the Joseph T. S. who has poems in the *Fugitive*[49] ("which qualifies for the Nashville Prize," won by Laura Riding Gottschalk).[50] The Harvard copies are Merrill Moore's.[51]

Speaking of Burke, the "dissection" in *Scrutiny* convinces me that the magazine is over-rated. I just saw that Auden said that Burke was the best critic in America (a few years ago); that's enough me. Why I am staunch I don't know; I don't like some of *Philosophy of Literary Form*[52] and I've only read *Attitudes Towards History*, part of *Permanence and Change*[53] and some incidental stuff.

I sit in on Richards' course in the Humanities[54]—Plato, New Testament,

Old Testament, Dante, and *Troilus and Cressida*. A wonderful person. Looks like Andre Gide from where I sit.

I'm very serious about teaching next year, or at least pretty serious. If I don't get a fellowship in Europe I need a job, and it might as well be pleasant—or do you think they would hire more than one young instructor? I really would appreciate your leads; if there's any place you want me to query—.

I added a little to my three lines:

Drifting under as well as farther, each piece
Of us that turns to island coherence
To dissolution, widens the water and hides
The beach. So the burying sands are hid.
Brief the service over these bones.
    Space
Had mattered before we did, coloring up
To wet and sand. Now take space along your hand
And draw us both horizonless;
Fling us both beneath the bend, planes
That shift the flat world's sense, called away
Over the edge (Sides Columbus will never Plane.)
    Each piece of us another print,
Shot in the dark, shifting our edges.
    Macbeth
Killed his separations, one by one
And no return.
    Here's a story that's more
Than simple: the other night, found in your arms,
I felt the belly turn to the moon; watched,
Astronomer, the breasts to comets; knew,
Explorer, this was star-gap; died, a gnat,
You were heavens, my brain's pieces, ends.

I think I told you I saw Stravinsky lead Stravinsky, Jr. and the Boston Symphony in a fine Stravinsky program.[55] Also, glared at Clifford Odets during *The Big Knife*,[56] which re-written once would be a passable bit of second-class theater. The key line is something like "The most beautiful thing in American life is failure." In fifteen years that's going to sink one more level into the populace. The church membership is growing, probably because of industrialism, n'est c'est pas.

My metaphysical teacher, Wanning (he reviewed *Boston Adventure* for *Partisan* and is a nice fellow)[57] thought that "sensuous apprehension" of thought meant flowers and springtime and perfume.[58] Nevertheless, no class is taught without reference to the New Critics: nevertheless, this doesn't do much good.

We are getting old. I can vote now and don't deserve to.

Mary Sledge and Joe Allen[59] are going to get married when they can scare up rent-money.

How did Edgar make out on the Rhodes business? One student here had Ransom on his committee a few years ago.

Everybody from Auden to Richards sincerely bemoaned Theodore Spencer.[60] There was a fire at Kenyon the radio just said, one killed, thirteen injured.[61]

I can't fill the page. Write soon.

> Love & may Paul bless you,
> Dick

> Private TS.

> March 4, 1949 | 1055 Forest Ave | Palo Alto

Dear Dick,

Thanks for your flattering interest in my story. I may yet do it with such encouragement. I wish I had you here (or, better, me there) to talk about such matters. You know of course that I wrote it first (1 fourth of it anyway) from the Negroes' point of vantage (sample first sentence: "This boy was as slippery black as the peeled branch with which the old man was driving the cows homeward."), but decided against it because I thought I needed something I might as well call a perceiving intelligence, i.e., the doctor.

The first two lines of the sonnet became:

Must you show still more fair the more you're bent
To try my love, rather than quit me straight?

And then the legal gas ran out.[62] So the whole sonnet then became:

Are you grown old in love and near to dying,
That with so many old complaints to right
You will voice none, all care of self denying,
Indulging me past loss of appetite?
Has time that sours our best then sweetened you?
Ah, but deathbed repenters never mend
Till all's done, and a richer world's in view;
So your conversion promises an end.
Even this new-put-on habit of devotion
Hangs less on love than on mortality,
And time's your master, for you step his measure:
As once time flattered you, you flatter me
But to corrupt me at the last with pleasure,
Thus stealing from me with no hint of motion.

Titled: "A Lover's Complaint of Too Much Attention." Winters liked it, though an old maid in his class thought it was "cruel." Even so, you may be right. But if so, how are we to recover the ruins of the past? Not in Eliot's piecemeal quotation manner, pray.

Your letters always "stimulate" me, set me going. They evoke the East, which I long for. If the East is decadent, the West is primitive. Out here even Henry Miller is literate. Which reminds of a story of John Ransom's currently going the rounds. To wit: John B.[63] was asked by the editor of a Frisco newspaper book page to do an article on West Coast writers, so diligently wrote letters to everyone including Miller, who replied with a list of names and addresses of fabulous unknowns whom John "must look up to make his story complete," ending with some fantastic foreign name who he said was so courageous that the publishers wouldn't print him as yet—but they'd "soon get his scent."

Yes, Jarrell on Ransom is fine. I was more than pleased since—this will be immodest—he said what I meant to say and did say a little of in my thesis, though I was less articulate and not clever at all. And despite what you say about my thesis ("perfect" is an ambiguous word), it still is lousy, and damnably naïve.

Of course one of Winters' virtues is naiveté (I can't spell that word), even if he does know French poetry, and a little Spanish (both of which he reads well; Edgar backs me up on this, for I wouldn't know on my own). Perhaps it's "the primitive West." Example: after he read my sonnet I asked him if he didn't object to the puns, and he countered, "What puns?" I pointed one out: he said: "Don't you think that's rather subtle?" So, smiling, he had me. By the way, I'm sure I've told you how magnificently he reads poetry in his false basso. If Harvard library has the Library of Congress recordings of him reading his own poems, you might be interested in hearing them; I haven't heard them, but they ought to sound grand, for he can make even Wordsworth's sonnet rhythms sound very moving indeed (on which sonnets he is very amusing, by the way, and the old maids sit gaping while he calls "like a nun / Breathless with adoration" trite.)[64]

Certainly *Scrutiny* is overrated. They are always harping on the necessity for standards (good in itself, but embarrassing) very primly, meanwhile writing in the most awful jargon, and getting as hazy as Babbitt[65] does when they come to defining what they mean (or as hazy as I get in class on the same points). I meant nothing by what I said on Burke but to call your attention to the article. Burke and Empson are both about as illuminating and full of insights as you can get, and Burke's style less hypertrophied, his counterwords not very maddening and clearer than some of Winters', and what I take to be his Marxism not particularly obtrusive. *The Philosophy of Literary Form* and *Grammar of Motives*[66] are, for me, by and large impossible. But my respect for him shot up tremendously yesterday when I saw Stallman's new anthology[67] with a couple of things from *Counterstatement*, I believe, the ones where he talks about the "psychology of the hero and the audience" and "qualitative progression etc.," both of which Winters has obviously read carefully.[68] I was rather excited by these two pieces myself. Have you ever tried his "novel"?[69] I have used it in my freshman classes to illustrate all the devices of 18th-cent. prose rhetoric, for which it is even more convenient than Dr. Johnson.

Your howler on Paul is the best yet; should we do a catalog?

Edgar didn't get the Rhodes; I thought I'd told you. His story (he has become consciously amusing, and a great talker) is that one of the board asked what he thought of R. P. Tris Coffin,[70] and Edgar was of course honest.

I read Richards on *Troilus* in the *Hudson* with pleasure;[71] it must be taken from the same course lectures or something of the sort. By the way, isn't *Hudson* annoying? The godawful poetry they print; and then never identifying their contributors, or where their selections come from (as in the case of Richards, and even worse, the selection from *Dr. Faustus*, I presume). Though Tate on Longinus showed that he hadn't lost his touch:[72] were you as pleased as I was that Tate remarked on the sameness of Winters' and Ransom's theories, which neither would confess?

As to teaching, I still haven't got around to mailing off any letters, except some to Miami asking if I can teach there one of the summer terms. But I have my form letter prepared, and am going to send it this very day to Auburn, Rollins, Florida Southern, and Emory. Have you any other suggestions? I'd like very much for you to try these places too, if you feel like it; then if we both got offers from the same place, everything would be set.

As for your poem, I am running out of paper, but would like to say that the rhythms are very interesting, rather impressive, and so is (a fresh start after all)—the language, for the most part, but I can't make out much of what the poem is about, and that's either your or my fault (of course I've only read it three times). It sounds, naturally, a little like Empson as you must know: Iago and his gennets?[73] There is probably too much wit in it, if that is possible. Most of the lines by themselves are moving, and I can make out some of the connections, but it still remains as a whole incomprehensible to me. I'll try it some more, though.

I also read the first part of Joseph Frank on "Space in Fiction" in Stallman's anthology;[74] as I remember, Lubbock points out very similar things about Tolstoy as Frank does about Proust, though Lubbock doesn't invent any fancy terms.

I am at work on my short novel, but it's nothing I can dash off. Nevertheless, I am much engaged with the idea, interested in the problems, and am still trying to solve them with the aid of my Tolstoy practically open beside me.

The quarter here is almost over; I'll have about two weeks of worktime free then and hope to be able to send you some results.

Keep us posted.

> Jean sends her love, having
> dreamed about you last night
> Don

Stern Papers, Regenstein Library 38:3; TS.

In the spring of 1949, frustrated by the burdens of his assistanceship at Stanford, Justice decided not to complete his PhD. The Justices left for the University of Miami, where for the next two years Donald taught and Jean worked in the campus library.

As Justice was leaving Stanford, Stern was completing his master's and preparing to teach abroad on a Fulbright scholarship. He taught for one year at College Jules Ferry in Versailles, and for another year at Heidelberg University.

Tuesday [May 1949] | [Cambridge MA]

Dear Don and Jean,

I can't read another word of "The Prelude"[75]—if any of its sixteen good lines sneaks herein I still apologize. I can maintain a psychic distance from the examination atmosphere anyway, though everybody's mouth shows sign of much biting and all the world is felt to depend on the unread pages. This is what Harvard calls the reading period—the undergraduates come back from Bermuda, the libraries are crowded, the Radcliffe girls disappear, the prizes are distributed. I made out mixedly in the last: "Ransom"[76] took second in

the Humanities division to an analysis of the Thanatos painter and his connection with Greek Vase decoration. This has left me with a certificate and
an offer of an assistantship. The latter I can turn down as the French govern-
ment has been successfully lied to about my knowledge of their language and
customs and I've been assigned to one College moderne Jules Ferry, a junior
college for jeunes filles at Versailles. It was the nicest assignment I believe
and everything seems alright. I get about twenty thousand francs a month
and will not bother to find out how much this really is until two weeks before I
sail (tourist on the Queen Mary, Sept. 14). I plan a modern illustrated version
of the *Sentimental Journey*.[77] The announcement said that assistants have
found it profitable to take along American folk music etc. The impression
given is that I am the representative of American civilization and one of the
two courses will be something like chattering to the jeunes filles about the
intimacies of American life. This does not faze me as much as the elementary
anglais; I've already purchased a cowboy hat and whaler's shoes.

I'm surprised at Warren, and at Bogan, and Swallow, too. William
Abrahams[78] is not only the perpetrator but the victim of miserable
poetry—(Dunstan Thompson, or somebody's elegy,[79] which Oscar Williams
prints in six of his eight anthologies, is dedicated to him). I remember Trimpi's
poem with brief disfavor. Phare Young[80] is out of my range. Maybe they didn't
read the poems. The story makes up for it all and more. Congratulations . . .
and for the Stegner legend[81] also. (The twenty bucks I don't need—better save
it in case I can't remember the word for food and have to eat at the Ritz—it
was poker money anyway and the luck I had that night was sufficient grace.)

I would like to get down to Miami more than anything but I'm pretty sure
I won't. If I do it might be between June 20 and 30—OK? My exams are over
the fifteenth and I have to be back at summer school (I'm taking German—at
Har.) the fifteenth of July. Maybe I can get a lift down with someone.

My landlady has been yelling about a Siamese cat thirty feet in a tree which
she wants since nobody has claimed it and it's worth a hundred dollars and
has asked me if I know how to climb trees. The tree is in the center of five or
six houses and there's an ambitious eye at every window. The cat is really
beautiful—bigger than that one of Dr. Cotten's[82] and black and white (or is
that the definition of Siamese).

I went sailing Sunday for the first time. It's the thing up here. It was at Marblehead and the boat for six of us was a "Marconi sloop." I surrendered my coat to one of the Wellesley girls and froze as a true agrarian. This was one of my rare social moments. We later saw *The Tempest*,[83] put on by the only intelligent acting group I've seen—the Harvard workshop. The only negligible work was Ferdinand who it turned out was Miles Morgan, grandson of J. P. Less deficient was Nancy Ryan, granddaughter of Thomas Fortune R.[84] who was Ceres, I believe. They burlesqued the masque, which was an error; outside of all this, it was very exciting.

What's *The Good Soldier*?[85] It sounds a great deal more congenial at Stanford as far as "fellow sufferers" go. There is an Emersonian pluralism at Harvard which is professionally tender to all attitudes and congenial only to one—however, I'm still in the limen, which Johnson,[86] an extremely nice instructor of mine, says is two years. He and his three thousand volumes go to N.Y.U. in the fall. I'll try and get him Ken's apartment as he's going to join Burke Shipley at Kansas. Ken wrote that Burke received a letter from T. S. Eliot saying that his thesis sounded "rather interesting."

Apparently teaching jobs are hard to get. Some bright light here, a lesser version of Mumford Jones,[87] is going to Hawaii for five years. Jones "wondered" if I was too busy to check a proof for him. I told him I was on my way to the lavatory if he'd like me to check it down there and he said he'd get someone else to do it no thanks—seems to be a nasty habit of his. I'm going to carry a copy of *Reason and Madness* around him. These miserable attacks are just what eat him away.[88] He solicits the destructive impulses.

Sounds from here as if Paul will marry Mary Lee (I don't know the rest of her name).[89] I think marriage will have a "perceptible and beneficial"[90] influence.

I played the greatest game of tennis in my career yesterday. You'd better not trifle with me if we clash in Miami.

> au revoir et a bientot,
>
> Dick

If I write a thesis it will be "Literature as Scourge."

Private MS.

c/o von Braun | Weherstrasse 13 Heidelberg | [February 1950]

Dear Don and Jean,

Have carried your letters since they came, but with rushing and preparations and my typewriter stuck at Saarbruchen for want of a trunk key have not given vent to what was a desire to respond immediately about the stories, Gay, plans etc.[91]

"Hope Springs'" beginning is out of the great comic literature of the world.[92] I'll go right on to the novel beginning. I'm beginning to stereotype my reactions to the Proustianism narrative of the southerners (grr) and may not be a fair judge. Really, Don, I think it is too easy now and very dangerous for the writer. You have so very much that lives (as far as the *mere* writing) on precision; *so* much of that was *glowering darkness*, or was it glimmering? And it hurts me to read the line about the recoverable past in that sentence (tho certainly recoverable rescued a little). I'd love to see the Tolstoi version. "Hope Springs," however, was so good that I tore up most of what I had written on my story. There's no use working until you can get something like that.

The picture of you is wonderful. The French won't resist a minute, même with the pidgin effects (every American talks pidgin French, I mean everywhere.).

I didn't get the assistantship here. Mr. McHealy[93] of Dublin is staying another semester. I went shopping & found a probable job doing something analyzing reports for the State Dept. Anyway, it's $4000 a yr. plus an apartment (maid service), so if it comes thru it'll be wonderful. Meanwhile there are teaching & secretary jobs for Gay (at $50 a week). (You live well on $100 a month. There's no doubt that you all can find something when you're ready to come here.) I'll work nights learning German & hunting for a PhD at the university here. I "sent for" Gay to come over at the end of the month and if all goes well we should be married within a month, either here or in Paris. Can't you come?[94] [Absolutely no present—now. You can buy us a dinner in Toulouse. I hope to have a car & we'll pick you up Christmas & go to Italy—the 5 of us. Tell Edgar to come see us here first.][95]

What can fill the parentheses? It's Gay (a family name—her first one's really Ruth) Clark from Darien, Conn., 17 months older than I am (so you should feel adjusted now), a sociology graduate from Wheaton College in

Mass., New England family undistinguished by anything but going to Yale, father's in the power & light or gas & electricity business, she's written poetry, but not really, and is just learning to read; she's very sweet & I do love her, so what more's sayable.

Maybe we'll have enough money to start a magazine—exactly like *Criterion*, except less crap in it. Do you think it's feasible? I only have you two & Edgar as contributors plus some dubious French, German & Italian lads (Transl. on the right hand side). Maybe a theater. All around things seem so loose. Call me Thelma—[96]

We can evacuate through Basel.

Please tell Norma Hello and include her in this communiqué. Tell her even if she owes me a letter from months, I'll break down and write her as soon as my typewriter comes.

Told Paul if I came home I'd see him in N.Y. Also told him to go see Gay. Whyn't you drop her a card & say hello 19 Oakshade Ave—Darien, Conn.—she's lovely—if you go to N.Y. & she's still there, Darien's right outside.

Is there anything *I* have to do to officialize marriage, anybody I must tell or are there banns to publish & what not.

At any rate I must write mein aunts und jetzt.[97]

So meine lieben kinde[98]—forgive this hieroglyph and write.

                                        Dick

Private MS.

                                        May 1 [1950] | [Miami]

Dear Dick,

It's been really awful of us not to have written for so long, especially to an expatriate, and especially to such a faithful sender of appreciated postcards. The catalogue of my mental tribulations since my last letter to you would be too tedious and the tribulations themselves too nebulous to amount to much. But I'll run through a few of the physical trials I've suffered, for your amusement. Coming home from a couple of hot sets of tennis one afternoon and being naturally overpowered by an unquenchable thirst, I consumed all the cokes in the house and then decided to open a can of peach nectar. I was so tired I couldn't make it to the drawer where the silver was kept; instead I reached to the top of the icebox for the icepick. You know what happened: I plunged the icepick through my thumb, all the way through, the point coming out of the nail. After recovering from that, I took up tennis again, playing nearly every afternoon. And every time I played I took a spill. I split two fingers on clay, the other thumb and both knees on asphalt. And still I played; in fact, I am typing this in tennis shorts and shoes (summer being quite early this year, here) while waiting for somebody to come by and play tennis with me. All this, not to mention the worst cold I've had for seasons, which is just now leaving me, and leaving me with a rather annoying cough. And then there's chess. I play fourth board on the Coconut Grove Chess Club, which is currently in third place in the city league, a pretty fast league which numbers among its players the state champion. Naturally chess takes some study. Then there are the races. I was just about getting a system worked out when the tracks closed and the horses were shipped north. Naturally that took study and time too. In short, I haven't done much writing.

But I've had some good luck. Herschel Brickell[99] is putting my story into his annual collection—you know O. Henry Prize Stories.[100] Apparently there's no money in it except possible but doubtless improbable royalties, and a chance at the prizes, not a very good one I suppose. But there are other things—it should make future sales easier, and it should interest publishers, etc. Of course I can be wrong.

I spoke to Halstead, the head of the English department,[101] today about getting the raise I'd been promised. I got a two-hundred dollar raise, but had been assured of another hundred. He passed the buck, and apparently with good cause. But I'm mad. In fact, I'm actively speculating on quitting, not even trying to get a job elsewhere next year, but just going to New York (where it's cheap to live if you know how, and where jobs are always available if the going gets too rough) there to settle down to writing. Jean is almost convinced. The time seems ripe: all I need to make ends meet would be a fellowship or working agreement with some publisher. And Houghton Mifflin and Little & Brown have both written me about the story, both faintly routine but also very flattering agents. Nothing I'd like better. Of course our minds aren't made up, but we're toying with the idea.

I asked Halstead, by the way, if they were hiring anyone new (since there's been a lot of bad blood about budgetary cuts, etc.), and he said they were hiring one person on a one-year basis, but didn't mention that it was you and I didn't somehow feel that that was the particularly fitting moment to ask, since I'd just been mildly fussing with him anyway. They are, by the way, letting four people go, and quite a few people are up in arms. The university, you see, continues to spend its money on buildings and artificial lakes rather than on teachers or books, and several departments have been on "emergency" bases for as many as five years now, with no relief in sight. So it may be a good idea for me to get out while the getting is good, and for you not to get in at all.

But anyway, what are your plans for the immediate future? Will we see you this summer, next fall, when? Write soon, and tell us all the news.

About your story. I haven't sent it out any place. I didn't feel like typing it up again. And besides—I do think you ought to be able to sell it, make more money out of it than you could in its present state. Why don't you wait till we get together and let us go over in concert?

Last time we heard from Paul he said he might come down and see us some weekend (by air), but we haven't seen hide or hair of him. Edgar inquires after you, and doesn't know what his plans will be for the future.

Saw *City Lights*[102] yesterday. Much moved by last scene—of recognition—but felt the passions were being exploited at the expense of the reason, since the fable and its meaning were too pat. A first-rate writer, for instance, would never try or be able to get away with anything like that.

Don

[September 1950] | 1829 N.W. 46th St. | [Miami]

Dear Dick and Gay,

I don't know how it's happened that we've waited so long to write—particularly when we are so anxious to offer you our congratulations and good wishes . . . We wish we could deliver them in person. We were certainly delighted with the news . . . got the announcement a couple of days after your letter.

We had a pleasant visit in North Carolina; we were in Hillsboro for nearly a week, and at Norwood for the rest of the time . . . got over to Chapel Hill on two occasions, but didn't see anybody we knew well except Nat Macon and Bill Thomas and his wife Sara Tillett[103] (he has gained some weight and she, some nervousness) and that old habitué of Danziger's you probably don't remember, Walter Campbell.[104] Everybody has a Fulbright; Nat, one to Holland, Monte Howell,[105] to somewhere. Had a disagreeable interview with Ab,[106] who told Peter that he had sold five copies of *A Woman of Means*[107] but that *A Woman of Property* had sold very well . . . Hillsboro is lovely. Peter and Eleanor made us go see all the old houses . . . one of them impressed me especially, an old place nobody has lived in for years—the owner won't sell—in a Faulknerian state of disrepair, with ivy all the way to the tops of the tallest trees, and some old carriages, one a closed carriage, still sitting out in an outbuilding. Their place is not that romantic-looking but is big and attractive and old enough to make us envious. We were even more envious when Peter revealed that he had got 3,000 for his last *N.Yorker* story. Ho-hum. (My brother James, who is at home most of the time now, between brief stays at Yaddo—he is always loaded with savory and unsavory lit. gossip these days—has been getting a thousand each but still complains bitterly.) These statistics have an unholy fascination for me; in view of them, of our penniless state, and what seems to be, alas, a natural aptitude for the job, I have tried turning out tales for the women's magazines. Probably I shall be relieved if none of them sells. It only took two and three days to write them anyway; I just hope that, if one does by chance sell, nobody tells me it's my forte.

The Zwerins are fine . . . Norma started an epithalamion for you back in the summer but gave it up . . . Don and Mike have been playing tennis . . . They are beginning to worry about the draft. The latest bulletin says all non-veterans under 26, regardless of wives, families, etc., are next. Don is looking anxiously at his osteomyelitis scars.[108]

We still feel pretty hopeful about coming over in February, though. Latest word from Edgar is that he still expects to sail in late September. We were going to stay in N.C. till he got home from Stanford in Sept. and drop by to see him . . . but we ran out of money . . . Which reminds me that I forgot to say we had a visit from Paul at Norwood—two days. He and Don disagree more than ever . . . We were glad to see him, of course. We went up to Salisbury to see Betty Anne, and Paul went back to see her after he left us—with the utmost secrecy, for some reason. (I mean, he didn't tell us he was going, and didn't mention it in his letter afterwards.)

Florida is fairly nice right now—the season of avocadoes and hurricanes. The hurricanes have unfortunately been skirting us, but it has at least been raining.

In glancing over such publications as *Redbook, Cosmopolitan* (to see what they're buying) I came across dozens of stories by one Richard Stern[109] . . . Also several by Don Stanford, one of Winters' old pupils—I assume it's the same one—and we also saw a murder mystery by him, to our surprise.[110]

If we do get to come over in February, Gay, I will write you a lot of questions about what one needs . . . I guess it's impossible to get a place where one can cook?

Don is writing too, so I'll leave the rest of the news, if there is any, to him. Mr. and Mrs. Justice send their best wishes along with ours.

Love,

Jean

September the Somethingth [1950] | Miami

Jean's letter seems to cover the subject, but I'll add my congratulations and best wishes and whatever random words occur to me.

Are you going to have to worry about the draft, or does working for the State Dept. exempt you, Dick? Here, all my 4-F friends from the last war are being called for examination. One of them—my chess partner—got out after his psychiatrist phoned the board, or whatever it is you phone. But he told me there wasn't any doctor on hand to examine eyes and ears—I don't know whether to believe this, since I think I've heard such a doctor is required by law—but anyway, some sergeant simply wrote down about his eyes—and mind you, he wears the thickest glass I ever saw—vision, 24-100, without even asking him to read the chart that I don't think was there either, or at least my friend didn't see it. Now his eyes are officially 20-1000, so you can see he was scared. So the stories go. Another—Eugene Rosenbloom,[111] who was psychotic or something in the last war—was asked by the psychiatrist, Are you religious? to which he replied, Jesus saves. But that's only his story. However, they have just accepted one of my parents' renters who was 4-F last time. So . . . We will be in France if the Santa Clara County Draft Board has misplaced my registration and if the Russian sub misses our ship, etc.

My story, I'm sorry to say, has gone the way of your novelettes. It is not to be read by strangers. It missed fire, that's all, and I'm pretty sick of it right now. Maybe, if we do cross, I'll bring it along and beg your help, but for the time being I'm trying to forget it.

Instead, I've been back at writing poetry. And sending it around. So far I've collected two notes from Karl Shapiro[112] at *Poetry Magazine* and one from Arthur Mizener at *Furioso*.[113] But no money. I still have about seven or eight out. *Partisan* mailed a few back with the plain rejection slip, but strangely enough, this rejection slip was not in my poems at all but in two written by a chap named—yes, you guessed it, Paul Engle. They weren't such bad poems either, considering the corn he has written.[114] And considering the crap *Partisan* prints. I'm at work on one now that I think will turn out to be fairly long. Since I've run out of other news, I suppose I might as well fill up the rest of the page (and maybe more) with samples.

From "*John Manley Stewart, Bachelor*"
(the long one, still roughish in spots, no?)

An old maid and a bachelor could smile
At other couples tangled hand and foot
In passion's knot, and legal ones to boot:

Bloodlines were stouter still.
Nor had we ever wished them looser tied
    Until the night she died. (Something has to be done with this line)
Although I spooned out half a pint of rum,
    And propped her in my arm,
And heaped on blankets in a foot-high pile,
And covered her myself in my despair,
Even my body could not keep hers warm.
And yet that coolness was the first to come
    Between myself and her.

∾

(A later stanza)
Now everything has fallen on my hands.
Too many apples, figs, peaches and grapes
Are ripening but to shrivel—let them fall;
Too many flowers, and with too sweet a scent,
Stars, dials, initials (Sister's doing)—most
Of these the weeds shall have, or else the frost.
There are too many fields to cultivate.
    Better it is to rent,
And better yet to sell, and best of all
To give, give all away. These timber-lands,
Marshes and streams—at my death let the state
Assume their burden, as my only heir,
And institute a wildlife refuge there. Etc.[115]

(And here's a revision of an old one you may remember—there's a second stanza, but I think I'll leave it off when I send it out again)

On A Shipload of Catholic Emigrants Which Perished Off the Eastern Shore

One day the sun looked down through cloud and mist;
Thereafter, looked on our small ship no more.

The sea which bore us in
Its open palm was closing up its fist.
And have you seen knots, being wet, resist
Unravelling? Learn how our hearts shrank then.
Pray all who can that we may sink no lower.[116]

An Oriental on His Deathbed

Who wouldn't grumble to have come so far,
Merely to spill perfumery on the straw?
What got us out of bed, at our age, pray?
That something which we saw, or thought we saw?
Sleepwalkers we, and had been many a day;
Old men, gone wild with gazing on a star.[117]

Epigram on the Wise Men

The wisest men of Christendom were lit
Their way upstairs by a celestial candle. (I know you don't like these two lines)
Fallen belowstairs in a dozing fit,
We late-arrivals dream that birth a scandal.

(I don't know if you ever saw my sonnets on the devil: Paul[118] hadn't, so here
they are.)[119]

A dwarfish, pious, country kind of fool,
Much too big-hearted to be any use
Around the house, half cherishing abuse
For breaking every little household rule,
That servant, who cracked forty plates a day,
Out of anxiety to serve, no doubt,
Never again will follow us about:
Just as the preacher warned, he's run away.
Dull and unclean enough he was, but still,
Not one of us had ever wished him ill.

Why, we had flowered to manhood in his care,
So used to him at last we'd stroke his hair!
He seemed in his own stubborn way above
Our wrath and God's, yet could not bear such love.

Who is it snarls our plow lines, wastes our fields,
Unbaits our hooks, and fishes out our streams?
Who leads our hunts to where the good earth yields
To marshlands, and we sink, but no one screams?
Who taught our children where the harlot lives?
They gnaw her nipples and they drain her pap
Clapping their little hands like primitives
With droll abandon, bouncing on her lap.
Our wives may adore him; us he bores to tears.
Who cares when to our dry and yellowing grass
He strikes a match or two, then disappears?
It's only the devil, on his flop-eared ass—
A beast too delicate to bear him well—
Come plodding by us on his way to hell.

Don

Stern Papers, Regenstein Library 38:4; TS.

Tuesday 12 [September 1950] | [Paris]

Dear Don and Jean,

We thank you both for the congratulations. I won't be more effusive till Toulouse or Heidelberg. I will tell you that the happy reason for our revealing the marriage earlier in the year was that we learned Gay was going—is going—to have a child either in the beginning of February or late in January.[120] We are now quite excitedly hunting down cradles and cribs and diapers and, at the moment, place to stay after Oct. 1 as Dr. Waly[121] has decided there will be no war for awhile and he can come out of the cave in Spain. It's too bad for it was a lovely place with a view. Over the river, over the old bridge, opposite the castle (Hemingway's new title)[122] and a corner touching sunsets at Mannheim (all this can be found in *Boston Adventure*). We need a room and a kitchenette. I hope we'll get them for under $30 a month. It shouldn't be too difficult.

We didn't buy a car for economy. We have a friend with a little Fiat station-wagon ($500), which is in my name as I get gasoline cheaper, but we don't get much use of it. With a baby it'll be better to make our trips by train if there aren't too many side ones. We figure next Sept. (if I save my leave, I get about 5 weeks) for Italy, southern Germany and back through France. We hope you'll share it with us. If you astound us by selling something to *Redbook*, Jean, perhaps you'll have an American car. It's worth the extra money probably. I think writing for their things is just as difficult as anything else. Unfortunately nobody has ever mis-mailed one of Richard Stern's checks to me.

Since the last letter, the job at the University has arrived. With the salary I shall be able to buy 2 of Dr. Booker's old collars and little else.[123] It will mean three hours a week on Poetry and Fiction, or as you like it. This compensates slightly for my grotesque non-State Dept. job with the staff message control. It's the army and I'm afraid there's no exemption here, nor will be if I ever land the job which I first anticipated, not, as I thought, with the State D., but with again the army. I receive about $3000 a year and it will cost us about $1700, I imagine, to live—perhaps much less. Next year I'll try and get a job in Rome and maybe we'll save enough money to get home and do a PhD.

All this of course is shadowed by your ominous bits about the draft board. I don't know whether that "institutionalized discomfort," as Paul Sherry says,[124] would be better or worse with the war. This last, however, affects me surprisingly much. I've dreamed about it six or seven times, great looming heads of Stalin blistered with columns from *Time* magazine. I wake up very angry and want to bayonet Henry Luce.[125] I think he's as good as any.

It's difficult to believe your story went the way of my scraps. I'm positive that it's retrievable. I should love to read it one way or the other.

It was nice seeing some good verse too. That Ransomian "John Manly Stewart, Bachelor" (incidentally, I never saw John Ransom[126]—he sent a

Cézanne post card inviting me for a drink but he sounded quite engaged by Parisian bachelor life, and though I should have liked to meet him I never went) I like very immediately—the stanza (have I seen it before) is pleasant in an obliquely balladic way and with the exception of "until the night she died" and the patness of the "wildlife refuge" line (and its rhythmic jerk—the way I read wildlife is spondaic) it looks like a real meaty narrative. The Yeatsian journal of the Magi "Oriental on His Deathbed" and "The Epigram," especially the first, are more pleasing than the sinking Catholic emigrants. The Audenesque sonnets on the devil (excuse their allusive but not condemnatory vice) are not exactly to my taste but, except for the questions which begin number two, are very useful verse and pretty exciting in the last six lines of the second.

Here are two old lines of mine which creep in anything I try, "The glands have wishes which puzzle our virtues / This though they feed them and club their malingering." Outside of this my activity is rather restricted. Temporary reason is reading dutifully such things as Parrington[127] and *Silas Lapham*[128] (which is worth reading) for my courses.

Paul's poetry is really no better; in fact, he's become only manneristic and sluggish. Nobody should read Allen Tate at 17 (though you did I think), let's say nobody from Chattanooga ought to. He was quite impressed at James Ross' playing professional ball and having Allen Tate as a return address.

The *New Yorker* must sell a lot of copies to pay Peter 3000 for a story. I thought it was a quality sheet.

Poor Mr. Rayford[129] just told me about a little German boy coming to him on the street yesterday with a pointed finger crying to his mother "Look, look a schwartzes Nigger." Mr. Rayford says he'd rather die than go back to Virginia and he calls Heidelberg "little Georgia." He has a German girl named Ruth Schmidt in Frankfurt and in spring he's going to drive the whole family over Germany in his 1950 Chevrolet.

We learned that the room we'll be leaving in two weeks was the library of a Rektor of the University (in about 1885). The students, said his granddaughter sadly, used to march up with torches on horseback singing "Alt Heidelberg" and "Gaudeamus Igitur." The room is stuffed, with hollow heads of Venus de Medici and wooden statues with misplaced parts. We'll be sorry to leave it.

Perhaps Gay can write a page when I take this to her to mail.[130] Write soon and don't get drafted, either of you.

Dick

(I'm playing in a Tennis Tournament this week too. Perhaps I can break a leg or do they examine you sitting down now.)

Private MS.

CORRESPONDENCE OF 1951 TO 1952

Dear Don and Jean,

Two ways to go about jobs here, the first being, I'm told, slow and unsure, namely writing to personnel depts in Washington. The second is to make direct contacts here either personally or by letter. The first nearly always works but I imagine the latter could be just as effective. For jobs in education, write Mr. Egbert Hunter, 7700 T.I. and E. Group, APO 757. (No German needed.) Posts are education "advisors" which involve setting up centers for the army and administering them—three years' experience required-teaching—. However, even I squeezed out three years. As for State Dept, one might write to Personnel, Hicog Frankfurt, APO 757 and see what possibilities are open anywhere in the "theater." If the unexpected happens and neither bears fruit, I'll look around. You, of course, should get the fellowship.[1] Didn't know it involved no "labor but writing."

I suppose you are a sort of "nihilist" as you put it. I'm surprised at Paul's facile despair, however.[2] (Despite the tone of the Magi poem,[3] I could say you're not particularly concerned with "beliefs," which is where all of us are more or less, despite Edgar's churchgoing—Paul is exempt, naturally[4]—and sweater-swaggering. Of course, we do believe without question of rightly or wrongly in the no discussion policy (which is post silver age Rome I believe). However, being anecdotalists, or nihilists, or pre-Christians (these talk tho) leaves us with such little tonal range; but again one can only accept this and perhaps, with slight violation of accepted aristocratic policy, state it. I wonder if it is this position which makes us such limited derivativists—. No, that's not so—humanism seems assuredly worse. But the absence of a Gide chez nous is interesting if important or not. As for the poems in the book,[5] I enjoy them greatly as you know. And the skill of the blank verse, also, tho you present the original edition in footnote. I don't think one would do this through a verse play with much success, however. There William C. Williams has a case.

Have just finished a short tour of Belgium and Holland. The Rembrandt, Vermeer, et al, with cities like Bruges and Delft made it very exciting and lovely. Nothing particularly extraordinary, tho a classic joke happened to me, namely asking a woman I knew was French (in French) where it was in the castle that William of Orange was assassinated and getting back "Je ne parle pas hollandaise. Je ne parle que francais."[6] The castle incidentally is really kept up, a sixteenth century first floor and an eighteenth century second, the former, in the usual terms of snobbism here, by far the better. The usual American professors from Wyoming University are around and, according to the same terms, pronouncing Goethe "Gaty."

Christopher returns the salutes as does Gay. And we look forward to times on a farm somewhere with you patting all our heads.

Dick

I'm afraid Paul-like tones are creeping into my letters. I am also putting on weight again.

(INCIDENTALLY our street address is NEUHAUS STR 7 FRANKFURT/ MAIN telephone 55517)

Private TS.

Hillsboro, North Carolina | October 1 [1951]

Dear Dick and Gay,

It was wonderful to get your letter and the pictures, and I feel that it was very magnanimous of you to write us another good letter after we've been such delinquent correspondents! We've missed hearing from you, very much indeed, and we'll try to do better this winter.

The address calls for a lot of explanations. First of all, the Stanford fellowship didn't come through.[7] Very disappointing, and I'm afraid, a little surprising to us. We planned at once to go to New York, write, get jobs when necessary, etc. Then Don went up a couple of weeks ago to look things over, and, after a week, decided the situation was intolerable. We have taken refuge here in Eleanor and Peter's house, while they are living in Greensboro for at least a while. We don't expect to be able to stay here all winter but expect to get some quarters either here or in Chapel Hill. (Don is thinking of getting the PhD after all, if he can get an assistantship next quarter.) Fortunately we don't feel the gloom that probably should go with all this uncertainty.

Hillsboro is nice, and is now very autumn-y—it seemed very fitting when, a few hours ago, the Episcopal rector's wife and I had an across-the-fence conversation in which she told me about the possibility of getting an apartment in one of the more revered local old-houses, called Burnside, which is going to be made into a duplex...

As to the summer—Don taught in summer school and I worked from April till August. My job was pretty entertaining, as my first venture into the business world (filing and some policy-writing for an insurance agency) and I almost couldn't make the break, especially since the dozen girls who worked there had instituted the loathsome custom of farewell luncheons, and as the turnover was fairly large, I knew what they were like. The girls were a revelation: they discussed things like whether Mexico is a territory of the U.S. and whether or not it's correct to address a Negro, via mail, as "Mr." Then there was the file clerk who constantly belched and always giggled afterwards, "Why bring that up?"—As you can tell, the place left its mark on me.

The pictures are awfully good—Christopher is very handsome; I wish we could see him... We get excited about going to Europe all over again, after talking to the Robie Macauleys,[8] who were here a few days during our earlier and more formal visit. They'd just returned from a six-weeks tour with the Lowells,[9] who're still over there, somewhere.

We stocked up on enough literary gossip to last all winter, while we were here before—consists mostly of divorces and mental breakdowns. Probably you knew Warren had divorced the formidable Cinina, who has been committed.[10] Now the Jarrells have just parted company,[11] and we feel the breakdown part may follow judging by the anecdotes of Randall—wearing coonskin cap around campus (made from coonskins got with some kind of coupons), doing ballet steps around the post-office, and going in for handwriting analysis. But maybe that isn't sufficient evidence... Robert Lowell is supposed to have been assumed he won't have any more breakdowns. All this sounds rather dull—I wish there were some really momentous piece of news, like Eudora Welty's eloping with somebody.[12]

We went over to Chapel Hill several times and on our last visit saw somebody we knew, named Pete Long.[13] He is somewhat fat and, complete with brilliant tie, is what he calls a "nigger lawyer." He related the complimentary things he told the F.B.I. about you (they finally called Don, by the way, during the summer). He has a suit going against James Street, in whose fishpond a negro child drowned, and was hoping to be appointed to defend the accused man in Chapel Hill's murder case, the slaying of an elderly eccentric, Miss Rachel Crook,[14] of Crook's Corner.

We hear from Paul often—couldn't go to the wedding, had expected to see them during the summer, but they returned to Minnesota right away. We planned to see Edgar too—he returned in August—but dates and places got rather confused, with a New Jersey forwarding address thrown in—(we are feeling the effects of our letter-writing habits!) He's going to teach at Stanford, though what, I'm not sure.

The Zwerins don't seem too pleased with New York, and Norma was contemplating a return to Miami till after the baby comes, in November or December, I think. They are living on Long Island. But she asked for your address, so maybe you have first-hand information.

Have you read *The Catcher in the Rye*?[15] We liked it . . . I've been reading just what's at hand, *The Mill on the Floss*,[16] which I read the way I read her last, in high school, and practically wept, like Dick Hagood[17] reading Dostoyevsky in his cups. I'm now on V. S. Pritchett's latest (I trust) *Mr. Beluncle*.[18]

I see Don has given you mailing instructions, so I'll add only, Please write, and do forgive our tardiness.

> Love,
> Jean

October 1 [1951] | Hillsboro

Dear Dick and Gay,

I've little enough to add to Jean's letter, as you will see, save for a few random comments, which are the little enough. I must say, however, that as the disappointments and difficulties mount up one toughens and sinks somehow into a slough of happiness or at least content—or so it seems after two days at Hillsboro.

Reading your letters at least keeps us sophisticated. I've put on Jean's beret, as a token, to type this letter; also with my new crew cut it keeps the fall winds out. And a week ago Sunday afternoon, when I recognized Auden coming in to the Greenwich Restaurant (6th Ave. and Waverly Place) where I was, like him, breakfasting, I didn't feel so bad, having just read your letter the night before describing your lunch with (of course yours was really with) Mann.[19] Mike and Norma by the way couldn't distinguish Mann from the Mrs. without turning on another light. Trying to put myself to sleep the other night by composing verses in the dark I turned out four lines re the breakfast with WHA:[20]

Four booths only stood between us
    And one narrow aisle,
And different faiths, and different tongues.
    Also your style etc.

But I prefer the refrain I thought of on the spot:

From chatting with Christopher, Stephen and all,[21]
You've come a long way, boy, you've come a long way.
He did look seedy, tweed jacket and all.

Let's play a game of intercontinental chess. I'll play White (for convenience) and move Pawn to King's 4th. We can finish the game when we see each other again (which from the general tone of your letter seems as if it may not be as far off as it was a while ago—if you'll pardon me for reading between the lines, or trying to). Perhaps we'll be getting the doctorates somewhere near or perhaps at the same college. Why not?

In the next few weeks or months I'm going to be writing a novel—at last. It's going to be an extension of my "successful" story—an extension in both directions. It will be easier to write than my "major work," of which you have seen one paragraph of the epilogue—that will be my second.[22] Now let us pray.

If you can get a letter back by the 15th of October we'll be still in Hillsboro, which is all the address you need; or a letter in care of Fred E. Ross at Route 1 Norwood will always reach us.

As ever,

Don

Stern Papers, Regenstein Library, 32:14; MS/TS.

While Stern was teaching in Heidelberg, Justice was accepted as a PhD candidate at the Iowa Writers' Workshop. In January 1952 the Justices took a bus from Miami to Iowa City, where they were picked up and toured by Paul Engle. In a letter dated February 4 [1952], Justice shares his first impressions of life in the Midwest, as well as his excitement about the Workshop and the assistantship he took. As many letters of this period also express, he was eager for Stern to join him there.

P.O. Box 26 | Hillsboro, N.C. | December 5, 1951

Dear Dick and Gay and Christopher,

Yesterday was a muddy rainy day, like so many days used to be at Chapel Hill. But this morning it was fine and clear; we turned the heater off for the first time in a week or two. Also, and even better: instead of the "boxholders" we'd been getting at the post-office, there was a good haul today. Your sola, for one; and don't ask me what a sola is, but whatever, we can surely use it; and I do think it is all we will need till February, when my little Iowa checks start (I got the letter confirming that the day before the rain); you see, we still have the car, though it has stopped starting, and it will be worth a couple of hundred probably, which should pay for the winter coats etc. that Iowa's snow will require; further, our living expenses are so low, what with the rent-free town house, etc.—not much more than a hundred a month at most. And for two, at the P.O., there was the following note enclosed with my chess story,[23] which came back from the *New Yorker*:

I am sorry to tell you that the decision is against "The Coming Thing" but at the same time I wanted you to know that we are interested in your writing and hope that you'll have another story to send us soon. We like the way you write but believe that this particular story is a little too static—at least for us. (Sic!)[24] In spite of your careful detail it (the details are remembered from my Village days & from my recent trips up to Marshall). But I didn't find out if the fountain in the square (Washington) is still left running with the water shortage. Does not seem to us that your old Mr. Marshall ("your old"—Ha!) quite comes to life (the point of the story was that he came to death, if you'll pardon the joke) and the story somehow does not seem quite lively enough to make the reader really care enough about him. I go into all this detail only because I really hope you will try us again.

> Sincerely yours,
> K. S. White[25]

Who is, acc. to the new book Ross and the *New Yorker*, one of the big guns. Believe it or not, I find this encouraging. As soon as Rita Smith sends my "Vineland's Burning" (which I may enclose with this letter)[26] back from *Mademoiselle*, I intend sending it to the *New Yorker*, along with a little "casual" I'm lackadaisically at work on about our experiences in an apartment in Coral Gables last year. In other words, bombardment is in order. Yesterday was a low point in other ways: I got so damned tired sitting at the typewriter making copies of things for the application I'm sending in for a Saxton Fellowship that I had to quit, lie down, etc. and read *Alice in Wonderland*,[27] from which I swipe the following "motto" for the novel—back to the one elaborated from the story you like, by the way:

> "But I don't want to go among the mad people," said Alice.
>
> "Oh, you can't help that," said the Cat: "we're all mad here. I'm mad. You're mad."
>
> "How do you know I'm mad?" said Alice.
>
> "You must be," said the Cat, "or you wouldn't have come here."

I'll enclose the carbon of the synopsis if I don't get tired making the carbon. About 4000 words beyond the original story itself are done, though this may not be enough to get me the fellowship.[28] I'll try to find Paul's letter with the translation in it too, and send that along.[29]

Here is a poem you may have seen an earlier version of:

Move you, O lips, to speak?
What more would you express?
Roundness is all you know,
Round lips, and rounder cheek,
And roundest nothingness,
   My all, My O!

Move not till you have pressed
Some roundness into these.
I am in roundness caught,
Round lip, and rounder breast,
And roundest nothingness,
   My all, my ought!

This may be too old-fashioned for me and you, though. By the way, I also got a nice note from Lisa Dyer (do you know her?)[30] of the *Hudson* about the two poems I sent her. But what the hell. Did I send you my epithalamic epigram? There isn't really much news from Hillsboro except about what we are writing, so you'll have to excuse my running on about it. I *have* discovered a nice walk through the woods down to the Eno river; and Jean and I have thoroughly investigated our favorite ruins; and the Taylors and we did drive down to Norwood together for Thanksgiving, and they, with Peter's mother, dropped in on us one afternoon last week; and I have written Edgar about a mammoth old house here with an almost even more mammoth greenhouse, where the local florist used to live, which is for sale, and which he ought to buy, for he has always hankered after growing camellias somewhere or other (his father being in the nursery business and all). Your translations do read nicely, though Edgar isn't available to check them for accuracy; I wish I could. Have you got enough for a book? There's a vague possibility that the people in Miami who printed my chapbook would be interested;[31] Paul sent some of his poems to them, though, and they turned his down, for which I was sorry; but they are anxious to put out another chapbook, and it wouldn't cost you anything but the postage, and of course there'd be no profit in it either. Jean, by the way, I have put to work as Colette's first—or was it her first?—husband did with her:[32] I have given her a daily quota of 420 words to write on her novel, which I am envious of; of course I'll let her use part of her own name unlike M. Colette. We are pretty certain she'll have enough this way to apply for one of the end-of-the-year prizes. I probably told you some time or other that her "motto" and title come from *Lucien Leuwen*,[33] paraphrased, and in English: In the provinces, there passion still exists. (p.132 of English translation—what's the French, by the way, if it's handy?) Come February or March, I'll give you an up-to-date, first-hand report on Iowa, and maybe you'll consider it even harder: I do know already, according to Peter's talented gossip, that Paul Engle and wife[34] have a farmhouse about thirty miles out at which they hold their wild parties, and though they installed plumbing, it soon broke down, so they erected an immense stone privy some yards from the house with room for twelve seats, toward which the guests must plunge through Iowa's sleet and hail to enjoy the unpartitioned conviviality of relief. Don't let this discourage you, though. The tuition rates are very low, and besides, unlike Stanford, these are provided with fellowships and so on; and I'm pretty sure you could get one next fall if you wanted to; it goes without saying I'd do what I could and we'd love to have you-all around. You ought to be able to whiz through for the PhD in a couple of years at most; it will certainly take me that long, what with having to learn German and brush up the French. Well, enough: I must get to typing the rest of the application material if I'm to get it off today. And many many thanks for the sola. And tell Paul Bowles[35] he has an admirer when you run into him (I mean of course an admirer of his stories), and may Ibn's Greyhound be fleet returning you. Why not try Morocco too?

Don

P.S.

You will be disappointed to hear that I rank in verbal aptitude acc. to the Graduate Record exams, in only the 98th percentile; in lit of course I hit the 99th. What language does Christopher "have"? Or what languages? By the way, I have only about 2 or 3 pages to go on a story called "Redwine & Sunflower"—about the Indians in Paris—which you *will* definitely have to check for details: I've decided to throw the Indian stuff out of the novel-to-be and the Paris epilog—that's what this story is. Yr friend Fixler[36] is Sunflower, but his role in Heidelberg is only briefly mentioned & somewhat changed. My God, but you ought to make some comment on how prolific I've become. Also am doing a poem called "The Nymph Grown Old," "Is there not one spare part for my repair" etc. I'm running short on paper, which explains the marginalia. Best to Gay & Kate from Jean too.

Stern Papers, Regenstein Library, J–R; TS.

[December 1951] | [Miami]

Dear Dick & Gay & Kit,

Write us at 1829 N.W. 46th St., Miami, where we are being forced to adjourn till February. I am doing a song with the wonderful dactylic refrain *Christopher Macomber Stern*; I wish I had it for Christmas.[37] Much love, etc.

Don

Song of the Nymph Bathing

My waist disappears in the sky:
Ankle, knee, and thigh
Naked to the quiver
Of water-snakes in the river,
And the smoothness of fishes.
I am all that the water wishes
As it curves round my breasts.
I perform what the water suggests:
Down in desire I sink;

That iron taste I drink.
Above my open eyes
Waterbugs, dragonflies
Skim, skate, and dive:
The water itself is alive,
Its grassy arms enwreathing
A young girl bathing.

On Breakfasting with Auden in the Greenwich Diner

Three booths only stood between us,
    And one narrow aisle,
And different faiths, and different tongues,
    Also his style.
That keener sense which poets boast
    May fry his bacon crisper,
Yet I enjoy mine more than he,
    For he can't whisper
That he is breakfasting with me!
    He frowns into the distance.
The joys of meeting are, I fear,
    Mine, not Wystan's.

Morning Song

Though lovers lock
Limb to limb,
At dawn the cock
Uncouples them.[38]

Rejoice in this!
If lovers learn
Too much of bliss,
Night may return

To each alone,
And each exhort
The cock at dawn
To start, to start.
Then praise his art!

Stern Papers, Regenstein Library, 38:3; Christmas card.

February 4 [1952] | 606 S. Johnson St. | Iowa City

Dear Dick & Gay et al,

The street called straight[39] looked more beautiful than anything here, esp. since a mid-winter thaw is on. However, aside from beauty, of which there seems to be no particular surplus (the ice-packed Iowa river will *do*, though), this place is wonderful. Paul Engle, who is our benefactor, has arranged for me to teach a course in fiction writing which meets but once a week; I also rate a private office in the Old Dental Bldg. We travelled by bus (as to Stanford) and are still extending a series of contrasts: of course the weather there was finer, & Winters was incomparable but otherwise I'll take Iowa City (as first looks go). Engle, in answer to a phone call, was at the bus station within 90 min. with a car-door open to speed us to an apt. he had arranged for (a nice, roomy, old one), then on a quick motor tour of the campus, peppered with apologies that he wld be out of town over the weekend & so couldn't entertain us in a fitting manner, & promises to call the asst. librarian about a job for Jean, which maybe he did, for she was offered a splendid job immediately. I go into such details for what must be obvious reasons: I'm overwhelmed by the attentions & decencies showered on us. In fact, unless it goes to 19 below, as everyone here boasts it did earlier this year, we will be quite comfortable; plus which we'll be self-supporting & -liquidating. Won't, in other words, need the money Jean wrote you for from Miami, and also *will* be able to start repaying.

This must of need be a preliminary report—I don't even register till tomorrow. (For such courses as PhD German & French.) Walter Van Tilburg Clark is the big bug currently in residence as a teacher: he wrote a nice story called "The Wind & Snow of Winter,"[40] among other things. *The Western Rvw.* of course comes out of here (as did even Grant Wood,[41] I believe, Dieu m'en garde) &, though I don't precisely know what will be expected of me, I certainly intend to worm my way onto & maybe into the magazine one way or another: if so, if I can get any voice in it, expect things to pop, by way of contributions expected from you & Edgar & so on. It's a giddying sort of prospect in a way, & a good reason for coming here.[42]

As a matter of fact, they seem to take pride in "encouraging the arts"—and I don't know why I shld put it into quotation marks, for it's hardly a thing to be ashamed of even if Grant Woods do come out of it. A symphony orchestra, paintings & sculptures on all walls & in all lobbies, a special bldg. for the writers, who seem to be numerous, a production of the *Beggar's Opera* this week, etc. A little middle-aged New York—or, rather, Chicago. Truth is, it probably beats Chicago. I know it beats Chapel Hill—and very likely Stanford.

After a couple of weeks of dull classes my enthusiasm may ebb—I do doubt it, though.

Consider it for your PhD, Dick. I mean it. One can write a novel for it, you know, if one has to or wants to.

Rejoinder about my "Nymph Bathing" poem: "Down in desire I sink; / that iron taste I drink," was supposed to have a similar effect to the one Winters comments on in "Prim. And Decad." Relative to Crashaw's rendering of the 23rd psalm.[43] Sorry it didn't.

Powerhouse[44] I will read if you all promise to come back to the states for a PhD.

In Miami, aside from driving a cab for 10 days, the only thing I did was to compose a suite of five pieces (Scherzo, Gigue, Andante Mobile: Canon, Alla Marcia, & Finale) for clarinet & bassoon—playing time, 90 seconds—and a trio for clarinet, oboe, & bassoon—playing time, 130 seconds—either of which, or both, I will gladly dedicate to Christopher (since his *real* name spoiled my poem-to-be):[45] they're both jolly & acrid: theme of trio [see fig 1.]:

Take your pick. A bassoonist friend of mine in Miami,[46] an excellent musician, promised me to get recordings (amateur) of them & send them to

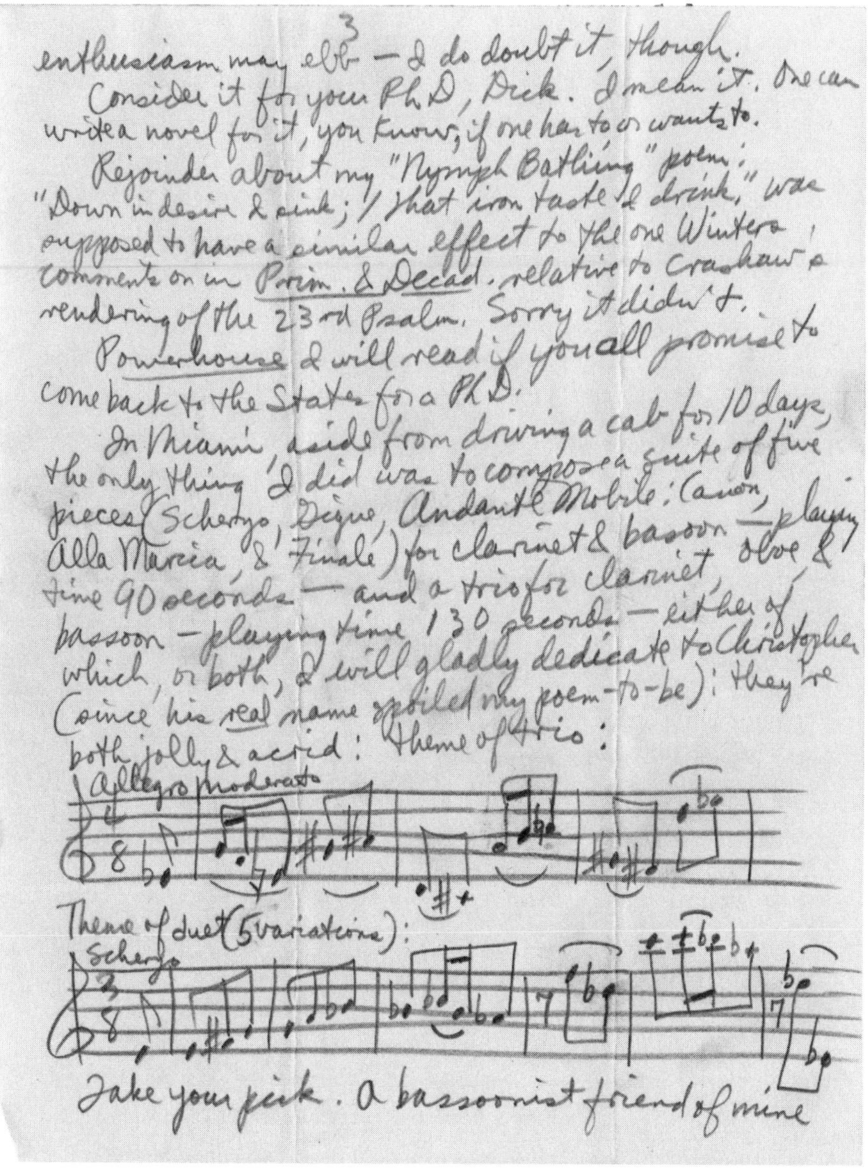

Fig. 1. Handwritten musical notation, theme of trio for clarinet and bassoon, by Donald Justice. Reprinted with permission from the literary executors of the estate of Donald Justice, © Jean Justice. Courtesy of the Special Collections Research Center, University of Chicago Library.

me; if I can get copies made I'll send you some. Ruggles, my old composition teacher (when I was 17–18) had a big piece played last season by the Phila. Orch.[47]—well received, surprisingly, since he is moderner than, e.g., his sidekick Ives.[48] You will observe that my musical interest has revived; I may even sit in here, if permitted, on a seminar in the 12-tone series, a modified form of which Ruggles taught me.

We expect to be near enough the Ramseys to visit & be visited occasionally once the ice goes.

Peter has a grand offer from the U. of Chicago for the spring quarter &, acc. to Engle—& Peter—will be invited over here for a lecture, so we'll see them too. Too bad, really, that Christopher isn't a year or two older, for I think he'd be wild about Katie Taylor—they'd make a grand match: but maybe the difference in age won't matter any more than it did to us (or to you all, as Jean reminds me). Oh, well—write soon, and love to all of you.

Don

P.S. A sample of Mid-Westerness: my parents having offered to buy me a suit (which I am dearly in need of), I stopped in the best-looking men's store here & asked for a 3-button single-breasted banker's gray flannel—the salesman said that type hadn't got this far West yet, only as far as Chicago, but he will order etc. Charmant.

Stern Papers, Regenstein Library, 38:3; TS.

February 12 [1952] | [Heidelberg]

Dear Don and Jean,

Christopher seemed really pleased with the themes as, searching Iowa City out on the big American map above the desk, we were with the first report. Engle comes close to the German angle (I am not even tempted to suggest there might be anything to that lapsus machinati, this though I am pleasurably in the midst of that definitive weigher of all angles, *Clarissa Harlowe*)[49] and that seems indicative enough of that west of the golden age where they have to wire to Chicago to ask about the three buttoned banker's flannel from New York. Very much indeed like Damascus, where my request to call England on Christopher's birthday was met with a somewhat saddened answer that they couldn't even *call* Cairo. (I think it was at your wedding that we wanted to call you in Norwood and I think it was the third operator who asked about the Rosses, said "she knew them and they lived out in the country and didn't have no phone," which I'm afraid I borrowed in altered form for my one time novelette. Not for local color Jean, but for the operator.) Golden or not, Iowa sounds like the place to be and if you continue with it as it's started with you, then we look forward to coming, say in September of '53. Maybe they could dig me up a course in the short novel or something. At all events, it's got thaws, which Harvard doesn't allow, and is cheaper and you can write a novel and most important of course, you'll be there. (If I don't have to know Latin I'll stop right now. If you get with the magazine, I swear a contribution. If Katie Taylor and Christopher don't object, we'll plight a troth.)

Grant Wood and Walter Van Tilburg Clark don't faze me tho *The Track of the Cat* did.[50]

Norma wrote about the possibility of coming to Europe en route to Israel. The latter strikes me as a dangerous business with three children. The food situation is very bad there and there is even more war tension than in the US. You're isolated as far as travel goes and you even have to look over at the old city (of Jerusalem) through barbed wire. The Mediterranean is nice there and they say the oranges are the world's best. I guess she has gotten more or less the same report from Mike by now.

I'm enclosing these eight snaps, which as much as any other eight will give an idea of the sort of tour that took in three times as many countries as it did weeks. I'll add a ninth to round it up with two Austrians, who spent a ten day vacation with her brother, a baker in Cairo, and whose posture gives the measure of the indolence and ennui which characterise the Mediterranean liners whose weekly stint, Marseilles, Genoa (Naples, Venice, Trieste), Piraeus, Beirut, Alex(andria) and back again is the Middle East belt. Unfortunately, my one shot of Venice is a misty view of a ship strut, which is too bad because sailing up the Grand Canal past the Lido and the Arsenal is one of the great scenic beauties of the world, I imagine. How one really misses Europe by then. Even absorbed by a couple of hours at Brindisi the Middle East needs Venice for the contradiction to its haphazard intricacy and *it* is so much there, the sun going down in all its pastel hotels and offices and palaces, the little white bridges leading to the "motoscafo" stops (no buses in all Venice) and the really thrilling square—about all I had time to see because by then I could hardly distinguish the postcards from the original.

The first picture is in the Kalemegdan gardens in Belgrade; the Danube is on the right and it meets the Sava to flow into I don't know what. This is about the only breathing spot in Belgrade, which is just what *Time* would say a communist city is like, no cars, uniforms everywhere, great clean grey buildings, a massive post office topped by Greek entablature, a massive new Byzantine church with nobody in it (tho they said it would be packed that night—Jan 6—for Christmas Eve), the feigned luxury of the best hotels (all very cheap—fifty cents a night and fifty cents for a meal), the rolls old, the roast pig suckled in milk depressed on a thick white plate—but it was freezing cold and I'm not sure of anything but that. It was still Europe. The next day getting on a train, which was cold enough to preserve oysters, my view of the East started when a peasant stooped into the third class wooden compartment, emptied his nostrils on the floor and about twelve filthy looking bundles into the racks. A wine peasant came on the next in slacks and advised me to sit in the dining car, the only place they had heat. I spent the next twelve hours there with, as we got more and more south, some of the strangest individuals I've ever imagined existed. In the first place the car filled up and everybody started off with hot slivka. That led to involved conversations with people six tables back and across the aisle. Not speaking three words of Serbo-Croatian didn't matter. I was often during that ride the theme of everyone's concern, especially as the passengers' opinions were just as valuable as the conductor's about the possibility of getting my train to Salonika. Serbians with black hair as plastered as the beret they wore, and mustaches, seemed particularly friendly, stopping to shake everybody's hand or looking wistfully at the little blue four leaf clover in my lapel, probably associating it with something religious, sharing their lunches (slabs of white butter, black bread—very good—swine chunks and sweet pastry) and finally descending at the tiny, miserable towns along the route. I had to change at Skopje and the engineer missed the station and had to back up two kilometers. I waited a few hours in a waiting room in which there were so many actual types of people that no one noticed me as anything but another one, tho I looked nothing at all like any of them. Serbs, Croats, Albanians, Macedonians. Greeks, Gypsies, Turks, Arabs, most with wine jugs and clay pots, many such a mass of rags you'd have thought they hadn't discarded a piece of clothing since their weaning and had simply added more rags as growth split the originals. All this in a mean white room with a small red communist poster, two hands with a hoe and rifle stretching up to a gold star. Everyone stopped talking when a policeman walked in to censure somebody or a neat little fellow with a cap walked in to sneer at everybody in general. But they are what is called hospitable, generous and courteous and the "they" means it's the way everybody in the east except the Snopes's acts.[51] As for politics, Tito is doing what Ataturk did in Turkey, Mohammed Ali in Egypt, Reza Shah in Iran[52] and every other one of these people east of Europe seems to be doing in their countries, conciliating or eliminating the independent nationalities, harnessing the farmer-peasants and coming out with that hopeful, new arrogance, which is not arrogance in the individual students or travelling salesman you meet, but only confidence, some self-pity and much braggadocio.

Anyway, the second picture is a four-foot marble group laid against an iron fence in back of the Greek agora in Athens with a thousand other leavings and the third is a self-portrait of a Macy's balloon and the Parthenon.[53] The Acropolis is a real "experience" and must include your preconceptions and expectations as part of what it's there for. There's a contemporaneity about its past which is the sun and the Acropolis is littered, as is much of Greece, with such meaningful fragments that you don't see how enough events could have been to stand behind all the commemorations and potsherds. And the new building is wonderful also, Floridian in the best sense, porches and spaces for the sun, square lines for a bright sun's outline in the clear days and all out of the rock which is everywhere, marble usually being the most available. The city has a luxury air, which Salonika even had to the lesser degree, luxury in building, goods and time. Backgammon parlors all over—in Turkey the barbers take up some of this excess time—and men sit there slapping the chips and drinking Turkish coffee for hours of what would be business time in the west.

The fourth is the Blue Mosque in Istanbul, which is nearly as wonderful looking inside, airy, blue mosaic, birds flying, boys chanting the Koran on the carpets. The muezzin is calling from the middle minaret but he's barely, and perhaps not, visible. This mosque is opposite Hagia Sophia, which I think is the first interior that ever made me feel what building means. Istanbul is a fairy town, mosques floating over it, cut in three by the Marmora, the Golden Horn and the Bosphorus, the last a soft, bending channel lined with fortresses and castles and part of which you see in the fifth snap, which I took incidentally from the seraglio, now a gorged museum where you can see the head and hands of John the Baptist or the biggest porcelain collection in the world.

Sixth is outside the east gate of Damascus, the old wall on the right and by the church which is erected by Paul's entrance into the street called Straight. The next is also Damascus, from the peak Mujareem from where I think it was that Mohammed said he wouldn't bother entering the city as he expected to enter heaven. The last is one of the streets of Old Jerusalem, which is a swarming mass of 40,000 Arabs, asses, goats, outdoor cooking and the smells of six thousand years surrounding Calvary (over which Constantine's mother built a dark, gold-stuffed church), the wailing wall, the great mosque, the temple, Pilate's etc etc.—the boy in the picture is a nice little fellow who doesn't believe in God, wants to go to America and says "here is where Our Lord was judged" etc for the tourists.

This letter was as exhausting as the trip, minute for minute, and I think as little pleasurable for both of us. I won't not send it, but excuse the Fitzpatrick, Kaltenborn[54] aspect. If I think about the trip as "material," which I do in that special sense, it'll be obviously "yes,"—there are a million anecdotes and backdrops and articles and relationships which make the "history" both of this particular trip and of anybody's relationship to such a pre-existing area as this. I don't think a reflective piece of art has come from any of the cities I visited except maybe Alexandria and Istanbul which are international in the middle east sense (Greek-Italian-French-Natives, with French as the second language and natives divided into original Christians—Copts or Maronites—Moslems and half-breeds).

But I don't want to say anything more, but write soon and I hope we'll be established in all senses and preferably headed away from Frankfurt by our next return.

Gay and C. enjoyed England and got fat and rosy due to the cold and commissary privileges.

> Best from all,
> Dick

The Hendersons,[55] satisfied with ancient but fed up with modern stone walls, are heading home. I mailed the sola just before I got your note but it can't hurt either of us.

Keep it for now or ever—

> Private TS.

[May 1952] | Iowa City

JUSTICE'S VERSION

Cooley leaned his head back on the chair and shivered a little. "Unbelievable," he said softly. "Unbelievable." He laid the book on the desk.

He had read for hours, straight through dinner to the last page, but only when he had put on his topcoat and was out in the nearly deserted streets, with the clocks sounding some half-hour he couldn't identify, did he realize how hungry the reading had made him. He headed downtown, to find an open café. But the cold air sharpened his sense of exaltation, and his mind kept turning on the book, going over it as a woman goes up and down the stairs of a new house. He had passed at least two lighted cafes before he remembered to go in.[56]

Dear Dick—

(1.) You can surely get into the fall term (I'm sorry I hadn't got around to sending the bulletin, etc., but I will enclose an application blank—you could probably get into the second summer session if you wanted, the starting date of which I will add to this later when I find out). (2.) The university has a hospital right in town (and there are two others also I believe). The university hospital has an extremely good reputation, they tell me. If you were enrolled as a student, you & Gay might get a cut-rate on the baby—I'll try to find this out too, & enclose the information. (Yes, you would.) (3.) I don't know what you think of as reasonable, but such an apartment could certainly be found (I suppose the hot running water is a European joke, for of course the Midwest has creature comforts). (Enclosed: univ. circular on housing.) Baths, however are often shared in this college town—not always. I estimate it would cost you $65 or thereabouts per month, unfurnished; maybe as low as $50, if it were a bus-ride out from town. Furniture, they say, is very easy to pick up during the summer, as are apts., supposedly. We know of a little house for rent for the summer for $60, just for an example, but it's way out, and by July it will probably be taken. (We pay $60 for one bedroom, kitchen, living room, shared bath & telephone—rooms roomy—on bus-line, 10 mts. walk—furnished.) However, we'll of course keep our ears & eyes open. (4.) We'll borrow a cot or something to set up in our living room for your temporary visit, & though you would feel crowded, it could be done. (5.) I have been discouraged about summer jobs, which I am told are almost impossible. I can't believe this, and surely you could find something if you had to, though it might not be pleasant. (A lot of the boys, for instance, worked last summer on a construction project.) A job in the fall would be easy. (6.) I know nothing of part-time help except baby-sitters; it might be hard to find, though so many of the students have babies & can't believe it's impossible. I will try to find out this afternoon & enclose the information. As you see, I started rewriting your story & then decided that your beginning might, after all, be better (after all, it is the logical *beginning*).[57] I liked your revision very much, though in a way it seemed you had thrown at least the diapers out the window. But I suppose now that your arrival is so imminent we can wait & do this together, which could be fun. I had started my complete rewriting of "Caboose-Red" (complete to the title, now "Feather Sighing"):[58] it all takes place on the featherbed, in line with some remarks of yours, I believe. I had started with the idea of doing it for the *New Yorker*, to pay transportation to Salzburg with the proceeds, but it was uncertain at best. Much better, undoubtedly, that you should come over now & get your PhD. We certainly will be happy to see you all (Paul will be glad to hear, too). —Let us know price range of apt. you're interested in & also if you'll plan on having or buying a car (not necessary, of course). I'll speak to Engle about you before he leaves although I doubt that he'll be able to get you a fellowship for this fall (too late & too few); next fall, of course, should be no trouble. You should have some writing to show him: some poetry (incl. translations, since he's interested in these) and your monastery story[59] if that's available—this is if you plan to be in writer's workshop, as I suppose you do, though there's no rush about this material. Ray West will be here next year; also—Robert Lowell is taking Engle's place for the year. Good news, this, I think, though I do like Engle. Jarrell, by the way was here last week for 3 days—made a good impression on everybody—said, in brief, that poetry ought to be about something you can tell your friends (cf. Rilke) and could afford to be sentimental (but not quite so baldly, of course). ("I'd like nothing better than to hear that one of my poems had made somebody weep." -Jarrell.) The parties here are good by the way: we had to miss out on most of the best Jarrell one because I was very sick—though briefly—during most of last week (which explains why I hadn't got around to sending your story or comments, etc.). I am in fine health & spirits now, though, & returned to my afternoon ping-pong session today with vigor (on Mondays it follows the poetry workshop, & all the "best poets" participate). You'll be sure to shine here as a student; I do, & you're a better. Again, Jean & I both are very much excited that you may be coming soon—we anticipate much that is fine, even, or esp. from Christopher.

Don

p.s. Just heard from Peter today that he's coming next week, for a lecture, etc. He said Jarrell "raved" about "Ladies by Their Windows."[60]

p.p.s. Lots of ex-Harvard men here, by the way.

1st summer session begins June 11th—it's the only summer session—can you make it?

Stern Papers, Regenstein Library, 38:4; MS.

CORRESPONDENCE OF 1954 TO 1955

In June 1952 the Sterns moved to Iowa City. For the next two years, Justice and Stern studied together at the Writers' Workshop. In 1954 they completed their doctorates.

Justice's creative dissertation, "Beyond the Hunting Woods, and Other Poems," included a number of poems that would later appear, in some form, in The Summer Anniversaries. *Stern's dissertation was a book of stories, many of which he published during his time at Iowa.*

Following graduation, the Justices traveled to Europe on a Rockefeller Foundation grant, and, after a stint in New York City, Stern taught for a year at Connecticut College in New London.

Friday [June 1954] | [New York]

Dear Don & Jean,

I guess Tom has told you about our trip.[1] It doesn't exactly pain me to think about it, but as long as you know the story, I'd just as soon refrain from writing it.

We are now in process of trying to buy a good, standard make car for five or six hundred buckles.

It was very sad leaving you that night.[2] I'm going to miss you both very much & I do already. I'll also miss Iowa City. Never did New York seem so disagreeable and the East so strait-laced. This must seem peculiar to you; perhaps my feelings stem in part from the rather disastrous entrance I made when all along I thought of driving up triumphantly to the various householders acknowledging the respectful loss of the non-drivers.

I've been to two publishers so far, one a new second cousin who, to my surprise, publishes only books in psychoanalysis (he's hit his first best-seller with the Jones biog. of Freud)[3] and then to Doubleday where I asked for Ken McCormick & was met instead by a glad-handing assistant who told me "Ken would have been so glad to see me but he's with the President." I was soon disposed of mostly because I was too obviously awed by the splendour of the surroundings & the misdirected kindness with which they welcomed me. I'll try a few more places because this cousin said that they were always looking for readers, especially for foreign books. I'm sure nothing will come of it.

Excuse my enclosing a note for Tom—I don't know his address.

This letter is mostly to thank you for everything you've done for me for the past two & a half years, Iowa, the degree & above all the writing. I'm sure

I'd never have written 3 coherent lines if you hadn't helped me. I probably won't again.

I'll write you when things have shaped up a bit around here. I may just start working on a book & if so, I'll tell you how that comes on.

> Best from all of us,
> Dick

I started rereading this letter & it's illegible. At least you'll know it's from me.

Private MS.

The Justices soon grew homesick. Moreover, they felt increasingly unable to afford Europe on a Rockefeller grant. Once again they returned to Miami to stay with Justice's family. They also spent a short time in Iowa City while Justice looked for work.

In 1955 Justice interviewed at the University of Chicago. The position was offered to him, but he turned it down in favor of another teaching job at the University of Missouri at Columbia. On Justice's recommendation, Stern interviewed for the Chicago position and accepted it. Unlike Justice, Stern was fond of city life, and of Chicago in particular. He taught there until his retirement in 2002.

February 27 [1955] | [Miami]

Dear Dick & Gay,

I started a letter to you a week or so ago telling you, among other things, of a race coming up at Hialeah the next day in which three horses were entered by the names of Dante, Plato, & Nickleby, all longshots, none of which in my opinion had a chance but which I supposed you'd be hunch-player enough to want me to bet for you; only I not only didn't mail the letter, I didn't go to Hialeah, and Nickleby of course came in paying a pretty fair price. (Ran again yesterday at small odds and trailed the field.) We've started listening to *Amos and Andy*[4] on Sunday evenings as you used to do at Iowa City. Do you still? Did you hear the one in which Andy, in a confidence game with the Kingfish, said, "Well, I'll be, if my name isn't Russel J. Simpleton!" The Kingfish: "Simpson, you fool!" I wrote to the man at Chicago mentioning Delora's name (this before your letter) by a lucky chance, and got a reply expressing interest;[5] he now has my credentials; no further word. Also wrote to Yale Press about the Yale Younger Poets Series: deadline turned out to be March 1 and they wanted a volume of between 48 & 64 pages. I checked the library, found Bogardus' volume didn't run that long, and after much hard work, managed to send in a volume (rough in spots, but only with poems I wouldn't mind seeing in a book) just a page shorter than Bogardus'.[6] I have, I think, 7 or 8 new poems that you haven't seen. This of course has kept me damned busy. I'm not going to type out all of them, for several reasons, but I'll put in a sestina because I want your advice about it, about the last three lines specifically, because I can't decide what to do about them. The background of precedent is, as far as I know it, this: the rule is that the seventh stanza (you know this I guess, but just in case it's hazy) runs three lines with the end-word 1 in middle of first line, end-word 2 at end of first line, end-word 3 in middle of second line, etc., and poets like Rolfe Humphries keep to this rule (and of course the classics) but Auden takes his liberties with this order and also with exact mid-line placement (as do most others nowadays) but always sticks to end-words at the ends of lines, and Pound leaves out two of the end-words but does end each of the lines with one. Now here's the sestina:[7] Jarrell even has one without last 3 lines.

I came by first light to a wood
Right in the shadow of a hill
And saw about me in a circle
Many I knew, the dear faces
Of some I recognized as friends.
I knew not how I came that way.

I asked how they had come that way.
They looked at me like blocks of wood.
They turned their backs on me, those friends,
And struggled up the stubborn hill

Along that road which makes a circle.
No longer could I see their faces.

But there were trees with human faces.
Afraid, I ran a little way
But must have wandered in a circle.
I had not left that human wood;
I was no farther up the hill.
And all the while I heard my friends

Discussing me, but not like friends.
Then through the trees I glimpsed their faces.
(The trees grew crooked on that hill.)
Now all at once I saw the way,
Above a clearing in the wood
A lone bird wheeling in a circle,

And in that shadowed space the circle
Of those I thought of still as friends.
I drew near, calling, and the wood
Rang and they turned their deaf faces
This way and that but not my way.
They rose and danced upon the hill.

And it grew dark. Behind the hill
The sun slid down, a fiery circle;
Screeching the bird flew on her way.
It was too dark to see my friends.
But then I saw them, and their faces
Were leaning above me like a wood.

In the moon's circle on that hill
I saw the faces of my friends
Change in a way that shook the wood.

OR: I saw the faces of my friends
    Change in a way that shook the wood.
    I fled that circle and that hill.

OR: The friends were fiends, the hill hell,
    The wood wide, and the way woe.
    The circle closed; berserk the faces.

The last, you see, violates everything. None keeps the proper order. Which do you like best? Or not any of them? I wouldn't blame you. Can you write an ending? (I noticed, by the way, in typing this up, and don't know why I hadn't noticed it before in all the labor I put in on this, that the order of the end-words in stanza two is screwed up, which screws up the whole order, but it's too late now to do anything about that.) Here're the first three stanzas of another sestina I started, using the end-words of a sestina by Weldon Kees[8] (who's a more interesting poet than I'd thought he would be, and sympathetic to me though not great or even outstandingly good); I spent five times as much time on this one without being able to get it to go any farther; could you take over from here?[9]

I often wonder about the others,
Where they are bound for on the voyage,
What is the reason for their silence,
Was there some reason to go away?
It may be they carry a dark burden,
Expect some harm, or have done harm.

How can we show we mean no harm?
Approach them? But they shy from others.
Offer, perhaps, to share the burden?
They changed the subject to the voyage,
Or turn abruptly, walk away,
To brood, against the rail in silence.

What is defeated by their silence
More than love, less than harm?
Many already are looking their way,
Pretending not to. Eyes of others
Will follow them now the whole voyage
And add a little to the burden.

Here's one I did finish, though, on a sestina-like basis, sort of.

As for the key, we know it must be minor.
B minor, then, as having passed for noble
On one or two occasions. As for the theme,
There being but the one, with variations,
Let it be spoken outright by the oboe
Without apology of any string,
But as a man speaks, openly, his heart
Among old friends, let this be spoken. Thus.

A major resolution of the minor,
Johann's great signature, would be too noble;
It would do violence, violence to our theme.
Therefore, see to it that the variations
Keep faith with the plain statement of the oboe.
Entering quietly, let each chastened string
Repeat the lesson she must get by heart,
And without overmuch adornment. Thus.[10]

And a lighter, *New-Yorker* type, which I include only because I thought of the
idea (if it can be called an idea) up at your place last fall; the kids' (pardon
me, neither Jean nor Gay likes that word much)—the children's influence
probably.

—The children that loved them so,
Where are they now? The dog,

So jealous, where is he?
And the indifferent cat,
That played all day with a spool?
And where can the children be?
The toys are coming to life
Under the Christmas tree.

—Better they should not see
That pretty walking doll
Despite her broken knee
Dancing all alone
Around and around the tree,
Nor the weeping doll, for she
Must weep real tears tonight
Under the Christmas tree.

Enough for now. More another time maybe. This week back to the play and a story I've got started. —Our landlady has told us she definitely wants the house back June 1st, which means, if we do have any money left, we will be coming up to Connecticut (or somewhere around there, if you're going to be elsewhere) and will be interested in the Jarrell house, if still available. Also, I think we'll be able to send you a little more money on our debt as soon as we get our income tax refunds; we applied a month ago. Living is turning out to be pretty inexpensive here, if a bit dull; we miss the good friends and the good times of Iowa City. Heard from Engle; no mention of a job there; he said he was writing poetry furiously. As for a part-time job at Connecticut—where would we get the rest of the money to live on? I've tried to think of an "angle" but without luck. Otherwise, damned good idea. We are still trying to win puzzles,[11] still fighting the fleas, still hearing the rat at night; now a dog has started howling, afternoons, somewhere in the next block. This is about all. Did go to a play last night, given by a pretty good amateur company: *Another Part of the Forest*.[12] I'm thinking of writing the director (whom I think I knew as an adolescent) and volunteering my services. The cold weather has gone from here; hope it has up there too. What have you been writing, Dick? What's the other news? My bedtime now.

Love,

Don

Ah, here's one more poem:

> It was down by the river I went walking
> To see the great ice-shoulders heaving,
> And stood on the bridge to hear them knocking
> At one another. Oh, they would be having
> Each his own way, to judge by the fury.
> I wanted to ask them what was the hurry,
>
> But watched them go without much feeling,
> As one might observe the back of a stranger
> Leaving a train and wish to be following,
> Knowing of course there wasn't much danger
> Of anything rash or suicidal,
> But letting my thoughts turn vaguely tidal.

Stern Papers, Regenstein Library, 76:2; TS.

---

908 E. Washington | Iowa City | April 15 [1955]

Dear Dick & Gay,

There's lots of news—I can give you the facts but am not sure of my emotions. First, this: I'll be teaching next year at the Univ. of Missouri, an assistant professorship, $4500. The way it came about: I returned from Chicago, dubious of the impression I'd made there, since I'd been tense, nervous, and inexperienced at such things, and sweated out their reply for five days. Then I got the offer, as I wrote you: instructorship, $4250. I was about to sit down & type an acceptance when I decided I owed myself a celebration; went down to play ping-pong, ran into Ray West[13] instead, who told me Missouri wanted somebody to teach poetry etc., that he'd told them about me & they seemed interested; will do no harm to inquire, thought I; I did; they wanted me for interviews; I, who'd sworn I'd never, if I could help it, go through such an ordeal again, drove down last Monday, had a much less tense time than at Chicago, came away Tuesday, got a wire Wednesday offering me above job, wrote letter to Chicago Thursday explaining the situation, got frantic wire this morning from Chicago offering me $4750 and promotion next year, immediate answer required; I didn't know what to do; last night, though, I'd written Missouri accepting, and besides, Jean liked the idea of living in Columbia much more than in Chicago, so I wired Chicago declining; Tom says they must have been shocked and will probably be even more so. I'm rather shocked myself at myself. The Chicago job, I know, is the best job I've ever heard of being offered to anyone in my nebulous position; probably the chance of a lifetime for me and all that; esp. this would be true if I were a teacher, thought of myself as a teacher; but I don't, I don't want to have to; people at Missouri seemed more interested in preserving me at least part-time as a writer, at least they so expressed themselves; also we know, or can pretty well predict, the kind of life we'd have there—a smallish college town much like Iowa City—and we know we like that kind; the Chicago is more a mystery & a challenge etc., but I think the wrong kind of challenge to accept. I know I've never felt more "wanted" in my life; it's a good but puzzling feeling. Did I give you any details of the Chicago interviews? Here are a few at random. Olson[14] told me he'd just had a letter from Wallace Stevens[15] sort of acknowledging him as a fellow poet and also that I wouldn't have to be an Aristotelian to fit in, despite propaganda to the contrary;[16] seemed friendly. Zabel was prissy,[17] bored by me as a person. One chap—an Australian[18]—asked me if I ever looked at the learned journals, just by way of small talk not as a quiz, and when I said yes, asked me if I didn't think MP had improved a lot since George[19] took over; I couldn't even nod agreement. I asked several about crime in Chi; one told me a tale of how a friend of his had been in town for several weeks unbeknownst to him until he read in the paper how the friend had been picked up a couple of streets away bashed and bloody; another said the talk of crime was much exaggerated; it turned out he lived in a suburb twenty miles out. The job would have been half in the English department, teaching advanced exposition, creative writing, perhaps a literature course in alternate quarters, half with a committee for general studies in the humanities where I'd have taught a course called Humanities 300 A, B, and C mostly involving the preparation of theses but including apparently some bibliography & methodology as well as committee work in correspondence, tutoring, and generally assisting the chairman of the committee, an interesting little man with a passion for General Custer.[20] At Missouri I'll teach 20th century British & American, the writing of poetry, narration, and a sophomore survey, with graders whenever I want them. In general the people at Missouri are a little friendlier, a little younger, I hope a little less demanding.

But thanks anyway for the Chicago tip. It's helped my confidence no end.

There's probably news of people here which you'd be interested in, but this terrific concern the last 10 days with my own job problem has doubtless wiped much of it out of my memory. Let's see: Evans[21] is taking a job at Brandeis teaching Old English. Tom is trying for something at Chicago, in the college (not the Division). Tom's doing stories for his thesis but so far hasn't got up nerve to show them to Ray or anybody. Quite a few new and supposedly interesting people here. We went to a party at Emma Swan's last week for instance;[22] maybe you've read some of her poetry in various places; seems she's a Swan Soap heiress; but so far she's struck me as rather dullish. We've played some croquet naturally; Tom becoming my partner and a new boy named Pete.[23] Don's[24] pretty gloomy some of the time; worrying about his comprehensives, his responsibilities in general, and his sins at large. Jeanine's the same. Tom and Jacky have a torrid romance, apparently.[25] Gertrude Buckman[26] strikes me as dumb; thought it was Hamlet who tried to stop the Queen from drinking the poison, insisted on checking it in a nearby copy, e.g.—We are enjoying ourselves and I think I'll be able to work better now that the job's settled.

Tell me more about the Princeton business; you've only mysteriously alluded to it heretofore.

Let us know about Macky's house as soon as you can.[27] Ray has offered us, tentatively, his house for the summer at reduced rents if we want it, but I told him we'd prefer Connecticut if we could get a house there.

We saw Paul Ramsey & family,[28] as I suppose I wrote you; Starr is very pretty & bright; the twins aren't bad for twins; Paul is his old self but a little subdued; I wish he could make a big success of himself at something quick so that he could stop justifying himself before the world; Bets is a good wife and we liked her.

The drive up was terrifying and tiring; I fear death every time I get out on the highway in a car.

I've just about decided to write a novelette instead of a play this summer; not quite decided yet; but a publisher through here last week said publishers were interested in very short novels now etc. Plays are unpredictable (just like me); maybe you can change my mind for me.

Write soon please.

Love,
Don

Stern Papers, Regenstein Library, 76:2; TS.

April 27 [1955] | Iowa City

Dear Dick,

It had crossed my mind that you might be summoned.[29] If you want it, I certainly wish you luck and ease. I don't know what advice to give. I know that I kept pretty quiet and was far from brilliant (my stomach was upset) but it seemed to work. It certainly is a teaching plum. And of course it would be nice to have you all in the neighborhood, roughly speaking. But think, do think of the life in Chicago. If you can possibly make ends meet on your present salary, remember the nice house you've got there, the nice drive in on a spring morning, the easiness of the courses you have to teach, the nearness to New York (and yet far enough away, maybe, from the bombs),[30] etc. On the other hand, there's the undeniable prestige, the possibility of various academic excitements etc. You'll probably have free time enough to look up the Belvins,[31] who have a big apartment; their phone number's been changed, but the operator will give the new one, and their new address is 6419 N. Lakewood, way out on the other side of town from the university. If you had time, you might come on out here for the weekend; everybody would be delighted; we have a roomy sofa; it would I think be pretty pointless (and beyond our budget) to come into Chicago; Tom might, if you could let us know in time.—They'll probably put you up at the International House, feed you in the Faculty Club, a somewhat dark & ancient building, being redone under Maclean's supervision (partly). Mrs. Blair[32] is very nice. They all seem to read the *New Yorker*; Maclean's enthusiasm is General Custer, but probably best if you don't seem too well prepared and pre-informed?

We have been wasting our time, having a good time, simmering down after the excitements of job-hunting. Jean, a little worried about stretching our money over the summer, has taken a temporary job on her own initiative, typing some sort of test results in the Educational Testing Center. She's nearly finished a story; I have a bet on with her that I'll finish mine first, but I hope she wins. Mine's rather an old chestnut, which of course I didn't bother realizing till I had it going: a doctor visits a strange house etc., but I've probably mentioned it before.[33] I didn't quite realize it in fact till I came across this quotation as a chapter-head in a Dorothy Sayers mystery:[34] "I who am given to novel-reading, how often have I gone out with the doctor when the stranger has summoned him to visit the unknown patient in the lonely house. ... This Strange Adventure may lead, in a later chapter, to the revealing of a mysterious crime."—In this case nothing more serious, as far as I know yet, than contributing to the delinquency of a minor.

I wish you would cull the best and send me on those stanzas by your students on my sestina and your own, if any; I need a fresh start, some new slant. I am really stuck. I promise not to copy and of course it probably wouldn't help, but on this I'm desperate. Can't sleep for running over the same maddening words, etc. Other days I try not to think about it. But the beginning is so good I don't want just to surrender. I may type out a sheet of alternative stanzas I've done, none of them satisfactory to me, and ask for your comments, your advice, your preferences. I worked a good deal in Miami on another poem too, which I feel pretty hopeless about, it being so Yeatsian—somehow I couldn't help it, though I know better; I may type some of that out too.

Yesterday I swiped a copy of the *Western Review* out of the office and read your story again and James Hall's and a few other items.[35] Your story and Jim's are both good. I've read your thesis too; the other Schreiber piece,[36] the one at home, was to the best of my memory new to me and very good too except for some unclear and apparently insufficient (or insufficiently indicated or suggested) motivation—Schreiber's sudden decision seems unaccountable in terms of this story alone; you have to think back to Felicite;[37] a few small changes I think would make it work on its own and get it printed and liked. The mother-in-law is a very amusing old soul. I think *Arrangements at the Gulf* is good too;[38] I'd seen—all I remember seeing—is a piece of this. A general though slight revision of this one charging it with just a little more excitement and perhaps suspense as well as slipping in just a couple more odd particulars (chiefly about the old man himself, perhaps, or about the resort hotel or the Thanksgiving dinner or something) while keeping the tone cool and quiet would work, I believe; I think the organization is right now and the end is really touching. I'm surprised the *New Yorker* didn't show more interest.

One of my ways of wasting time has of course been croquet. Pete Everwine, the new fourth, plunged $20 into a new set—the old balls were sadly chipped; rubber-tipped mallets, thin, English-type wickets, etc.

Wouldn't houses other than Macky's be too expensive for short-term summer rental?

I can't remember if I told you the risk I'm taking at Missouri. (Needless to say, don't mention this at Chicago.) It's only a one-year job, taking the place of Don Drummond,[39] but I was given mild assurances of its perhaps developing into something permanent. Of course Chicago would have been a risk too.

Well, we hope you can afford a quick stopover here; please try. And again, good luck, and love to all the family from all of ours.

Don

Leaving the harbor eased the burden,   At First it hardly seemed a burden
If not for long. Behind lay silence;   OR:
And all before them lay the voyage.   They are accustomed to the burden.
O may it lead them out of harm   Children, they played apart, in silence,
Unto that country not like others,   And read old maps and dreamed of voyage
The musical tongue, the new way!   etc.

To them it may not seem a burden
After so long. Probably silence
Is what they like best on a voyage,
And, just because they dread some harm,
Are they so different from others?
They only want to get away.

But what if love should prove a burden?
The only safety is in silence,
As they knew long before the voyage.
Spoken too freely, <u>thou</u> can harm.
They see it now, observing others.
Love must be told, but not that way.

What anodyne will ease the burden?
I know that it will not be silence,
And, very likely, not the voyage.
More likely it will do them harm.
Bound for that country not like others,
They ask you, "Does it lie that way?"

Others touch hands to ease the burden,   OR: I think they meant to leave the burden,
Or stroll, companionable in silence,   To stroll, companionable in silence etc.
Under the stars which bless the voyage,   X X X
Nor hear the foghorn speak of harm   X X X
X X X   To grow daily more like others,
X X X   Nor ever relapse to the old way.

X X X
X X X
Some friend, perhaps, prescribed a voyage,
Thinking it could do no harm.
But they are not at all like others;
They can never get away

How can I help to ease the burden?
X X X
X X X
See that they do themselves no harm,
Remember tomorrow to ask the others
Not to look at them that way.

(For Stanza Five)

O may they waken far way,
The birds crying their sweet burden,
In that country not like others
etc.

But everything along the way
Reminds them somehow of the burden:
That island, so remote from others,
The cold, the icebergs drowned in silence,
OR:
The icebergs in a world of silence,
The foghorn speaking all night of harm

A pleasant red-haired man,[40]
Noticing my red hair,
Predicted a great career
But for the asking mine,
But whether of sword or pen

Confessed he could not tell,
So cloudy was the ball,
And how could he have foreseen,
A stranger met in the street,
That words from a stranger's mouth
Should seem the simple truth
To a boy of seven or eight?

    later:
O recreate that hour,
Divine Mnemosyne,
When all things to the eye
A dawning splendor wore,
And I was wheeled in a chair
Past vacant lots in bloom
With goldenrod and with broom
And all the yards in flower,
X X X
When the simple voice of a bird
Or a housewife from her yard
X X X

Stern Papers, Regenstein Library, 56; TS.

---

336 S. Governor | June 14 [1955] | [Iowa City]

Dear Dick & Gay,

Thanks for the confirmation. The Chicago job I don't think will be a mistake
for you. You'll surely be in the thick of things and are sure to prosper there.
I was a little dazed while there, I didn't get the impression that I'd have the
sort of schedule you'll have: I inferred I'd be working more directly and
eternally with Maclean. The standards of teaching there would, I fear, be too

high for me; certainly too high without a great deal of elaborate preparations you won't need to make. I counted up the distance on a road map the other day—as I remember, it's just under 400 miles from Columbia, Mo. Not too far for [a] week-end now and then, I hope. Columbia's 250 from Iowa City and if the Petersens[41] are here next year (there seems to be a little doubt) Tom and we are planning to come for some football game or other. Moreover the rumor is (though Tom hasn't mentioned it himself) that Tom and Jackie may get married next fall when she comes back from France: the wedding would be a nice opportunity for a get-together too, wherever it takes place (some question of Chicago or IC, I understand)—don't, as they say breathe a word of it, though, till you hear it from Tom himself. There's many a slip . . .

We're moved into the Wests' now—thank God. The last few days at the Bakers'[42] were maddening. Noise constantly; screaming; dogs yowling; people coming in to look at the apt. The bed had one of those slopes and I had one of those slumps, so couldn't sleep at all. Became extremely nervous, short-tempered, and a little depressed. The West house is big and quiet, though, everything fine. (It *is* a house, by the way, not the apt. you remember; there's even a garden, a lawn to mow, etc.) It's the first time I've had a study of my own. And a piano. Also TV in the study. The only thing lacking is the Sterns. Two stories to the house; stairs on the same side entering as Peter's house in Hillsboro; reminds me very much of the months we spent there. The weather's about the same so far, too—cool throughout the house. In fact, it's been amazingly cool here—only about three hot days, widely spaced, so far this summer, and Sunday it was down to the forties and no higher than the mid-sixties. Incredible, when you remember how hot it already was this time of year when you first arrived out here. Ray has as you know thousands of books; it's been an orgy with them since Saturday, when we moved. Cowley's *The Literary Situation*[43]—he's a maddening gnat; many books of poetry I hadn't seen before, most impressive being Nemerov's *The Salt Garden*;[44] *Hart Crane's Letters*[45]—a really moving book. It's having a curious effect on me, this last one, I don't know how to describe it; I think I want to experiment some, branch out, grow bigger. If possible. Of course his poems are as chaotic as his life—but it's quite a legend; a marvellous story; many mysteries. I feel (like you) that I could write better if we were nearer you-all; I need a ready, critical, sympathetic audience; Jean is ready and sympathetic, but she likes everything. I'll enclose some stuff later.

I've written letters to Berryman[46] and George Nauss[47] asking for contacts with publishers; Nauss says Scribner's in the person of Wheelock would be interested, but that even if he took the ms. it wouldn't appear till fall after next and of course it would be with the work of two others. One of the others, Louis Simpson, who's all right.[48] I've also spoken to Paul,[49] Marguerite,[50] and Ray about the problem of publishing a book; and Cal[51] spoke to me of his own accord (as I may have written you, saying he'd mention it to his editor at Farrar—he's moved from Harcourt along with his editor—and to Catherine Carver[52] at Harcourt—I somehow don't trust her though—she turned down "Patient B").[53] The trouble is that I probably won't have enough poems that I'm satisfied with by the end of the summer, which I've set up as a sort of mental deadline: 30 or 35 pages. Now this would probably be about enough for the Scribner's enterprise, but not for anything else. What's your advice? I know it's not supposed to be wise to rush into print, but God knows I haven't done so; I cast away poems all the time; keep only the cream; also I'll be 30 this summer; isn't that time enough? I wish I could talk to you, have you help me decide about what poems to go in, what arrangement, etc. I do think some publisher is likely to print them, esp. after what Lowell said. But—One practical reason I'd like to have a book is that it'd help me keep a job; this besides all the mystique related to the mere fact of publication.

For instance, should I include the two poems that were in *Accent*?[54] I don't want to. Should I include "Aboard! Aboard!" From *Poetry*[55]—you know, the locomotives, the one with your phrase? I don't want to. What about "Homecoming"? No, say I; I still once in a while have a vague hope about doing something more to that one. The stanza you say Christopher and Kate have memorized—what about it?[56] It was meant to be part of a longer poem that still isn't worked out, and now, in fact, the stanza form of the other pieces is changed, and it doesn't fit in. Doesn't the fact that it's so Yeatsian automatically eliminate it, despite its graces?

The *New Yorker*'s had a comic piece on murder mysteries (I probably told you before) for 3½ wks. now—what do they mean? *Poetry* has had two poems for weeks also. Still no word from BO direct.[57]

Good luck on the novel. I wish we could have written a play this summer. Maybe next. What about a couple of houses on the Cape? Tom and Jackie would like one too. It would be a fine time. Tell me more of the ideas for the novel as they shape up.

We had duck stuffed with wild rice last night and again, just now, for lunch; wish you could share. The Bamboo Inn had degenerated, by the way. Petersen is taking Bantron[58] to cure himself of cigarettes; he has his ups and downs of moods (going back about two years, I guess, they're mostly downs), but we still play poker about once a week; I no longer feel like showing him any of my work, can't trust his judgment. Reed Whittemore[59] and Jim Hall will be here this summer teaching; Hall got a Rockefeller (did you apply?) as did Marianne Hauser,[60] May Swenson,[61] and Robt. Hivnor.[62] Either Snodgrass[63] or Hellman may also get one or split or get part of one.

Love from both of us to all of you. Keep the letters coming.

Don

PS

Glad your poem finally to appear;[64] I've almost forgotten it but think it will be sure to create a small sensation in the coffee closet of "the Division" at Chi.

The *Hudson* took "Thus" and the following, but turned down the Dantesque sestina:[65]

A woman I knew had seemed most beautiful
For being cold and difficult of access.
Have I not seen the cleverest man of us,
But at a word from her, honey or gall,
Blush and look elsewhere like a boy at school?
And others also, followers of the chase,
Look up or down but not into that face,
Owing to the perfection of the skull?
I knew this lady a dozen years ago.
Since, that she has to two or three been kind,

After long siege, and these not of her sort,
And that she has both given and taken hurt,
Hearing all this, and more, I call to mind
That high, improbable bosom, which was snow.

This is too Yeatsian, also, I suppose; anyway Petersen says so; it has a nice flow, though, is well organized, and speaks plainly; so I think. And you?

Here's a stanza of a sort of birthday poem (for the 30th, in Aug.) that I've worked on ever since Miami; the children's stanza was to be part of it, the stanza just preceding this one, but you'll see the form's changed; I'll add after this one, which I like, the substitute stanza for "the pleasant red-haired man" and the beginning of the succeeding stanza.[66]

At ten I was wheeled in a chair
Past vacant lots in bloom
With goldenrod and with broom,
And all the yards in flower,
The simple voice of a bird
Or a housewife from her yard
Flowering in my ear
Until it seemed I heard
The growing sound of life;
Root and blossom and leaf;
And in myself also
The vigorous shoot broke through.

Stanza I, a little rough:

Great Leo roared at my birth;
The windowpanes were lit
With stars' applausive light;
And I have heard that the earth
As far away as Japan

Was shaken again and again
The morning I came forth.
Some took it for a sign.
Huddled about the bed,
The tall aunts prophesied,
And cousins from afar,
Predicting a great career.

Stanza III, beginning:

By fifteen I had guessed
That the "really great loneliness"
Of James's governess
Was why she saw the ghost
On the other side of the lake

(I just remembered how it goes on)

And certain that my own ache
Was similarly vast,
I too began to pluck
Images out of the air
And shape them to my desire;
Shutting the door to my room,
I lived from dream to dream.

The last stanza was to begin thus, but is currently abandoned, obviously:

At thirty I look out
The window beside my desk.
There, boys in the summer dusk
Of green Connecticut
Kick, up and down, their ball.

Out of this, though, grew the following, which I intend, tentatively, as part of a series, to be called something like "From a House in Florida."

These are all meant to have a kind of pastoral simplicity:

The neighbor boy who climbed our wall
In search of something like a ball
Will not recall, will not recall

The urgency with which he crossed
Or even what it was he lost—
Only that something beyond cost,

Which nobody shall ever find,
Once rolled off somewhere out of mind,
Beyond a wall, with brambles twined.

Is another stanza necessary? The ending seems anti-climactic every other time I think about it, but the image doesn't.

Here's the first of the same series, begun; of course you may say that the Frost here comes out too clearly; I hope not; at least I don't think it does until the third stanza; if you say so, I'll start over with the 3rd.

The tree was there—it must have been—
For Yankee birds to winter in
And treat the backward Southern kin

To morning and to evening song.
Sung as it was by such a throng
It seemed unlikely to be wrong.

Oh, when the day was still in doubt
That confident unison rang out;
And night could not come in without

A chorus of welcome, no less ___ (gay?) etc.

Or, starting with line 3:

> And teach the backward Southern kin
> A more sophisticated song.
> Sung as it was by such a throng,
> It seemed both overloud and long. (or loud and overlong). Etc.

A third member of the series, which needs, I suppose some stupendous ending:

> The cat we kept, whose wounds were such
> She didn't want a stranger's touch
> Or even to be looked at much,
>
> Hearing us come, would run and hide,
> Shy as Susanna or a bride.
> The fact is, <u>we</u> were terrified,
>
> Still nursing our old wounds of her—
> Scratches, not deep. Of course they were
> Trifles compared to her torn fur.

If there's to be a fourth, it will probably be about the boys shooting the birds from the trees with Christmas B-B guns.

This one's Baudelairean, I suppose, and you may remember a wholly different version:

> Risen from rented rooms, old ghosts
> Come back to haunt our parks by day,
> They crept up Fifth Street through the crowds
> Unseeing and almost unseen,
> Halting before the shops for breath,
> Still proud, pretending to admire
> The fat hens dressed and hung for flies

There or perhaps the lone, dead fern
Dressing the window of a small
Hotel. Winter had blown them South—
How many? Twelve in Lummus Park
I counted shivering as they stood,
A little thicket of thin trees,
And more on benches turning with
The sun, old heliotropes, all day.

Old men, who wear against your chests
Torturous flannel undervests
All winter long, and yet are cold,
Poor, cracked thermometers stuck now
At zero everlastingly;
Who bend like your own walking sticks
As with the pressure of some hand,
Surely God must have thought you strong
To lean on you so hard, so long![67]

I'm not quite satisfied with "torturous" or, indeed, with that couplet, or quite certain the apostrophe should begin this and include both the images it does; what say you? I left out some further lines of description:

Hands fluttered on their laps, brown leaves
Of autumn blown just there by chance;
Their foreheads had a moon's canals.

(There were more; I can't recall them.)

I've also done 11 more lines on the sestina you liked the beginning of; have only 7 lines to go.

End of report.

Stern Papers, Regenstein Library, 76:2; TS.

July 2 [1955] | [Iowa City]

Dear Dick & Gay,

No news to speak of, just a friendly missive (I almost wrote missile).

It's finally turned hot here, though it's still far from as hot as when you first came. That summer keeps recurring to me; the ones afterwards blend together. Our sleeping habits have gone from bad to worse, partly in order that we can take advantage of the cool of the night for working; we retire at dawn, arise mid-afternoon. However, we've decided to reform; today we cheated ourselves on sleep and already, though it's not yet midnight, I am beginning to nod. Mean to turn in when I've finished this and mailed it—a little spin in our Olds in the night air, down to the post office. They're repairing College St., by the way, have it blocked off; you remember those bumps? The Capitol has lapsed into its usual summer doldrums; now playing *Laura*[68] (for probably the 10th summer) and some other feature even less memorable. We watch Groucho, *Person to Person*, and I the fights—on Ray's TV. Which gives me headaches—I had a fierce one the other night after poker (*not* because I lost $2.41 either) and not an aspirin in the house; at 7 o'clock I finally went down to Racine's, the only place open so early, and got the Asperline,[69] that being all they're allowed to sell here in Iowa at places without a pharmacist. This seems to have turned into an Iowa City paragraph; I don't know why. Thinking about the spin in the night air, I suppose. Well, to hasten on, then. I revised a little of the Yeats out of the sonnet and sent the revision to the *Hudson* to substitute. I sent the *New Yorker* an odd sestina I dashed off this week; I don't think it's any good, and it doesn't seem like me (to me), but it might be their type. It begins like this; if you want to see the rest, let me know.[70]

> They have climbed the mountain.
> There's nothing more to do.
> It is terrible to come down
> To the valley
> Where, amidst many flowers,
> One thinks of snow,

As, formerly, amidst snow,
Climbing the mountain,
One thought of flowers,
Tremulous, ruddy with dew,
In the valley.
One caught their scent coming down.

The good line, which comes later, is: Meanwhile it is not easy here in Katmandu. (The *good* in it being, according to my view, the "clever" use of *do*; this is what I hope Moss[71] will see and get hooked on.) I've almost got my "good" sestina finished too, the one beginning "I often wonder about the others."[72] Tell me, is it Auden? Sometimes I don't know. Is the Satan poem Auden or Baudelaire?[73] Is the "Old Men of Lummus Park" Baudelaire or who?[74] I honestly hope you exaggerate the extent of my influences; I meant to write "honestly think" but my typewriter may have been too honest for me. According to your plan for arranging a volume, that is, with the more or less original pieces coming last, which ones, pray, would they be? I'm in doubt. Should I try to do a blank-verse narrative of "Vineland's Burning"?[75] You know I started that once, and the beginning was good; it would fill out a book if I *could* manage it; but I'm not keen.

Edgar has finally condescended to write us a letter. I'm still peeved by his long silence but have replied. He has submitted to what he terms his "fate" and has got Swallow to bring out his poems; they appear in October.[76] May be driving through Ct. in July; wanted to visit us there; I had the nerve to suggest he call on you.

When will you all be moving to Chicago—the first of Sept. or so? What about housing there? Are Higgins[77] and/or the University at work on it? The U. of Mo. was supposed to arrange housing for us—in their faculty housing, duplexes, rather grubby-looking on the outside—but I haven't heard a word yet.

Jackie has arrived in France by now; didn't like the *Ile de France*, according to a letter from Tom. The more I think back on it, the more I enjoyed the crossings (excluding the first abortive one),[78] esp. the one coming back.

A terrible lot of plaster fell on our—rather, the Wests'—refrigerator a couple of hours back—what a crash! Jean thinks they'll be vexed because of our negligence—but how were we to know that that only vaguely sinister bulging crack was anything serious?

The next morning, or rather afternoon: We managed to get up at 10:30 today, a real triumph. No spin, after all. The Levangs[79] dropped in at 11:30—being aware of our previous habits—and kept us awake till 2.

I think each of us should write a short novel this year and then collaborate on a play next summer.[80] Rent "cottages" in New England somewhere and work on it every morning. I think I'll write my novel about a high-school teacher, naturally in a small Southern town, not worry much about form or style, just get it done. You know, a severe regimen of say two hours a day. With only 2 classes to teach at Chicago you ought to be able to do same, unless Maclean wants you as Custer's orderly. What did you and Elder Olson talk about? Did he tell you Stevens had written him a letter about his (Olson's) latest book of verse, for instance?[81]

Enough running on. It's too hot and still this afternoon. Oh, oh, some more plaster just dropped. Write soon. Our love to all.

Don

Stern Papers, Regenstein Library, 38:4; TS.

1328 Anthony | Columbia, MO | Sept 22 [1955]

Dear Dick & Gay,

I typed a letter to you a week ago today but having no envelope kept forgetting to mail it.

Many thanks for your letter, by the way. I will act on those suggestions which I can—and which feel right to me. Could you be a little clearer about your views on arranging the poems? And what about sending me the address of the *Paris Review*—the American address, that is? Berryman, from whom

I heard today, thinks I should try Scribner's, their Poets of Today series, since the volume is so small; he sounds pretty encouraging. I just read his Stephen Crane book and agree with you that it is marvelous;[82] I've read his Shakespeare essay again and agree on that now too. I think he may actually be writing a biography of Shakespeare, though his allusions to what he's up to are so roundabout I can't be sure;[83] he's up to something, though; and his Bradstreet book is coming out with illustrations by Shahn.[84]

Jean is working on poems now. A small anthology of lines: (1) "We make our seasons but unmade by some"; (2) "The yellow toy airplane is beached on the woodshed roof."

Problems of teaching occupy my mind in moments of idleness; so far it's hard to think of writing, even of revising, though I've done a little, a very little. I have a narration class, about a dozen students, totally without promise; this is supposed to prepare them for the advanced writing seminar. There are thirty in my twentieth century survey—so far we are still on the "Wreck of the Deutschland" and I am enjoying that. I had to recruit students for the modern poetry seminar—only one had signed up for it at registration and it was about to be cancelled; I now have five and we're reading verse drama.

Social life begins tomorrow with an outdoors dinner party at the home of the Beowulf teacher.[85] Next day a picnic with the 42 instructors and the 12 "senior members," including me.

Hardin Craig[86] pretended to remember me but had, I think, been briefed. Also pretended to remember Jean when I told him she & I had both been in his class; said she was a good student. He may actually have remembered. He definitely remembered you, asked about you. The only difficulty: he called you Dick Steele. I said, plucking his arm, "Oh you mean Dick Stern; he lived in Steele."[87] But deaf as always, he continued to call you Steele and I really couldn't correct him again. He sends his very best wishes—and when he sees you please remember to answer to your name. He even said, later, "It's funny—Dick Steele lived in Steele."

I wonder if our old Olds would make it any better than your Chevrolet. Right now the master cylinder is leaking, whatever that is; it means we have no brakes and of course can't afford repairs. Luckily I'm within walking distance of the school. Anyhow, if you're sure you can't make it at Thanksgiving, we may try.

Meanwhile, love to all.

Don

Got proofs for 2 poems in *Borestone Mt. Poetry Anthology* yesterday—no word about prizes.[88]

Stern Papers, Regenstein Library, 44:9; TS.

December 10 [1955] | [Columbia MO]

Dear Dick & Gay,

Well, when do you want our visit to begin and when to end? Our vacation starts here the 20th, I believe, and ends, I think, the 3rd. We wrote the Petersens, asking if they knew someone who might be leaving an apt. vacant the last week of vac, but have received no reply. If we stay longer than a few days with you, we naturally share expenses. Shall we bring the Chinese checkers as well as the Mozart sonatas? I think we'll be coming by train or bus not car: I'd have to buy a new tire, which I can't do. Not only that but I'm in terror of the roads.

I'm glad they're keeping you on; but there was never much doubt in our minds about that. I'm however in much doubt about my status here. It appears now to depend on Drummond's decision, and he's incommunicado in the Philippines. Peden[89] has promised to let me know as well as he is able before Chicago. If you hear of anything good, keep me in mind.

Your old men story must have gone at least to Mrs. White,[90] unless she's dead or completely retired. I think that's about the maximum time they ever kept one of mine—and that occasioned the letter from her. As for only 4 of 11 having been published, the watchword is, Remember Shirley.[91] Powers'[92] last story was a lot better than the Salinger. I thought. Though he was only repeating himself.

In the verse drama course, we have now read all of Eliot (except the *Clerk*)[93] and incl. the *4 Quartets*,[94] most of Yeats in verse (emphasis on *Purgatory*),[95] all of Auden (& Isherwood) except the *Dog*[96] (of which there were no local copies) and incl. the *Orators*,[97] and all of Fry[98] (too much). No text. The only verse drama anthology I remember is an old one by Kreymbourg[99]—out of date by now. I don't think there'd be much demand for one, so you must have meant just a modern drama anthology in general. But if you meant one in verse, there'd be little question about what it would contain: *Sweeney*,[100] *The Conf. Clerk, Paid on Both Sides*,[101] *The Ascent of F6*,[102] *Purgatory* (and perhaps *The Herne's Egg*),[103] *Phoenix Too Frequent*,[104] *Him*[105] (?), and *Under Milkwood*[106] (?). As for a drama text in general, I'd suggest *Purgatory* or *Words upon the Windowpane*,[107] and the *Conf. Clerk* and perhaps *Phoenix* among these, plus *Come Back Little Sheba*[108] (my favorite among Broadway plays for all time, I believe) and of Odets prob. *The Country Girl*,[109] something by Hellman,[110] prob. *Streetcar*,[111] prob. not *Death of a Salesman*[112] but of British plays I just don't know; I doubt there's much. Much more useful I think would be an anthology of 20th cent. literature that would include substantial helpings of the good poets and good short-stories, perhaps also a few non-fictionists like Adams & critic.[113] I'm much handicapped in teaching this survey by lack of good text.

Here's a poem, meant to be long, that I've been working off and on without much luck:

> Something of how the homing bee at dusk
> Had seemed to ask, perplexed, how there could be
> No flowers there, not even withered stalks of flowers,
> Conjured a garden where no garden was
> And ghostly trellises too frail to bear
> The memory of a rose, much less a rose.
> Some oak more monumentally an oak now
> Than ever when the living rose was new
> Cast shade that was the more completely shade
> Upon a house etc.[114]

A hexameter for line 3—quite a liberty for me. One of the later lines is a tetrameter.

I'll bring what I have of the play along.

We heard from the Wilners this week;[115] he's teaching at Yale now; his novel was rejected by McGraw Hill and is now making the rounds; he plans to begin another in spring. They had another child; Nancy was sick afterwards. A nice letter. Said nothing about being in Chicago for MLA though.

I have heard nothing from Paul Engle about the Scribner's thing; and nothing from the Princess[116] about those poems of mine she's had so goddamned long, though I wrote her another letter a month ago, demanding action. What should I do? She did write me last summer that she was accepting 2 but failed to mention which 2; I hate to ask for them back and yet I want some action. I haven't mailed any other poems anywhere; I can't feel satisfied with any.

I read Donald Hall's book;[117] he appears to be a good politician—his picture in *Time*, his book receiving the Lamont award, etc.: but he's a better politician than a poet. The poems, I'm afraid, are just plain dull taken all together.

Craig wants me to choose a book for Ellis-Fermor's[118] Christmas present—something modern and American. I suggested Eliz Bishop's new book of verse;[119] he countered by suggesting some anthology.

Has Olson ever told you about having to decide not to be a concert painist—no, pianist?

Yes, we will all begin to dislike literature; would that we were teaching mathematics or a foreign language. I realized suddenly Thursday night (about midnight) that I was teaching *A Portrait of the Artist as a Young Man*[120] the next morning and that I hadn't read it since I was fifteen (except for parts); that's no fun.

We can hardly wait for school to be done and to see you all again.

Love,
Don

Stern Papers, Regenstein Library, 44:9; TS.

CORRESPONDENCE OF 1956 TO 1958

In 1956 Justice took a teaching position at Hamline University in St. Paul, Minnesota. He taught there for one year, and in 1957 returned to the Iowa Writers' Workshop as a lecturer.

After ten days return to | Don Justice, Apt 306 | 1293 Grand Ave. | St Paul 5, Minn
                                                                October 8 [1956]

Dear Dick & Gay— I've written two duty letters tonight and have not enough time to get down to anything really worthwhile & pleasant—this is the nearest I can come.

The sonnet "A woman I knew had seemed most beautiful"[1] I cannot get permission from *Hudson* to reprint since those slow bastards haven't got around to printing it themselves yet. For "Ladies by Their Windows" & the other sonnet these 2 credits lines are obliged to appear: "Copyright 1954 by *The Hudson Review*, Inc. Reprinted by permission from *The Hudson Review*, Vol. VII No. 2, Summer 1954." I'm very sorry to foul you up like this. For the 3 poems from *Poetry*, the copyright is being assigned to me (for a fee). I suppose some credit line might be used, whatever you know or suppose to be customary, something like: Copyright 1953, 1954, 1956 by Donald Justice. Reprinted *Poetry: a Magazine of Verse*.[2] (?)

All right.

I can't remember the new sonnet well enough to quote and don't feel like looking it up right now.[3] I can try, though, with the added reservation that some of it needs reworking, the 1st line probably, for instance:

Father, because this day the death to come
Looked naked out from your eyes into mine,
Almost it seemed the death I saw was mine
And that I also shall be overcome,
Father, and call for breath when you succumb,
And struggle for your hand as you for mine
In hope of comfort that shall not be mine
Till for this rest of me the angel come.   (?) on 2 counts
But, father, though with you in part I die
And glimpse beforehand that eternal place
Where we forget the pain that brought us there,   (?)

And, father, though you go before me there,
Yet while I breathe, you shall not wholly die.   (?)

I've been experimenting with a (for me) new kind of thing too. Some Chinesy
(and probably old-hat) things:

1. The evenings are growing short. The sensible people
   Have had their storm windows up since Saturday last.
   Happening to look up, I see the first
   Goose of the season, bearing South to my homeland.
   (Goose is supposed to be ambiguous, a double mood)
2. For RGS
   My friend writes of the pleasures of last summer,
   Not excluding the Famous Dispute of the Easy Chair.[4] (5 beat lines)

And here's something very odd which I can't write unless I can think up the
proper story and perhaps take a vacation in the Caribbean (the story I ought
to go with is one Bob Vaughn has for a short novel—a search by a kind of
vagabond captain and crew for Columbus' bones—a wonderful idea when
you begin to think it over, but more for a long poem than a novel):—

I, Henry Tomkins, cook,
Formerly of the Guadeloupe schooner La Coquita
(As the people here in St. Thomas will remember),
And before that of many others of all sizes
Both in the islands and farther north,
A good cook, able to keep a watch soberly,
And the other things around boats when necessary,
Knowing not only the principal ports but the others,
And the chief bar for sailors in all of them, yes,
And where to go for women and the best music,
I, Henry Tomkins, aged 30, known as "The Shark"
(On account of this scar, I think, and my teeth showing),
Declare that this is the whole truth of that matter
To which I am the sole surviving witness,

And swear to it by God and the other gods,
And hope that Mr. Dufour (with his education)
Will put it down with as much comprehension as elegance:

As follows:—

You are my barometer, my sensitive instrument, which tells me I am
fair & warmer or cool & cloudy. So?

Jean and I are seriously considering making her stories (2 of them) into
television plays.[5]

We had a pleasant evening, or rather morning, with Berryman and his
fiancée; he's planning a divorce from his wife:[6] he called here at midnight
inviting us to a party right then, had just been in town 24 hrs.

Did I tell you I have classes 6 days a week—on T, Th, S's at 8 in the morning? Nevertheless I seem to have a little more time than at Missouri. I'm
hoping to get back to the play & maybe a story any day now.—As for your
play, maybe to lay it aside for awhile would be wise, while you do the novel,
but please don't throw it, don't even think of throwing it away. I think the
novel really ought not to be too hard to put together; the only worry I'd have
over it is whether people who can read *Don't Go Near The Water* & think that
funny (I read a page of it in *Life*) could possibly appreciate your wit too.[7]

There are more Republicans than I ever saw before in my life—that is,
among a faculty. Still, the Democrats outnumber them. The weirdest & most
vociferous Ike-fancier of them all is the other young "chap" in the English
dept. a friend of Paul Ramsey's from "the U."[8] (He once knew some member
of the Dulles family and calls R P Warren "Red"[9]—Paul had admitted this
boy was a name-dropper, but most of the names he drops you just never
heard of at all.)

Well, it's past bedtime, tomorrow being an 8 o'clock morning. Have you
had to start teaching your class yet? (Spoken without any bitterness at all.)

Jean thinks you are making that up about Pat Wolf[10] becoming a Hellman.
The game here, by the way, is volleyball.

Love to all,

Don

Stern Papers, Regenstein Library, 76:2; MS.

March 6, 1957 | [Columbia MO]

Dear Dick & Gay,

Your letter was a pleasure, as always they are. I'm waiting for a copy of your ms.—in between publishers if necessary.

Jean's been doing all the writing in our family. She has about half a dozen stories either finished or just about—one long one that looks very good to me, maybe because the main character acc. to me but not her, is modeled on me—a kind of fatuous intellectual who almost chokes his idiot baby.—*The Western Review* sent back her really good story without so much as a note—their stupid readers apparently didn't even show it to Ray (I had advised her it wasn't necessary to include a letter to Ray and so must take part of the blame).

I've sort of holed up for the winter if not for life. We've abandoned the car in the alley behind the house—we never see it from day to day except by chance, when it looks almost buried under the burden of snow. (Now and then I think, Ah you & me, brother.) Thus we go everywhere by bus, which is to say practically nowhere except perhaps a concert at Hamline now & then. Of course I go still 6 mornings a week to school but most of the time I naturally try not to let it seem real. And meantime I've found the nearly perfect dream world to hole up in—music paper. I've covered pages, as Jean evidently wrote you. The charm of it is that it has nothing to do with life—not only is this (mainly) true aesthetically, but practically—I mean no connection with career, money, etc. True play and far more exciting than solitaire. The main impetus is the good Hamline music dept., which puts the rest of the school (except for the basketball team—and me) to shame; all an inheritance from Ernst Kreneck's[11] having been here in the 40s, for what reason I can't imagine. (He lived in fact, in the same apt. bldg. we do—and is now in Calif.—which may be a good augury.) Well, I've been reading books, listening to records and studying scores and recovering a lot of what I'd forgotten in the last 15 yrs. and learning more besides—I can almost hear a score now, though I must go slowly—all of which is of course just faintly pathetic at my time of life. But good therapy. Though I've finished no poems etc., I have finished a piece in 3 short movements—8 minutes all told—for a solo piano and 10 wind instruments and some percussion—a sort of mock concerto. We've rehearsed it once and, after about 20 more (since it's kind of complicated), ought to be ready for a spring concert where it'll be performed. I'll try to get it taped; I think that can be arranged. It's not great music, but if I were 17 it would perhaps be considered promising.

Now and then from this refuge I send a letter asking for a job—one to Paul, one to Cornell. Nothing doing. I've also got my application in for a Saxton fellowship (with the first act of the play), but this is not very much to hope from since they were pretty discouraging about considering a play as the basis for an application.

I bought *Scarecrow Christ* and liked many of the poems—he *is* better than I'd thought.

What are Tom and Jackie doing? The Heisermans?[12] Did Jean remember to thank Christopher[13] for his nice Valentine?

I hope you can use the money. I won't say anything about how shameful it's been of us to put if off so long. If this doesn't square with your recollection of the right sum please speak up. Cash it quick, before we change our mind.

Love,

Don

The University of Chicago | Chicago 37 Illinois | Department of English |
1050 East 59th Street
March 17, 1957

Dear Don and Jean,

I had been feeling awful for about a month (a little longer than my usual cycle) when your letter arrived and took me out. It wasn't the excessively munificent repayment (a part of which I am now in debt to you for I'm sure), though that certainly wasn't painful, just the sadness of the letter. When you reported your words to the Oldsmobile, I joined in with you, Ah, you and me, brother. But failing music paper or an artificial universe, I finished off the second and wrote the last act of the play, and tonight I'm typing it to send to the agent Bessie[14] told me about last summer. (I wrote and got a cold answer from a subordinate, but what else is there.) I think it's all right. I'll send you a copy this week and then you can determine what part of it you wish to accept as yours and how you want to be known with respect to it, co-author, "based on a scene from RGS and DRJ," revisor, translator, or just in for a percentage (minimum a quarter, maximum seventy-five percent). It's great to have out of the way—if this is what it is, and I've worked so fast on it, getting it out of the way apparently means something. Olson read an act and a half, thought it "charming," but "needs action," Maclean ditto on eight pages—I don't agree. I think it's a "development of Chekhov"—or is this an easy way out? Art Heiserman is the other reader—and he was very enthusiastic.

Maybe I can get back to the novel,[15] now that Little Brown sent it back saying the characters were unsympathetic. I feel that way about the whole book, but I shall try to hack it out. I also kind of feel like writing a poem—a rarity with me and about as much related to my life as you say music is to yours. Now, saying this, my ambition stoops with fatigue. What a cold unfriendly world this is. And *Western* turned down Jean's story. Incredible. But your poem in the *New Yorker*—that recognition belated also—revived us.[16] The first poem that has sullied their pages in some time. And so sad too. But it's good to hear that you're thriving in the cold, Jean. I must confess to thinking your story of the fatuous intellectual choking his idiot baby based on me, but I hope your fiction will take care of even the tendency, the occasional tendency.[17]

Well, it's spring. And I think you will like Bellow[18]—a most unusually friendly fellow. Called up here and spoke for the first time in his life to Gay: "Mrs. Stern? How are you? This is Saul Bellow. How's everything?" etc. I *think* that's nice. He told me that the Berrymans are "expecting." Did you see the picture of half-mad Lowell in *Life*, a baby encased in a royal bassinet between him and a weary-looking Elizabeth?[19]

You ask about Tom and Jackie. Tom seems to become even more involved with college politics. He also works diligently and continuously. The week's vacation we begin now is heaven for him. At the end of the next quarter and before the summer quarter, when he teaches, he and Jackie are going away for three weeks and they mentioned your using their apartment. OK?

Maclean and I had our first real argument the other day, and since have been treating each other very gingerly and even with careful intimacy. He read me—or rather showed me, the oration he delivered at his best friend's funeral two weeks ago, and talked again about his stunted career (his own). I hear more confessions from Williamson, Sirluck and Olson.[20] I do like Olson and Sirluck—and Maclean too—tho, but I feel soggy after a session of this sort and they helped compound my depressions.

I read the other Kingsley Amis novel[21]—it's about as good as the first and, on Wilt's[22] instructions, invited him to come over here next year. I also accepted an invitation by the Riverside Church to help screen poems for a national contest! Fifty dollars. A propos, let me add to your burdens by saying the choice of judges was slid out of my hands this year and so you lose seventy-five bucks.

I hope things warm up on Grand Avenue.

Love,

Dick

When I shift out of low next, I'll write of it and pull you out of yrs. This way we might keep going for a few years.

Justice Papers, University of Delaware, F386; TS.

February 14, 1958 | [Iowa City]

Dear Dick and Gay,

I don't know why it has taken me so long to getting around to writing you. I suppose that one's energies decline over the years and under a cold—my record of having or catching a cold every Christmas is still unbroken. The football game languishes now on top of a closet and the darts board is virtually unused. What have we been doing? It is hard to say. Trying to remember the way it was, it seems that as soon as I shook the Christmas cold I settled right down to the ambitious schedule I resolved on there in Chicago[23]—4 hrs. a day writing, 2 hrs. a day at the piano, and 2 hrs. for work. That lasted several days and then Gene Lichtenstein[24] came into town. When he left, there had accumulated a whole pile of correspondence (official) and manuscripts to read, not only of my own students here but of maybe half the amateur writers in the country, all of whom do want to get in the workshop next year and most of whom write long tedious novels about the occupation forces and soldiers getting involved with native girls. With that out of the way there's at least a week lost somewhere, but then I started work on the review for the *Western* I'd been postponing for years—it's not done yet but I have a good start.[25] Also I've got the long poem, which we talked briefly of at Christmas, under way, if you can call the three opening lines any way at all; there are several other lines for later and a much clearer idea of the whole thing, though. Here's the "plot." (As you'll see, it's a kind of blend of *Under Milkwood*[26] and Peter's story "Bad Dreams," and an old story of mine about Great-Uncle Billy.)[27] A family has gathered in an old house in the summer; they are waiting for the grandfather to die; one rather stormy night, some nights after a July 4th party at which the older people set off the remaining fireworks at night after the children were in bed (this, I hope, will keep getting referred to in the course of the poem), everyone in the house suddenly wakes up, for no real reason, strangely, unaccountably, and one by one a selection of these people tell what woke them and what they were dreaming about: the servants (together with a chorus), a boy, an adolescent girl (both sleeping in "the children's room"), a widowed aunt, a bachelor uncle, the boy's mother, maybe a couple of others, and last of all the dying grandfather; perhaps a dog will tell his dream too. There will probably be narrative interruptions or choric commentaries by the servants (lying downstairs away from the others). It could go on to be quite a long poem, as you see. The first three lines are thought by the servants:

Why do we turn in our beds,
Neither waking nor sleeping?
We did not hear any thunder (etc!)

If I can get, say, the first 50 lines done I'm going to apply for a Saxton fellowship again.

Paul is still being coy about next year. Vance Bourjaily wants to come back too, and we have entered a sort of friendship pact—either we both come back or neither of us does. We're also thinking of offering ourselves as a team to some college that wants to start a writing program.[28] Do you know of any such places? He's a very nice person. His third novel, which I've just finished reading in carbon, is quite ambitious and pretty successful; it tries to be Tolstoyan in some ways and in some ways succeeds but is a little thin in places and a little too saga-like in others and structurally impure; but very interesting and incidentally full of the things which ought to make it somewhere between a critical and a popular success, maybe both. There's a long sequence (with which the book begins and to which it returns about halfway through) concerning a production of *Hamlet* by a group of children between 8 and 16, approximately, directed and starred in by a girl of 14, interpreted too by her in a pretty interesting way. And all sorts of funny and sad things, and a complicated plot. Title: *The Violated*. Did you try his first two books?

I've had a couple of letters from publishers in New York—at last. Scribner's invited me to submit, but I'm not going to. Instead I sent a manuscript off yesterday to Hudson River Press. This is a new outfit planning to publish paper-backs (well-made ones) of new poetry, translations, long short stories, and short plays; to be distributed as widely as they can manage; to sell at either 50 or 75¢; to pay the author 15 to 20% royalties. They expect to break even on between 400 and 500 copies and say that the City Lights people have not sold less than 2000 of each of their paper-backs. It all sounds European and promising, just the sort of thing I would like to get behind and in. The man's name is Jerome Dennis Rothenberg[29] and the address is 50 Broadway, if you're interested. Rothenberg very nearly assured me that my book would be taken and printed this year. I called it *The Summer Anniversaries*. Does that sound all right to you? I used an epigraph—after all—but one I made up:[30]

O recreate that hour,
Divine Mnemosyne,
When all things to the eye
Their downiest splendors wore.

Jarrell, who's apparently Poetry Consultant again (or still) at the Library of Congress, wrote me asking to record some of the poems for their "archives" if I planned to be in Washington "in the next few months";[31] otherwise they'd pay for a local reading.

I'm going to teach here this summer—which will mean some money in case I can't find a job for next year. Not enough for a year, but perhaps I could pick up a fellowship or something to go with it.

And that's about all the news from here.

Tell Tom, if you like, that I will still be here this summer but that it would be nicer for everybody if he would finish his novel and get the degree out of the way—that is, unless they want to move here this summer for him to finish it. That would be very nice for us. How is his toe?

Oh yes, I meant to tell you above about a curious experience of ours this week. Tina Bourjaily[32] went to the hospital Monday night to have their second child (a boy, it turned out) and they left their four-year-old girl with us overnight. She demanded a story and the only one, when it came right down to it, which I could remember and which she hadn't heard was *Beowulf*: I didn't even think how scary it might be for her, esp. since I was so desperate to think of any story at all; later on she called me upstairs to tell me she'd just seen *Papa* Grendel. She may have been pulling my leg.

I'll type out on another sheet a couple of extended versions of poems which you haven't seen in this form.[33]

Let us hear the news from Chicago. Hello to Christopher and Katie.

> Love,
> Don

Stern Papers, Regenstein Library, 56; TS.

March 22, 1958 | [Iowa City]

Dear Dick,

I'd have written before but that I fell to what's called in the South "the flu," and it has been even longer and harder than usual to stand up again. In fact, I still have a fever sporadically, this after 9 days. All this is nothing compared to the novocaine and the other cane, but it prevents or at least hinders reading and typing out of letters. It also gives me an excuse to do nothing but write and sleep, happy pair. I've had, in fact, a very good writing week. Finished the first section of the long poem,[34]—see enclosure—written 13 lines of a sonnet, just for practice, and done a section of the long poem in prose, a poem "en prose," I think, though I may decide to break it up into more or less regular lines after a while. The prose piece written last night in fever—perhaps a good state for composition, for I remember writing the first 14 lines of "On a Painting by Patient B"[35] while in the infirmary, burning. Also did another song a couple of weeks back, before being stricken. This song and an earlier one, both to my poems, will be sung April Fool's Day as part of a program of poetry readings in which I'm involved here. I hope to get tapes.

I hope you're wrong about the Guggenheim. I'd like to hear, in fact I'd have liked to take part in, the tapes of the plays; save them. Thanks for giving the agent my name regarding my own plays—I'll do something about that when I'm feeling better. And thanks for the news about Berryman. I hope he will do the review for *Poetry*: you and he together will have made my reputation, if ever it should be made.

I have a lot of correspondence still to get out of the way; I've let it pile up again, while indulging myself in this ailment. I'm tired. But I will write you again later.

P.S.—I read Boussard's[36] (?) poems and recommended that Paul get her a fellowship if he could. Because you seemed to think that your involvement with her application might make things delicate, I have refrained from further activity, but will if you think it best. Even should she not get one in the next month or so, there would still be a chance next fall, by the way. She seemed original but wild to me; talented surely.

> Best lovingness to all,
> Don

THE SERVANTS:

We have not heard any thunder.
We have not seen the lightning
Flash upon the horizon.
We have heard only the weathercock
Turning as usual, the clock
Wheezing before it strikes.
It is three o'clock in the morning.
Why do we turn in our beds,
Neither sleeping nor waking?
We should be used to the dark.
We should not mind so much
The absence of moonlight. We have only
To turn the light on again
To restore the shape of the attic.
We have only to wait for daybreak
To restore the fields to their places.
Why do we turn in our beds,
Neither sleeping nor waking?
We have not taken the journey
Of which, just now, we were dreaming.
We have not left, after all,
A world made more or less tolerable
By the addition of curtains
And photographs of the children.
We are the servants only,
To whom nothing much ever happens.
Soon shall be cockcrow. Soon

Shall be birdsong under the rafters.
We shall descend the stairs
The back way, making no noise.
We shall perform the chores
To which we have grown accustomed.
We shall not lack for occupation.
We are the servants only,
To whom nothing much ever happens.
An old man is dying
In another part of the house.
We can do nothing for him.
It does no good to remember
How, after the celebration,
Long after the children were sleeping,
He stood in the back yard pointing
The last of the roman candles
Skyward, over the arbor.
An old man is dying
In another part of the house.
Why do we turn in our beds?
We are the servants only.
We can do nothing for him.

Minor alteration and readjustments, particularly of the refrain lines, may follow, but this is *almost* it. I hope you find it as formidable as I do.

Stern Papers, Regenstein Library, 33:1; TS.

Wednesday [March 1958] | [Iowa City]

Dear Dick & Gay,

The photograph of the Mike Todd[37] funeral scene in the Des Moines paper had a head of hair and forehead that looked like you, Dick; of course we were looking for some resemblance. And at least you saw Sugar Ray[38] work out.

Mike Z.[39] I'd like to hear from, but I guess I'll have to write him first, since I owe him a letter. If he is bitter about Norma, as you say, the reasons are mysterious to us; everybody keeps everything from us, it seems.

I am sorry to hear that Bob Mack died.[40]

I haven't heard anything more from Rothenberg. I don't know what's happening about the book, but I assume no news is good news and that it may well be off to the printers by now. I hope he will like your play. I suppose I mentioned that Gelfman[41] wrote me inquiring about mine.

What have you blown your $225 for? How did they arrive at that very odd looking figure? The only thing I can think of is that it is one quarter of a thousand, though it must have other associations.[42]

I had a letter from Bob Vaughn; he is in Puerto Rico. I don't know how he manages to live; he and his girl, called D.,[43] have a house, he says; and apparently he has more free time than I (and you) for he says he is writing; the only mention of financing came out when he said that D. had sold a couple of paintings for a couple of hundred bucks each. Virtue is its own reward. Its own excuse for being too, I guess.

Mainly I wanted to reply to your objections about the chorus. I guess they must be serious ones. Jean too thought of *Murder in the Cathedral* right away. The chorus you are thinking of is the first one in which the refrain "Living and partly living" occurs, which is also in a 3-beat line, though loosely. I naturally don't think there is much connection except the accidental and necessary. For instance, the 3-beat line is anybody's, Yeats', Auden's, Eliot's, mine, if that series is not too aggressive. Also the commoner-mentality for a chorus is anybody's—Greek tragedy's, for instance. At least in the translations, the habit of thought, the kinds of expressions of many of the choruses in the tragedies of different people sound very much alike. The point is that the chorus is just that person or group which is deprived by nature from participating in the great events, and which can thus be only vaguely disturbed, instinctively responsive to them, if at all, and which can more or less report the facts objectively and not go overboard. Eliot, I think, fakes this a little on the plane of reality: the poor women of Canterbury are made up, and they get awfully damned excited and poetic. Whereas, I would argue, my servants naturally belong to the scene of action, the business of the real life of the house, and speak naturally. Because the content of their speech and its diction are so very ordinary, in fact, I have felt that a dramatic rhythm was justified, necessary. All of the parallelisms are also part of the conventional rhetorical garb for such things, and might be justified even further in terms of the psychology of the dream or half-awake state maybe, though I'm a little dubious of such things. Furthermore, there are no real borrowings. The likenesses are the likenesses of a kind not of a particular thing. Still, I'll agree, that even that may be too much in this age. The context may take away part of the sting, because I don't think it will sound very much like anybody: again I may be wrong, though. And by the way, Auden likes to begin with the 3-beat line too, in "For the Time Being" or "The Sea and the Mirror,"[44] for instance, and he has speeches of the commoner-mentality in which there are similar echoes of Eliot, though perhaps not so much of the essence of the thing all at once. One last suggestion: try substituting "you" for "we," and see if you think that is any better. It works well enough, I think, hastily, in all the stanzas except perhaps the first refrain "An old man is dying."

It is three o'clock in the morning.
All night now we have listened
For a sudden footfall, a whisper,
Half forgetting at times
What it was we expected
Or even that we expected
Anything out of the ordinary.

I have to hurry the rest of this letter in order to make a conference on time. So I will just say that Section II, which follows, I am not yet decided about, that is, whether it should be printed as prose or verse or some combination of the two—I'll try it here as verse, in a mixture of 3, 4, 5 and 6 beat lines; the prose version would be worded very slightly differently.

> Slowly now from their dreams the sleepers awaken.
>   And as, slowly, they grow aware of the light,
> Which only by very gradual stages invades their rooms,
>   Timidly at first, testing the sill, and then
> More boldly crossing the floor, regarding itself
>   Brightly in mirrors (which seem, indeed, to bloom,
> Under such a gaze, like shy girls of the country,
>   Or like small ponds which, dry all summer,
> Brim all at once with the first rains of autumn),
>   It seems to them, half awake as they are,
> That someone has left a light on for them,
>   As a mother might for her children,
> And that it has been burning there all night, quite close,
>   Even while they were dreaming that they slept
> In dark, comfortless rooms like these, or, in some cases, caves,
>   Damp and airless, or a tunnel, extremely narrow,
> Through which a train was expected momently, thundering.
>   And the light left on seems to them perfectly natural,
> And in fact necessary, for they have not yet remembered
>   Who they are, and that they are no longer children.
> And as, slowly now, they open their eyes to the light,
>   It is in time, though barely, to glimpse their dreams
> Already disappearing around the last corner of sleep,
>   The retreating tail of the monster winking and flashing.

I dashed off a sonnet too, for relief and practice. See backside.[45]

Speaking of Islands

You spoke of islands, where the fishing boats
Sleep by the docks like men beside their wives,
Content all night, while under them the waves,
Arching their backs a little, purr like cats
And rub against them peacefully. Some nights,
You said, nothing in all that harbor moves
Except those boats with motion of those waves
And a few sleepy gulls with cries like flutes.

You spoke of islands as I speak of you,
Sea-circled and remote, an island too,
And of such latitudes as islands keep,
And languorous airs, and fragrances offshore,
And blue approaches to desire and sleep,
O my belle harbor, my San Salvador!

Must go now. Write soon, and love to all.

Don

Stern Papers, Regenstein Library, J-R; TS.

May 24 [1958] | [Chicago]

Dear Don and Jean,

Forget when I last wrote, what I'd covered, and what not. We were all very happy about the *Es-quire* sale; I think it was as good, and in some ways better than selling a story of my own. Congratulations to you, Jean, aren't in order, but they are to literature and the goddamn publishing world.[46]

And did I thank you for the care and speed with which you took care of those Mann awards,[47] Don? If not, herewith. Your judgements took the day, of course. (Delmore Schwartz,[48] writing on some sort of wrapping paper, couldn't remember what he was judging, and said, "I'm not sure of my judgements at this time.") Other judge, Jim Hall.[49]

Mike has been through and told you of Norman Mailer's[50] explosive visit; I'll amplify when I see you. I just put "Lillian" (I'd better say Hellman) on the plane last night, and am looking forward to spending some time in "the Vineyard" with her and Lenny (Bernstein),[51] Averill (Harriman)[52] and Jeesie Christ.[53] But the sweetest little bourgeois aunt I ever saw—that she wrote the plays, was a lush for fifteen years, saw the Russians take Moscow in '44, was in Spain in '36 etc. and I do mean etc., is about as believable as the Grimm brothers' collection. More when see.

Hawk's Well wants to do the book of stories—is worried about copyright for Rothenberg feels fiction might well sell over 1500 copies and copyright problems are complicated (five years only etc.) Verlin Cassill rewrote (apparently) the story about the college instructor for one of his sex mags[54]—I told agent "not too much" but "ok" and expect $150.00 minus agent's fee. I guess I told you that the novel is off (I think it's by far the best thing I've done—though it could be rewritten again and again—I was doing it till an hour before I sent it off—nine months after I began), the agents seem very enthusiastic, Funt has tried to see ms. but agents don't want to show it to him and don't want me to until contract with publishers is signed.[55] Nothing more on play, tho I'll send it to Hellman's office (I told her about yours also). BBC returned TV play. Have been really busy for a change and haven't done any work on the *Schreiber* which must, I see, be rewritten and rethought completely. You must help me. Am on TV Thursday with Wilt[56] and half of a very nice new couple we know here—you met them at the party (the Shils).[57] On Angry Young Men.[58] Then I make speech to alumni on same. Have read a lot of their crappy books, *The Contenders*[59] being one of the newest and worst. *The Entertainer*[60] is better than *Look Back*[61]—have you read it? Amis' last might as well be a collection of anecdotes or "thoughts about the times."[62] Saw *End-game* last night (with the Bway. cast including Alvin Epstein[63]—we gave [a] party for cast and Hellman after the play—H. didn't come because she hates the director and didn't know—she said—it was our party). Runs about two hours, should run half an hour—it's funny and instructive in a number of ways, but nearly as repetitive and irrelevant as O'Neill.[64] It's built like variations on a theme—the theme here being the "end-game." There's not an inexplicable word in it, just some foolish mistakes.

Have made tapes with Mailer and Hellman. Would you ask Ralph Freedman[65] if he'd be interested in Mailer's for *Western*. I think Mailer will have it transcribed (it's a fantastic thing—Mailer turns hipsterism into a kind of Manichaenism), and *Chicago Review* wants him to cut it—and he won't, I'm sure. He wants to use it as last of his short pieces in a collection to come out next year.

I thought your review of the poets excellent, tho feel funny about being known as bad-tempered reviewer. Perhaps I won't be. (Olson met Hall—thought him a disgusting sonofabitch. Liked Tony Hecht,[66] James Wright,[67] a kid.)

This should cover the year's work in England.

Love,

Dick

Rothenberg has quite good taste—disliked "Nine Letters," liked "Arrangements at Gulf."[68]

Justice Papers, University of Delaware, f386; TS.

Oct 6 [1958] | [Iowa City]

Dear Dick & Gay,

I just finished getting ready that Ford Foundation nomination of you and can finally feel it is okay to write you. Also, at last finished my review of T. Williams for *Poetry*.[69] Still to go, among numerous small matters, an article on recent developments in poetry for something that calls itself the *American People's Encyclopedia* and my introduction to Kees. A week on each, at least, it will take me. Then to poetry, I hope. I will include two short ones I finished about two days ago; one, I think, is good, the other a fair try at something. Jean is putting the finishing touches (we both hope) on her story about the collector of folk songs.[70] We are both glad to be back in Iowa city of course; we've both put on a little weight, for instance, for which I'm glad (of mine) and Jean's sorry (for hers); I weigh nearly 150 now, for the first time in my life. Of course, I've had my usual psychosomatic cold at the beginning of school term, but it's almost done now. The only blot on the week-end was the tie game of football, a great disappointment. I'll be going to New York, as I'm sure I wrote you, to read at the YMHA on Dec. 11.[71] We hope to be able to stretch the vacation from that date to the 5th of Jan. Have you made plans? I'd hope to spend some time in NY. Any suggestions? Would there be any excuse for you all to be there over Christmas? Or would there be an apartment available near you in Chicago for perhaps a week or at least a few days? We'd like to hear about your surely fantastic summer. And, of course, see the children and so on, since we've caught only glimpses for some months now. —My little book of poems ought to be out soon; it only waits for the Lamont announcement,[72] sure to be a disappointment, though not an unbearably great one. —By this time, I know, you must have heard about *Golk*. But what? We are very eager, not to say anxious, to hear also. And what about your second?[73] (Amazing.) When will you know about it? Etc. You must have been working very wildly indeed. Even Tom appears to have caught it, is working again, they write. (Including a very funny account of a night spent in Auden's apt. about which you've surely heard.) They plan to come out for a week-end. What about you? —Almost forgot to recap the Miami part of the summer, but actually there's not much to say of it—I still liked Miami pretty well (as I had the previous summer) but not as much: the trouble was the people, of whom Norma was representative, in that although all likeable and liked they seemed enervated and fairly depressed; what was depressing for me, among other things, was that most of them seemed to have good reasons for being so. —About the Mailer interview: Ray should by this time have read it; he was slow getting to it, though prompted by me and Ralph too I think, probably because he just got back in time for school and approached everything, including his loved *Review* (no sarcasm intended) with a very natural reluctance. If there is no pressing need there for the tape or the play, I'll keep them until we come on a visit or you do; let me know otherwise. And many thanks for their use; they pepped up my summer class, which was on its last weary legs by the time we got to them. —Poems on the other side.[74]

                                    And love to all of you,
                                    Don

1. Your face more than others' faces
       Maps the half-remembered places
   I have come to while I slept,
       Continents a dream had kept
   Secret from all waking folk
       Till to your face I awoke,
       And remembered then the shore
       And the dark interior.

2. But these maneuverings to avoid
   The touching of hands,
   These shifts to keep the eyes employed
   On objects more or less neutral,
   As honor, for the time being, commands,
   Will hardly prevent their downfall.

   Stronger medicines are needed.
   Already they find
   None of their stratagems has succeeded,
   Nor would have, no,
   Not had their eyes been stricken blind,
   Hands cut off at the elbow.

                      Stern Papers, Regenstein Library, 38:4; TS.

CORRESPONDENCE OF 1959 TO 1961

January 16, 1959 | [Iowa City]

Dear Dick & Gay,

I meant to write long before this. By the time we got back here I was coming down with my traditional Christmas cold, a little delayed this time; after that there was the Kees preface to prepare,[1] and some library work to do on it; and then the pile of manuscripts held over the vacation. I have today my first really clear day in weeks.

Jean probably told you in her letter that she preferred *Golk*: at least that was my impression in talking to her about the two novels. I mention this first because I conformed to what you said was majority opinion in liking *Europe* better. *Golk* is more original probably, but its very originality seems to me to put such a burden on the invention that it sometimes buckles under. I still think this is especially true of the first chapter, that is, following the wonderful beginning in the rug shop. I simply cannot see this bookstore business with Hondorp as a potential Golk,[2] even as it is "justified" later—for one thing, the justification is after the fact. The chess scene, too, though much improved over the first version, still strains my belief. Some of the sex seems gratuitous to me. And the style—though this may have been straightened out, at least for the most part, in the "600 verbal changes"—doesn't seem to me quite to sustain itself. By this I mean that some of its propositions are overelaborate, that some of its small jokes aren't necessary, that sometimes its Jamesian roundaboutness fuzzes the point, and that the diction relies too much sometimes for its humor on the long and fancy word—now this last effect is very good at times, esp. when it is possible to see the other factor in the style, the oddly intrusive low-class or even vulgar word sticking its nose into a high-class context, but not as so constant a diet, I think. I am in love with the whole conception just as I was at the beginning, but I do have these reservations about the way it was carried out. Papa Hondorp[3] seems very good almost all of the time, and Golk and Hondorp seem good most of the time; even the higher-ups have their moments, but the others in Golk's crew don't seem to come up to their potential—as they would, say, if this were the *Moby Dick* of the television industry—except maybe for Hendricks[4] when she and Hondorp go into the country, and when she leaves him. The sense of New York, its geography and landmarks, is good and satisfying all the way, too. It's so savage and original and at times so funny that it ought to be published and to get some notoriety, though. Even so, I'd think you ought to be willing to work on improving it if any publisher had not merely ridiculous suggestions, ones that would change the whole rather than the parts. The problems of structure in *Europe* seem to me to be solved: that must have been one of the hardest things to do, but the structure ends up seeming natural and unforced to me. In fact, very neat. There are only a few parts that I would criticize. The first part of the first chapter seems to me to scatter its effects in random perceptions and small jokes: the details of the life are so densely given that it leads one to expect similar treatment of everything, and this promise is not carried out (which is probably good). I think the weakest scene, though, is the scene in Gladys's[5] apartment, the dinner at which she is insulted: the motives of the characters, particularly of the insulter, aren't visible to me. The "philosophical" discussions, the comments about German national character, in other places seem to go on too long. The discussion about the art of the novel, which you seemed worried about, seems more interesting to me, though definitely questionable: personally, I am inclined to give you this, though others may not be. I find it interesting (though not really necessary). Ward[6] *is* a little disappointing, esp. in the next to last section dealing with him, but not too much so. I lent the book to a friend here who enjoyed it but who had this criticism to make, if you're interested. I don't think I share his view, by the way. It was a novel of careers, but the careers, their developments, were pretty apparent at the outset, so that the sense of change was less present than the sense of fulfillment of destiny, and therefore, there was not much surprise except in the particulars of the fulfillment. I've forgotten what you said about the novel of careers when you were talking about Pasternak's book, but I'll read the review.[7] I hope all this isn't going to seem too shattering. Understand that I like both novels very much—but that I think they both ought to be more perfect. What's the news on them from New York?

When we got back here, in addition to the batch of Christmas cards, there were a few letters of more interest. One, for instance, was from some underling at *Mademoiselle* who said she'd been at the reading and found it "masculine, passionate, and controlled." Jean interpreted this as a mash note. My first. She went on to say that she'd like to show some of my poems to the editor. So I sent a couple. They just came back rejected. Another was a letter from *Harper's Magazine*, the new editor[8]—I think he's new—asking also for poems. I sent him four short ones. Well, they didn't come back, but a check for $125 did. I was flabbergasted at the size of it.

Other news from here is that I'll be back here next year if I want to and that there's some chance of my getting a more nearly permanent appointment. Also I'll be teaching half-time this summer—a satisfactory compromise. Ray, as I told you, is leaving this June for San Francisco State. I don't think the following item is supposed to be public information yet, so please don't start writing letters about it, but he will probably not take *Western Review* with him. For one thing, it appears to "belong" to the university; for another, he doesn't seem at all reluctant to leave it here, in fact, says this would be his first choice. He might start another out there, a different kind, if he could find the money. The *Western*, in that case, might die; or it might continue under the editorship of someone here, or under the editorship of someone brought in especially for this purpose.[9] I'll let you know when all this is decided. The issue with you and Mailer ought to be in the mails today.

By the way, Vance says Mailer would like to come back to Chicago if he got invited.

We're packaging the novels in a separate container and stuffing in Cozzens[10] and *Famous Trials*[11] along with them. I'll register the package; I wouldn't know how much to insure it for, but I'll make inquiries. Okay?

Best to all of you and to the Rogerses and Heisermans.

Love,

Don

P.S. I bought Landowska[12] playing a couple of Mozart sonatas; she dots some of the eighth notes etc. but I found out a few things from listening. How is 4 No-Trump?[13]

Stern Papers, Regenstein Library, 32:13; MS.

August 23, 1959 | [Iowa City]

Dear Dick and Gay,

Shameful of us not to get a congratulatory letter off sooner, and the fact is that I did get one started last Monday, whereupon the phone rang and Edgar was calling us to come pick him up at the Cedar Rapids airport. Which, of course, we were very pleased to do. A nice visit we had with him, though many of the people he might have enjoyed meeting, and many of the things we might have done to while away the time, were unavailable, this being the dread interim period when even Kenney's[14] closes down and muttering wraiths are abroad upon the streets. In fact, it turned hot with his arrival and has been debilitating since, though not as bad as '52 and '55, the first of which I'm sure you will never forget, nor the second, we. Anyhow, Edgar left Friday and is off for Europe the fifth of October, will tour France with the (Marvin) Mudricks[15] and visit (Don) Hall in a 15th century priory at Thaxted (England), and doesn't know where he'll settle down eventually over there. He is, much as ever, the same fine person, very agreeable, though with a 2% reserve which no longer, after all these years, seems strange. And then yesterday was our 12th anniversary, which we celebrated by eating out at the Bamboo Inn, practically the only restaurant open here now—and by wishing to go to a movie, there being no decent ones playing. And so now that Sunday has come round, here is, at last, the congratulation. But it goes without saying, really, how pleased are we to hear that *Golk* has found admirers who also are in the publishing racket. The George Elliotts[16] say that since Criterion publishes few novels they probably can't be expected to push any they do print, which one understands is what is needed. Though I won't be surprised if it makes a sensation, it is so original (even though, as you know, I don't like all the parts of it, the more fantastic ones anyhow). And where does this leave *Europe*, I mean the novel? Will Criterion, for instance, print it if *Golk* goes well? Anyhow, it's about time, and more than deserved. Who would ever have thought—or did you say this before?—that both of us would have to wait till 1960 to publish our first books? May there be many more. And, by the way, the snatches you quote from the current one sound very intriguing, in two senses.

As for us, neither of us has written a lick all summer, except a review I did for *Poetry* of Housman.[17] Jean however is touching up her present-tense story to send out again;[18] she appears determined to try the little magazines first and the paying ones later, an odd reverse. And even I am working on a story, sweated over it all afternoon, in fact, a present-tense one too, by odd coincidence. But no poems done for months now.

We haven't much money, but in a week or two may take off for a week or week-end somewhere lakey north of here, in which case we might drop through Chicago for a couple of days, especially if we can count on your being there. When will you return? Drop us a postcard. And in the meantime, go to a couple of plays for me and take a long cool dip in the brine.

Love,

Don

Stern Papers, Regenstein Library, 38:4; MS.

Monday May 17, 1960 | [Chicago]

Dear Don,

The poetry reviewing is fantastic—I never really noticed before, being fooled by the Lowell reviews. Well, I trust you'll have one: I called Pak[19] at the *Chicago Review*, and he says that he will make an effort.

I have been widely, but Lord knows, not well-reviewed—intelligently I mean. The best was a girl named Didion in the *National Review*,[20] and a quite decent one in the NY *Post*,[21] but all the reviews that count, NYer,[22] *Sunday Times*,[23] have been brutal, or they haven't been printed (*Time, Newsweek*). Sales pictures is hard to talk about: Murray doesn't think more than fifteen hundred so far, but if so, most must be in Chicago, for a number of stores have been out of it and have reordered. (I've been on TV a number of times as you know, etc.) There've been about twenty altogether.

I'm about to get back to work, tho again I've been oppressed by office work as I haven't been since coming to Chicago. *Harper's* wants me to write a piece on Chicago—I might.[24] And I'm even trying a song or two for the night club, Second City.[25] First verse:

> I remember a time when I used to wake up
> And the streets would be calling me to come out.
> There was a great deal of sun and lots to do.
> The world stuck together—I was the glue—
> And everything spelled out ME.
> And everything spelled out ME.

See you in a few weeks.
Love to you both,
Dick

Justice Papers, University of Delaware, f386; MS.

Feb 23, 1961 | [Iowa City]

Dear Dick & Gay,

I'm sending under separate cover, as I think the cliché goes, Coulette's long poem based on the Fuller book.[26] Could you send it back when you've done with it, please?

Meanwhile I enclose with this a letter which I'd like your advice about. The last 3 reviews of my book I've seen really have driven me rather wild. I begin to feel paranoiac, suspect a conspiracy, etc. The Galler review was just too awful for me to be able to respond to.[27] But the sniffish little paragraph by Fitts in last week's *Times* was, in a way, the last straw.[28] I feel like getting into the literary war. The damned West-Coasters have captured not only the journal—see, for example, the front page piece by Rexroth in the issue of the week before[29]—but the minds of damp and spinsterish little jerks like Fitts as well, though they're probably only half aware of it at best. Gunn, as far as I know, is about the only man doing fairly steady reviewing who can be counted on not to repeat these faddish clichés about academic poetry and the rest of that crap.[30] And that's not enough. The letter is what's meant as a snide but light-spirited reply to Fitts and may not be right. Would you mind deciding? If you think it's justified and otherwise okay, would you simply mail it off? If not, just burn it or something. Here's the text:[31]

> To the Editor:
>
> I once began a poem with the line, "Your face more than others' faces," and called the whole thing "Love's Map," rather wittily I thought at the time, if somewhat obviously. Now along comes Dudley Fitts, your reviewer, to claim that I am deaf to the "latent" absurdity of this.
>
> Well, I am glad he saw my little joke and sorry he didn't like it, but if he had read as far as the second line—"Maps the half-remembered places"—he might have discovered that I was the one who put the joke there for him to find. Blatant, maybe; not latent.
>
> Yours,
>
> end of letter

More background. As you may've seen, my book is one of the final 13 in the running for the NBA[32] in poetry. And Fitts is one of the 3 judges. Which I take to mean that I haven't a chance, even aside from the great merits of some of the other 13 books, or the fact that Snodgrass (who, last I heard, still liked my poems a lot) is a judge as well as the so-far-as-I-know uncommitted Kimon Friar.[33] That's the picture. You be my advisor.

And, just by the way, where did they drag up some of those fiction choices? Where, in other words, is the great god golk? The literary racket needs re-stringing.

Jean is feeling fine and we hope Gay is too. Jean's started another story, and I'm really writing a lot of lines these days on a whole lot of different poems, which means it's rather hard to get any one thing done at the moment but good for the future.

More in a quieter time.

Love,

Don

PS Got a raise here to $7500 and assurances from Paul that I could stay on as long as I liked—so naturally elected to stay.

Enjoyed seeing you all very much—of course.

Stern Papers, Regenstein Library, 38:4; TS.

December 10, 1961 | [Chicago]

Dear Don and Jean—

My typewriter just broke down—just as I was starting—after 4 frustrating months—to write something and had, in preparation as 'twere, last night, reread old letters including some you had written from as far back as 1946.

Wellaway (*sp*), it will be very good to see you—tho odd at the Palmer House[34]—if you can endure a household like ours—we will be delighted to make the appropriate shifts. At any rate, you will be here.

8:45 is a terrible time. I will try and be there, but it might get by. I will find you down there—or leave a room message with you—but I'll see you. NO! I will be there!

I've meant to reply to your very good letter about *Europe*, but now there's too much to write about.

I wish Jean and Nathaniel[35] would be here—oops, I may be down there—shall I stay with you?—in a week or two—trying to HUNT!

Love,
Dick

Justice Papers, University of Delaware, f386; MS.

SOURCE ACKNOWLEDGMENTS

The letters of Donald Justice to Richard Stern are reprinted with permission from the literary executors of Donald Justice, copyright © Jean Justice. Courtesy of the Special Collections Research Center, University of Chicago Library.

The letters of Donald Justice to Richard Stern dated March 3, 1946, March 20, 1948, October 15, 1948, October 1, 1951, June 14, 1955, and October 8, 1956, first appeared in "The Literary Correspondence of Donald Justice with Richard Stern," *Hopkins Review* 2, no. 1 (Winter 2009): 70–96.

The letters of Richard Stern to Donald Justice are reprinted with the permission of Richard Stern from MSS 191, Donald Justice Papers. Courtesy of Special Collections, University of Delaware Library, Newark, Delaware.

The letters of Jean Justice to Richard Stern are reprinted with permission from Jean Justice.

"A Map of Love," "Anniversaries," "A Dream Sestina," "Sestina on Six Words by Weldon Kees," "Here in Katmandu," "Southern Gothic," "Sonnet to My Father," "Love's Stratagems," "Thus," "Speaking of Islands," "Bad Dreams," "A Winter Ode to the Old Men of Lummus Park, Miami, Florida," "Two Sonnets," and "Sonnets About P." are from *Collected Poems of Donald Justice*, by Donald Justice, copyright © 2004 by Donald Justice. Used by permission of Alfred A. Knopf, a division of Random House, Inc.

NOTES

ABBREVIATIONS USED IN THE NOTES

CS   Dana Gioia and William Logan, eds. *Certain Solitudes: On the Poetry of Donald Justice*. Fayetteville: University of Arkansas Press, 1997.

DJ   Donald Justice

RS   Richard Stern

SA   Donald Justice. *The Summer Anniversaries*. Middletown CT: Wesleyan University Press, 1960.

INTRODUCTION

1. Richard Stern, "A Very Few Memories of Don Justice."

2. Stern, *What Is What Was*, 42.

3. Stern never published a collection of his poetry, nor Justice the novels he began to draft.

4. Stern, *What Is What Was*, 45.

5. RS to DJ, February 7, 1946.

6. DJ to RS, February 29 [1948].

7. DJ to RS, February 27 [1955].

8. See Harp, *For Us, What Music?*; Charles Wright, "Jump Hog or Die," in CS; Mark Strand, "A Reminiscence," in CS; and Strand, "Mark Strand on Donald Justice." Unlike others who have written about Justice's competitive streak, Strand insists that it did not find its way into the classroom or workshop.

9. Stern published twenty-two books, including novels and collections of short stories, essays, and what he called "orderly miscellany."

10. For example, his early novels *Europe; or, Up and Down with Schreiber and Baggish* (New York: McGraw-Hill, 1961) and *Stitch* (New York: Harper and Row, 1965).

11. Peter Taylor was married to Jean's sister Eleanor Ross Taylor, becoming Justice's brother-in-law in 1947. Through Taylor, Justice was introduced to the poets Ransom, Tate, and Robert Lowell as well as others associated with the Fugitive group.

12. Cowan, *Fugitive Group*, xv–xxiii.

13. Searle, "New Criticism."

14. CS, xviii.

15. Justice, "Fugitive-Agrarian Myth."

16. DJ to RS, February 15, 1949.

17. DJ to RS, April 14, 1949 (Stern Papers, Regenstein Library, 56:2).

18. Justice was awarded not a fellowship but a teaching assistanceship, a position that paid little and demanded much.

19. See CS, 206; see also David Galler's review "Four Poets," originally published in *Sewanee Review* 69, no. 1 (1961) (reprinted in CS, 212–13) and George P. Elliott's "Donald Justice" from *Perspective* 12, no. 4 (1962) (reprinted in CS, 214–15).

20. RS to DJ [February 1949] (Private TS).

21. DJ to RS, December 27, 1948.

22. DJ to RS, June 14 [1955].

23. RS to DJ, Tuesday [May 1949].

24. DJ to RS, June 14 [1955].

25. Eliot's early poems "Ode" and "Before Morning." See "Correspondence of 1949 to 1950," note 30.

CORRESPONDENCE OF 1946 TO 1947

1. This being the first extant letter, which book he refers to is unclear. Justice worked on several novels during his correspondence with Stern, though none were ever published.

2. Justice was born in Miami, Florida, on August 12, 1925. He died in Iowa City on August 6, 2004.

3. The rhymes of this idiom are reminiscent of his poem "Women in Love" (SA).

4. Stern's "showyily" is a playful misspelling. Both writers took pleasure in wordplay and enjoyed the puns and exaggerated meanings that sometimes resulted from typographical errors.

5. At the time of this letter, English poet, critic, editor, and playwright Stephen Spender (1909–95) was the author of several books of poems, including *Twenty Poems* (London: Blackwell, 1930) and *The Still Centre* (London: Faber, 1939). See also DJ to RS, October 1 [1951].

6. Virginia Hunter was Justice's girlfriend during the semester he spent as an undergraduate at Chapel Hill.

7. Justice's "Poe and Virginia." See DJ to RS, February 5, 1946.

8. To the right of the original Gothic letterhead, Stern wrote, "I wanted these letters to be Gargoyles—they did the best they could."

9. Auden's poem "Petition," lines 13–14, lends Stern his metaphor: "Harrow the house of the dead; look shining at / New styles of architecture, a change of heart."

10. Justice met Jean Catherine Ross in a graduate Chaucer class at Chapel Hill. They were married on August 22, 1947.

11. After working briefly at a clothing store in Evansville, Indiana, Stern took a job with Paramount in New York City. There he did publicity work while training to join the international sales force. In a later letter he describes working alongside the grandson of Paramount founder Adolf Zukor (1873–1976).

12. Stern was engaged to Jo Bledsoe following graduation. Her mother disapproved and ended the engagement.

13. The reason for the omission of a letter in "life" is unclear; it is likely that Stern was punning on the magazine of this title, to which he and Jean subscribed.

14. An allusion to lines 3–4 of William Blake's "London": "Marks of weakness, marks of woe."

15. An inside joke between Stern and Jean Justice.

16. Allen Tate (1899–1979) and Robert Penn Warren (1905–89) belonged to the Fugitives at Vanderbilt University and helped produce the magazine that was the group's namesake. Later Tate and Warren became proponents of New Criticism. Cowan, *Fugitive Group*, 36–63. In 1949, when Tate was teaching at New York University, Stern attended his lectures.

17. The poet Edgar Bowers (1924–2000) served in the U.S. Army until 1946. That year he attended Chapel Hill, where he met Justice and Stern. In 1947 Bowers began his PhD at Stanford, studying under Arthur Yvor Winters (1900–68), and he encouraged Justice to join him there. Harp, *For Us, What Music?*, 56. Bowers's first book of poems, *The Form of Loss* (New York: Swallow), was published in 1956.

18. At the University of Miami, where Justice took his first teaching position, a one-year appointment as an instructor of English.

19. Edith Wharton, *Age of Innocence* (New York: D. Appleton, 1920).

20. Stern gave the Justices a copy of Winters's *In Defense of Reason* as a wedding gift, along with a coffeemaker. The following year Justice applied to Stanford, where he took an assistanceship and studied under Winters as an auditor. Frustrated by a teaching load that slowed his progress as a student, Justice left the program without completing his degree. Harp, *For Us, What Music?*, 13.

21. In "Primitivism and Decadence," Winters proposed an approach to criticism that denounced Romanticism and what he termed "the fallacy of imitative form." *In Defense of Reason*, 62. When Justice here alludes to his own "conversion," to absolutism, he is referring to the influence of Winters's book.

22. "Big Shot No. 2" and the "two friends" referenced here are unidentified.

23. The religious poet and critic Paul Ramsey (1924–94) met Justice and Stern at Chapel Hill, where he wrote a master's thesis on the poems of George Herbert (1593–1633).

24. Ezra Pound, *Personae* (New York: New Directions, 1926).

25. William Faulkner, *Go Down Moses* (New York: Random House, 1942).

26. In the style of the poetry of Robert Lowell (1917–77).

27. "The sun makes shadows of us all." This line from Stern's "Poco Commedia" impressed Justice, who later requested permission to publish the poem in a small anthology. See DJ to RS, April 3, 1948.

28. In an unpublished letter dated January 30, 1948 (private MS), Stern wrote that he had shown Justice's poems to the editors of the *Hudson Review*. Stern joked, "I didn't particularly like 'Letter to a Romantic'—so I added six lines to it before I showed it to them—'The moon makes minute men of mice' etcetera." This line, written in jest, echoes Stern's line in "Poco Commedia" and in the "companion piece" excerpted here.

29. Franz Kafka, *The Castle*, trans. Willa and Edwin Muir (New York: Knopf, 1930).

30. Thomas Mann, *The Magic Mountain*, trans. H. T. Lowe-Porter (New York: Knopf, 1927).

31. Rainer Maria Rilke, *The Duino Elegies*, trans. J. B. Leishman and Stephen Spender (New York: Norton, 1939).

32. F. Scott Fitzgerald, *Tender Is the Night* (New York: Scribner's, 1934).

33. F. Scott Fitzgerald, *The Great Gatsby* (New York: Scribner's, 1925).

34. Henry James, *The Wings of the Dove* (New York: Scribner's, 1902).

35. In the 1930s the fiction writer Peter Matthew Hillsman Taylor (1917-94) studied at Vanderbilt under John Crowe Ransom. See "Correspondence of 1948," note 34. Under Ransom's influence, Taylor became associated with the Agrarians. In 1943 Taylor married Jean's sister, the poet Eleanor Ross Taylor (1920-2011), whose six books of poetry earned her a number of distinguished awards, including the 1998 Shelley Memorial Prize and the Ruth Lilly Poetry Prize. In 1948 Taylor published his first book, referenced here by Stern, *A Long Fourth and Other Stories* (New York: Harcourt).

36. Unidentified.

37. Leo Tolstoy, *War and Peace* (1869).

38. In the original letter Stern drew a single vertical line to the left of lines 3-5; in the margin he wrote "(Thanks)." From the last line he drew an arrow pointing to the parenthetical that follows.

CORRESPONDENCE OF 1948

1. Stern worked for Bon Marché, at the time a division of Bloomingdale's.

2. William Empson (1906-84) spent a number of years in China and Japan as a professor of English literature. From 1947 to 1952, during the Communist siege, he delivered weekly lectures on Shakespeare at Peking National University. In 1947 Empson spent the summer months teaching at Kenyon College in Gambier, Ohio. Haffenden, *Among the Mandarins*, xx.

3. English poet, playwright, and critic Derek Stanley Savage (1917-2007) devoted much of his life and writing to the politics of pacifism. Savage was a frequent contributor to the earliest issues of the *Hudson Review*.

4. Following the death of editor Maxwell Perkins (1884-1947), poet John Hall Wheelock (1886-1978) took over as senior editor at Scribner's.

5. Around the time of this letter, Tate introduced Lowell to John Crowe Ransom (see "Correspondence of 1948," note 34), whom Lowell later followed to Kenyon College. Beck, *Fugitive Legacy*, 68-69. There Lowell also met Randall Jarrell (1914-65) and Peter Taylor, through whom he and Justice became acquainted.

6. Influential New Critic and poet Richard Palmer Blackmur (1904-65) was a friend and supporter of Fugitive poets Cleanth Brooks (1906-94), Ransom, Tate, and later John Berryman. Beck, *Fugitive Legacy*, 89-90.

7. Joseph Bennett (1922-72) and Frederick Morgan (1922-2004) met at Princeton University, where they studied as undergraduates. After serving overseas in the Second World War, Bennett and Morgan cofounded the *Hudson Review* in New York City. The first issue appeared in the spring of 1948, featuring

poems and essays by, among others, R. P. Blackmur, D. S. Savage, and Wallace Stevens (1879-1955). Morgan, "*Hudson Review*'s Early Years."

8. Frederick Morgan, "William Carlos Williams: Imagery, Rhythm, Form," *Sewanee Review* 57, no. 3 (1949): 675-90.

9. Peter Taylor.

10. Poet and translator William Arrowsmith (1924-92) was also a founding editor of the *Hudson Review*. However, he remained on staff for only a few years.

11. Cornelia Claiborne was the managing editor of the *Hudson Review* and Ellen M. Violett (1925-) was the associate editor.

12. *Factotum* was a small literary magazine produced by Paul Ramsey at UNC Chapel Hill beginning in 1948. The magazine published four issues over two years.

13. Writers Kenneth Rothwell (1921-2010) and Burke Shipley were members of the literary club Stern formed at Chapel Hill. Shipley was the son of Stern's high school English teacher, the former Fugitive poet Joseph T. Shipley. See "Correspondence of 1949 to 1950," note 49.

14. Stendhal, *The Red and the Black*, trans. C. K. Scott-Moncrieff (1830; repr., New York: Modern Library, 1925).

15. Stendhal, *The Charterhouse of Parma*, trans. C. K. Scott-Moncrieff (1839; repr., New York: Modern Library, 1926).

16. Théophile Gautier, *Mademoiselle de Maupin* (1835).

17. Anonymous, *La Princese de Clèves* (1678).

18. Meaning, at these addenda, "the Master would look askance."

19. I hope it will happen.

20. *Volpone* (1941), based on Ben Jonson's satirical play, was directed by Maurice Tourneur.

21. *Shoe Shine* (1946), Vittorio de Sica's neorealist film.

22. Charlie Chaplin's comedy *Monsieur Verdoux* (1947).

23. In December 1947, after leaving his job in Orlando, Stern stayed with Justice's parents in Miami for a few days—the only time he ever met them. That month's issue of *Life* featured a photo spread of Miami Beach, which, the article reported, was growing in popularity among the young and well-to-do. "Miami," *Life*, 29 December 1947, 31-42.

24. Justice's unpublished novel in progress, "The Animated Dead."

25. "How huge must be that whole which corresponds / To such a part." Dante Alighieri, "Canto XXXIV," lines 33-34, p. 181.

26. Percy Lubbock, *The Craft of Fiction* (London: J. Cape, 1921).

27. Gustave Flaubert, *Madame Bovary* (1857).

28. Edith Wharton, *The Writing of Fiction* (New York: Scribner's, 1925).

29. Balzac's novel *Le père Goriot* (1835), the first in which he used recurring characters to tie his works together.

30. Honoré de Balzac, *Eugénie Grandet* (1833).

31. Henry James, *The Ambassadors* (New York: Harper, 1903).

32. William Faulkner, *The Wild Palms* (New York: Signet, 1948).

33. Justice refers to his poem "Holy Saturday in Venice," a draft of which is printed here following his letter dated March 20, 1948.

34. The Arts Forum took place March 11-13 in Greensboro, and the influential poet and teacher John Crowe Ransom (1888-1974) was expected to attend. Ransom was one of the original Fugitive poets, who later associated with the Agrarians. In 1939 he founded *Kenyon Review*, which Justice and Stern read often.

35. Stern was unable to attend the Arts Forum.

36. Lyman Cotten (1901-91) was an English professor at UNC Chapel Hill. Stern studied modern poetry with Cotten, who also acted as Justice's thesis adviser. Cotten and Stern kept in touch following Stern's graduation.

37. H. K. Russell, Jean's thesis adviser, taught modern fiction at UNC Chapel Hill.

38. Hardin Craig (1875-1968), literary critic and historian, taught English at UNC Chapel Hill after a fourteen-year professorship at Stanford.

39. In an unpublished letter dated January 17, 1948 (Stern Papers, Regenstein Library, 32:14), Justice wrote, "As for Stanford, we're still dying to go. For instance, we made up this little line—which we haven't had the nerve to relay to Edgar yet—'O to be in Stanford, now that Winters there.'"

40. *The Fugitive* (1947), a drama based on Graham Greene's (1904-91) novel *The Power and the Glory* (New York: Viking Press, 1940).

41. *How Green Was My Valley* (1941), a drama based on Richard Llewellyn's novel.

42. *Tobacco Road* (1941), a drama based on Erskine Caldwell's novel.

43. *The Grapes of Wrath* (1940), a drama based on John Steinbeck's novel.

44. John Huston's 1948 western, *The Treasure of the Sierra Madre*.

45. Stern met Robert Boardman Vaughn, an old friend of Justice's from Coconut Grove, Florida, while he was living in New York. Vaughn's friends knew him as an odd, bohemian type, and his adventures inspired some stories and poems. Justice's "Portrait with One Eye" is about Vaughn's loss of an eye when a man in Kansas City, who promised to take him to Charlie Parker's mother's

house, mugged him instead. Following Vaughn's unexpected death, Justice wrote "In Memory of the Unknown Poet, Robert Boardman Vaughn," published in *The Sunset Maker* (New York: Atheneum, 1987).

46. Betty Anne Ragland Stanback (1926–77), Jean's roommate at the Woman's College of the University of North Carolina, Greensboro, and at Chapel Hill, went by her initials, B. A.

47. From 1947 until his death, Randall Jarrell was a professor of English at the Woman's College where the Arts Forum took place. Burt, *Randall Jarrell and His Age*, 13–17.

48. Isaac Rosenfeld (1918–56) was a well-known writer in New York literary circles as well as a critic. He published stories and one novel, *Passage from Home* (New York: Dial, 1946).

49. Robert Lowell's nickname.

50. Norma Troetschel (1925–92) was an old friend of Justice's from Miami. In 1948 the Justices introduced her to Stern. They too became close friends. For a time Norma was married to Michael Zwerin (1930–2010), a jazz trombonist and bass trumpeter and in the 1960s a music critic for the *Village Voice* and the *International Herald Tribune*. Zwerin is mentioned in later letters, though his marriage to Troetschel ended in 1958.

51. The poem by Edgar Bowers, "Two Poems on the Catholic Bavarians," was published in Winters, *Poets of the Pacific*, 8–9.

52. A draft of Justice's "Holy Saturday in Venice" can be found in Stern's papers at the University of Chicago's Regenstein Library and is included here. It is not clear with which letter the draft was sent.

53. Laurence Donovan (1927–2001) met Justice at the University of Miami, where Donovan later taught for many years. Donovan illustrated Justice's early chapbook with his etchings; much later, Justice wrote a preface to Donovan's *Dog Island and Other Florida Poems* (Sarasota FL: Pineapple Press, 2003). Harp, *For Us, What Music?*, 6.

54. The North.

55. Stern's poem, a response to Justice's "Holy Saturday in Venice," was not found with this letter.

56. The words "I will be blunt" were underlined in the text of Stern's letter as well as in the version enclosed by Justice. Perhaps Justice intended to call Stern's attention to these lines specifically; the underlining could also be Stern's, marking the typographical modifications to which Stern alludes.

57. *Waterfront at Midnight* (1948), film noir directed by William A. Berke.

58. Stern's "snicker" might be an allusion to Eliot's "The Love Song of J. Alfred Prufrock": "I have seen the moment of my greatness flicker, / And I have seen the eternal Footman hold my coat, and snicker, / And in short, I was afraid" (lines 84–86).

59. Stern refers to the film adaptation of *The Great Gatsby*, to be released by Paramount in 1949, starring Alan Ladd (1913–64), Betty Field (1913–73) and Nicholas Joy (1884–64).

60. The Austrian American psychoanalyst Wilhelm Reich (1897–1957) sparked controversy in the late forties when he announced his discovery of orgone, a sexual energy that he believed could be collected and rented out to patients suffering mental and physical illnesses.

61. Peter Taylor, "Allegiance," in *A Long Fourth and Other Stories* (New York: Harcourt, 1948), 59–69.

62. "The grave's a fine and private place," line 31 of Andrew Marvell's "To His Coy Mistress."

63. Empson's *Collected Poems* (New York: Harcourt) was not published in the United States until 1949.

64. Poet Louis MacNeice (1907–63), whose collection *Holes in the Sky: Poems 1944–1947* (New York: Random House) was published in the United States in 1949. The same year, Justice and Stern enjoyed listening to his radio-play translation of *Faust*, which marked Goethe's bicentenary.

65. R. P. Blackmur: see RS to DJ, January 14, 1948.

66. Justice's "Holy Saturday in Venice."

67. The Stevens poem "In a Bad Time" was published in the *Hudson Review*'s first issue.

68. Jean Ross Justice came from a literary family, including her sister, the poet Eleanor Ross Taylor (see "Correspondence of 1946 to 1947," note 35), and her brothers, both novelists: James Ross (1911–90), author of *They Don't Dance Much* (New York: Houghton Mifflin, 1940), and Fred E. Ross (1913–93), who won the Houghton Mifflin fiction prize for *Jackson Mahaffey* (New York: Bantam, 1951).

69. Allen Tate, *The Fathers, and Other Fiction* (Baton Rouge: Louisiana State University Press, 1938).

70. John Peale Bishop's poem "Perspectives Are Precipices."

71. Oscar Williams (1900–64), anthologist and editor of the *Little Treasury of Modern Poetry* (New York: Scribner's, 1946).

72. A production based on Ben Jonson's play (1610).

73. Italo Svevo, *Confessions of Zeno*, trans. Beryl de Zoete (New York: Putnam, 1930).

74. Copies of *Factotum*. See RS to DJ, Monday [November 1947].

75. In May 1948 Lowell and Tate joined the poets Marianne Moore (1887–1972) and Louise Bogan (1897–1970) in giving a reading at the New School in New York City. Frank, *Louise Bogan*, 343.

76. Auden taught at Barnard College for Women in New York City in 1947. In the fall of 1948 he taught a course on Meaning and Technique in Poetry at the New School. Auden, *W. H. Auden*, x.

77. Stern wrote the novelization of Lewis Allen's drama *Sealed Verdict* (1948) for Paramount.

78. *The Adventures of Casanova* (1948), an adventure-romance directed by Roberto Gavaldón.

79. Orson Welles, *The Lady from Shanghai* (1947), based on the novel by Sherwood King.

80. In an unpublished letter dated May 4, 1948 (Stern Papers, Regenstein Library, 56:2), Justice asked if Stern had met Jerome Weidman (1913–98) or Jackson (unidentified), writers in the story department at Paramount. Stern often recommended stories for film adaptation, including Taylor's novel *A Long Fourth* and Tate's story "The Fathers," which Jackson decided would be too expensive to produce.

81. John Peale Bishop (1892–1944) worked for Paramount Pictures from 1924 to 1926. Before that he was managing editor at *Vanity Fair*. In 1948 Scribner's posthumously published his *Collected Poems*, edited by Allen Tate, and his *Collected Essays*, edited by Edmund Wilson (1895–1972).

82. Kenneth Rothwell and Burke Shipley. See RS to DJ, January 14, 1948.

83. On James Ross, see "Correspondence of 1948," note 68.

84. For a synopsis of Justice's story "The Older Generation," see DJ to RS, December 27, 1948.

85. Justice refers to an incident in which Bowers withheld his most recent poems from their friend, Paul Ramsey. In an unpublished letter dated August 16, 1948 (Stern Papers, Regenstein Library, 32:14), Justice described this withholding as "one of the most devious ways of insulting a former friend I ever heard of."

86. See DJ to RS, August 1, 1948, for a draft of "Here Lies Love," published in *Poetry* 73, no. 2 (1948) and in SA.

87. See DJ to RS, February 29, 1948, for a description of "The Animated Dead."

88. Stern briefly dated the writer Geraldine Shavelson, the sister of Mel Shavelson (1917–2007), a screenwriter for the entertainer Bob Hope (1903–2003).

89. Eric Bentley (1916–), playwright, essayist, editor, and anthologist of theatrical works.

90. Wanda Hendrix (1928–81) was a minor film and television actress. In 1949 actor Audie Murphy (1924–71) saw her on a magazine cover and suggested they meet. They were soon engaged, but the marriage lasted less than a year.

91. Gwyned Filling appeared on the cover of *Life* on May 3, 1948. The accompanying article, "The Private Life of Gwyned Filling," earned her minor celebrity status. Stern met Filling once at the Quaker Ridge Country Club just before her engagement to a member there. With her in mind, he wrote "Prothalamium" and later his short story "The Illegibility of This World," reprinted in *Almonds to Zhoof*.

92. E. E. Cummings, *Him* (New York: Boni and Liveright, 1927).

93. *The Sainted Sisters* (1948), a comedy directed by William Russell, based on a play by Elisa Bialk.

94. *The Blue Angel* (1930), Josef von Sternberg's drama starring Marlene Dietrich (1901–92).

95. On Peter Taylor's stories, see "Correspondence of 1948," note 80.

96. Jean Stafford, *Boston Adventure* (New York: Harcourt, Brace, 1944).

97. Bette Davis (1908–89), American film actress.

98. *Berlin Express* (1948), a film noir by Jacques Tourneur.

99. Justice's "Here Lies Love."

100. Jean's unfinished graduate thesis explored points of view and time shifts in Faulkner's *Light in August* (New York: Smith and Haas, 1932).

101. In his 1943 essay "Four Quartets," first published in *Sewanee Review*, Lowell wrote of Eliot's "purple passages," including "part one of *Dry Salvages*, the unrhymed terza rima section in *Little Gidding*, the lyrics *The wounded surgeon plies the steel* and *The Dove descending breaks the air*, and possibly *Time and the bell have buried the day*." Lowell, *Robert Lowell*, 48.

102. *M* (1931), a German thriller directed by Fritz Lang, starring Peter Lorre (1904–64).

103. Siegfried Kracauer (1889–1966), cultural critic, film theorist, and author of *From Caligari to Hitler: A Psychological History of German Film* (Princeton NJ: Princeton University Press, 1947).

104. *The Paleface* (1948), Norman McLeod's comedy-western starring Bob Hope and Jane Russell (1921–2011).

105. On Stern's recommendation, Paramount's David O. Selznick (1902–65)

considered producing an adaptation of Fitzgerald's novel. Selznick eventually sold the script to Twentieth Century-Fox.

106. *The Rake's Progress* was written by Auden in collaboration with poet Chester Kallman (1921–75) between 1947 and 1948; the libretto was set to the music of Igor Stravinsky (1882–1971).

107. *The Last of Mrs. Cheyney*, the 1920s Broadway comedy written by Frederick Lonsdale, was later turned into a film starring Joan Crawford (1908–77).

108. A phonetic misspelling of "bright," meant to imitate Francis's famous speech impediment, as was Stern's misspelling of "breezy," to follow.

109. In an unpublished letter dated September 1, 1948 (Stern Papers, Regenstein Library, 56:2), Jean wrote to Stern that they could not afford a trip to Chapel Hill—Justice had just been accepted to Stanford and they were saving for that trip.

110. Richard Jones (1886–1965) was head of the English Department at Stanford until his retirement in 1952.

111. "Plain living and high thinking are no more," quoted from Wordsworth's "In London, September, 1802" (line 11, p. 460).

112. Wesley Trimpi (1928–), a Stanford scholar and poet, met the Justices through their mutual friend Bowers. Trimpi later married another Stanford poet, Helen Pinkerton. Together they appeared alongside Bowers in Winters's 1949 anthology *Poets of the Pacific*.

113. The heroic couplets that follow, meant to imitate George Crabbe (1754–1832), were read aloud by Winters to Justice's class. Harp, *For Us, What Music?*, 13.

114. "And would it have been worth it, after all, / Would it have been worth while," from Eliot's "The Love Song of J. Alfred Prufrock," lines 87–88.

115. Howard Wilson Baker (1905–90) was a poet and novelist of agrarian sympathies. New Directions published his first collection of poems, *Letter from the Country*, in 1941.

116. The unidentified classmate associates Justice's "Old Man to Young Woman" (*The Old Bachelor and Other Poems*) with Plato's *Symposium*.

117. To illustrate his disappointment with Stanford thus far, Justice borrows a metaphor from George Herbert's "The Pilgrimage." In Herbert's poem, the speaker travels great distances to reach the top of "the gladsome hill, / Where lay my hope, / Where lay my heart." Once there, he is disappointed by what he sees: "When I had gain'd the brow and top, / A lake of brackish waters on the ground / Was all I found" (lines 19–24).

118. Jean's letter, if enclosed, was not found.

119. Harvard University.

120. At Harvard, Stern wrote the short novel "A Justing Time" for a course taught by critic and novelist Albert Guerard (1914–2000). The novel was never published.

121. Perhaps a reference to Flaubert's *Trois contes*. Nothing came of Justice's suggestion.

122. In the style of English historian Edward Gibbon (1737–83).

123. English author, editor, and critic Samuel Johnson (1709–84).

124. Herman Melville, *Moby-Dick* (1851).

125. English poet and historian Thomas Babington Macaulay (1800–59).

126. Stern described Justice's "A Woman Growing Old" as "a fine cut of Southern Stevens." Unpublished letter, RS to DJ, Saturday 1949, private MS.

127. Cuban-born French poet José-María de Heredia (1842–1905). Winters's translation is from *Les trophées* (1893), Heredia's collection of 118 Petrarchan sonnets.

128. Stern's article on F. Scott Fitzgerald was not published in *Factotum* 2.

129. "*Factotum* no. 2."

130. Peter Taylor, "Middle Age," *New Yorker*, November 6, 1948, 29.

131. *Hika*, Kenyon College's student-run literary magazine.

132. Peter Taylor, "Casa Anna," *Harper's Bazaar*, November 1948, 137.

133. George Eliot, *Middlemarch* (1872).

134. Justice's unpublished story "The Older Generation," a synopsis to follow.

135. American jazz clarinetist and composer Artie Shaw (1910–2004) was married eight times.

136. The southern fiction writer Katherine Anne Porter (1890–1980) held a residency at Stanford during Justice's time there. Beck, *Fugitive Legacy*, 171–87.

137. Henry James, *The Turn of the Screw* (1898).

138. Joyce scholar William York Tindall (1903–81).

139. Justice was reading *The Notebooks of Henry James* (Chicago: University of Chicago Press, 1947). It is likely he had also read Edmund Wilson's essay "The Ambiguity of Henry James," originally published in *Hound and Horn*. Wilson offered a distinctly Freudian reading of James's novel, proposing that the ghosts seen by the governess are merely expressions of the symptoms of sexual repression. Justice evokes this reading of *The Turn of the Screw* in his poem "Anniversaries": "By seventeen I had guessed / That the 'really great loneliness'

/ Of James's governess / Might account for the ghost / On the other side of the lake." *SA*, lines 25–29.

140. The modernist novel *Nightwood* (New York: New Directions, 1946), by novelist and poet Djuna Barnes (1892–1982), was first published in the United States in 1937, with an introduction by T. S. Eliot.

141. On Peter Taylor's stories, see "Correspondence of 1948," note 80.

142. *The Collected Poems of William Empson* (London: Hogarth Press) was not published until 1949. Justice may have ordered Empson's previous collection, *The Gathering Storm* (London: Faber, 1940).

143. José-María de Heredia, "Le chevrier," in *Les trophées* (1893).

144. Communist.

145. A joking reference to John Keats (1795–1821), "Ode to a Nightingale": "Forlorn! the very word is like a bell" (line 71).

146. Fiction writer Ellen Glasgow (1873–1945), whose novels often focused on the lives of southern women.

CORRESPONDENCE OF 1949 TO 1950

1. The letter to follow, RS to DJ, Sunday [January 1949], gives Stern's reading of Empson's poem "Invitation to Juno." Stern had enclosed the poem, along with another early poem by Eliot, in a letter that I have not found.

2. Unidentified.

3. The first line of Empson's poem "This Last Pain," which continues, "They knew the bliss with which they were not crowned" (line 2).

4. In Stern's story "Cooley's Version," the title character (named per Justice's suggestion) translates from the French the novels of the fictional Mlle Trèves. Stern's story depicts a reversal of the roles of the translator H. T. Lowe-Porter (1877–1963) and the German author Thomas Mann (1875–1955). Stern's story was published in *Kenyon Review* 16, no. 2 (1954): 257–67, and in his much later collection *Almonds to Zhoof*.

5. As children, Larry Goldsmith and Dick Simmons attended summer camp with Stern in Belgrade, Maine. Goldsmith became friends with Justice at Stanford.

6. Recalling Antony's words, "I am dying, Egypt, dying," from Shakespeare's *Antony and Cleopatra* (act 4, scene 15, line 41).

7. "Desire under the Elms," in *Three Plays of Eugene O'Neill* (New York: Vintage, 1958): 3–60.

8. Betty Anne Ragland Stanback: see "Correspondence of 1948," note 46.

9. The Bowdoin Prize was awarded to Harvard students for unpublished essays.

10. The New Critic Kenneth Burke (1897-1993) was admired by Justice and Stern for his frequent contributions to the *Hudson Review* and *Accent* and for his numerous influential collections of theoretical essays.

11. Kenneth Burke, *Attitudes toward History* (New York: New Republic, 1937).

12. Harry Levin (1912-94), a scholar primarily of modernist literature, was editor of *The Portable James Joyce* (1947) and author of *James Joyce: A Critical Introduction* (1941). Having received a number of awards for his work in the humanities and modern literature, he advanced quickly from his instructorship at Harvard to become chair of the Department of Comparative Literature.

13. Peter Viereck, *Metapolitics: From the Romantics to Hitler* (New York: Knopf, 1941).

14. See the previous letter, DJ to RS, January 17, 1949.

15. Unidentified.

16. Poet and playwright Edwin Arlington Robinson (1869-1935) was a three-time Pulitzer Prize winner and one of only two American poets to feature in the New Critical teaching text *Understanding Poetry* (1938; 3rd ed., New York: Holt, Rinehart and Winston, 1960) by Warren and Brooks. Beck, *Fugitive Legacy*, 50. In 1946 Winters published a book-length discussion of the poet's life and influences, *Edwin Arlington Robinson*.

17. *The Collected Poetry of W. H. Auden* (New York: Random House, 1945).

18. Stern might here be teasing Justice for resurrecting his title "The Animated Dead." It was taken from a line in Tate's poem "The Oath": "There's naught to kill but the animated dead" (line 5).

19. A word invented by Stern to diagnose Justice's obsession with titles.

20. Stern inserted the clarification "mixed marriages." His original wording, which he crossed out, was "Desdemona and Othello."

21. In explaining Empson's "Invitation to Juno," Stern references lines 9-12 "Courage. Weren't strips of heart culture seen / Of late mating two periodicities? / Did not at one time Darwin / Graft annual upon perennial trees?"

22. French poet and Huguenot Guillaume de Salluste Du Bartas (1544-90), advertising executive and politician Bruce Fairchild Barton (1886-1967), and theologian and missionary Jonathan Edwards (1703-58); each of these, Stern points out, believed in the spiritual roots of social progress.

23. Perhaps a riff on Justice's comment, "It's something about the wheels."

24. While students at Chapel Hill, the Justices, B. A., Paul Ramsey, and Stern

were invited to join a literary club, formed by Edgar Bowers and Ken Rothwell, known as the Saucers, because they met weekly over coffee at Danziger's. Harp, *For Us, What Music?*, 11–12. The members took turns choosing a book to be discussed. Justice chose *Walden.*

25. French author André Gide (1869–1951) won the Nobel Prize in literature in 1947.

26. *La symphonie pastorale* (1946), a film adaptation of Gide's novel of the same title, directed by Jean Delannoy.

27. In the original text an arrow points to "imaginative."

28. Keats scholar Hyder Edward Rollins (1889–1958) taught English Romantic literature at Harvard.

29. Thomas Wyatt's "They Flee from Me."

30. As a student, Eliot submitted the poems "Ode" and "Before Morning" to the *Harvard Advocate*. In 1949, without Eliot's permission, these and other early poems were reprinted in the *Advocate* as "The Undergraduate Poems of T. S. Eliot." In 1967 the poems, emended by Eliot and edited by John Hayward, were published in *Poems Written in Early Youth* (London: Faber). The poems have been omitted here.

31. Justice's criticisms demonstrate Winters's influence. Winters proposed a revised canon of Elizabethan poetry, excluding Shakespeare's sonnets.

32. "Ah yet doth beauty, like a dial hand, / Steal from his figure, and no pace perceived," from Shakespeare's "Sonnet 104," lines 9–10.

33. The joke in "Sonnet 87" is the pun *dear*. Thomas Thorpe's (1569?–1635?) edition of Shakespeare's sonnets, published in 1609, concluded with the longer poem "A Lover's Complaint." For a later draft of Justice's inspired sonnet, "A Lover's Complaint of Too Much Attention," see DJ to RS, March 4, 1949.

34. Edgar Bowers, "The Stoic: For Laura Von Courten," in Winters, *Poets of the Pacific*, 16.

35. Leo Tolstoy, *Anna Karenina* (1885).

36. "A Hopeless Case," described in DJ to RS, January 17, 1949.

37. The December 1948 issue of *Scrutiny*, the quarterly literary review founded and edited by New Critic F. R. Leavis (1895–1978), featured an essay by *Hudson* advisory editor Marius Bewley (1916–73) titled "Kenneth Burke as Literary Critic," the "dissection" to which Justice refers.

38. Unidentified.

39. Gilbert White, "Natural Observations at Selbourne," in *Five Kinds of Writing*, ed. Theodore Morrison (Boston: Little, Brown, 1939).

40. Laurence Olivier's 1948 film adaptation.

41. In "The Fire Sermon," Eliot used a series of heroic couplets to imitate Alexander Pope's *The Rape of the Lock*. Eliot tells of the lady Fresca going to the toilet, a parody of Pope's Belinda *making* her toilet. In a much later review of *The Waste Land Annotations of Ezra Pound* (New York: Harcourt Brace, 1971), critic Richard Ellmann (1918–1987) noted that Pound cautioned Eliot against the couplets, "since Pope had done the couplets better, and Joyce the defecation." Ellmann, "First *Waste Land* I."

42. Comparing the first-person narrative of Justice's "Negro" character to Faulkner's Benjy, the mentally disabled narrator of *The Sound and the Fury*.

43. Intellectual historian Perry Miller (1905–63) taught at Harvard before and after serving in the Second World War.

44. Referring to Jarrell's essay "John Ransom's Poetry," which appeared in *Sewanee Review* 56, no. 4 (1948): 378–90. The issue was titled "Homage to John Crowe Ransom" and was composed of essays written for the occasion of Ransom's sixtieth birthday.

45. Novelist Kathleen Thompson Norris (1880–1966).

46. Paul Valéry (1871–1945), French poet and philosopher.

47. Albert Guerard, *Robert Bridges: A Study of Traditionalism in Poetry* (Cambridge MA: Harvard University Press, 1942).

48. W. H. Auden with Christopher Isherwood, *The Ascent of F6* (New York: Random House, 1936).

49. Joseph T. Shipley (1893–1988), Fugitive poet and father of Burke Shipley. His poem "Can I Believe" appeared in the *Fugitive* 2, no. 7 (1923).

50. The poetry of Laura Riding Gottschalk (1901–91) first appeared in the *Fugitive* in 1923. The following year she received the magazine's Nashville Prize.

51. Fugitive poet and psychiatrist Merrill Moore (1903–57) lived and practiced in Cambridge, Massachusetts. The "copies" mentioned here may refer to Moore's copies of the *Fugitive*.

52. Kenneth Burke, *The Philosophy of Literary Form* (Berkeley: University of California Press, 1941).

53. Kenneth Burke, *Permanence and Change* (New York: New Republic, 1935).

54. An early proponent of practical criticism and close reading, the English critic and rhetorician Ivor Armstrong Richards (1893–1979).

55. Russian-American pianist and composer Igor Stravinsky (1882–1971) and his son Soulima Stravinsky (1910–94), the younger of whom was often appointed

to play the *Capriccio* at this and other performances. Joseph, *Stravinsky Inside Out*, 82-83.

56. Playwright and Hollywood screenwriter Clifford Odets (1906-63) wrote the play-turned-film *The Big Knife* (New York: Random House, 1949).

57. Stern's professor Andrews Wanning (1912-97) reviewed Stafford's novel in *Partisan Review* 11 (1944).

58. Eliot's words with respect to the poets George Chapman and John Donne: "their mode of feeling was directly and freshly altered by their reading and thought. In Chapman especially there is a direct sensuous apprehension of thought, or a recreation of thought into feeling, which is exactly what we find in Donne." "Metaphysical Poets," 63.

59. Unidentified.

60. Poet and Shakespeare scholar Theodore Spencer (1902-49), author of *Poems, 1940-1947* (Cambridge MA: Harvard University Press, 1948) and *An Acre in the Seed: Poems* (Cambridge MA: Harvard University Press, 1949), taught at Harvard from 1927 to 1949.

61. On February 27, 1949, a fire that started in a chimney flue of one of Kenyon College's dorms killed nine students.

62. It is unclear what Justice is referring to.

63. Meaning not John Crowe, but John B. Ransom (1920-2000), whom Justice described in an unpublished letter as "the great man's cousin once removed." DJ to RS, February 12, 1950, Stern Papers, Regenstein Library, 32:14. Following his service in the Second World War, John B. earned a master's in American literature at Stanford.

64. Wordsworth, "It is a beauteous evening, calm and free": "The holy time is quiet as a Nun / Breathless with adoration" (lines 2-3).

65. Irving Babbitt (1865-1933) influenced the critical perspectives of New Humanism, which, like New Criticism, eschewed Romanticism in favor of more conservative, classical traditions.

66. Kenneth Burke, *Grammar of Motives* (Berkeley: University of California Press, 1945).

67. Stallman, *Critiques and Essays*.

68. Referring to Burke's "Psychology and Form" and "Lexicon Rhetoricae," reprinted from *Counter-Statement* (New York: Harcourt, 1931).

69. Most likely referring to Burke's novel *Towards a Better Life* (New York: Harcourt, 1932).

70. R. P. Tristram Coffin (1892-1955), author of sixteen volumes of poetry,

including *Strange Holiness* (New York: MacMillan, 1935), which won a Pulitzer Prize in 1936.

71. I. A. Richards, "'Troilus and Cressida' and Plato," *Hudson Review* 1, no. 3 (1948): 344–61.

72. Allen Tate, "Longinus," *Hudson Review* 1, no. 2 (1948): 362–76.

73. *"Gennets for germans* sprung not from Othello, / And Ixion rides upon a single wheel," lines 7–8 of Empson's "Invitation to Juno," the poem that inspired Stern and confounded Justice. See also RS to DJ, [January 1949].

74. Joseph Frank, "Spatial Form in Modern Literature," in *Critiques and Essays in Criticism, 1920–1948*, ed. Robert Wooster Stallman (New York: Ronald Press, 1949): 315–28.

75. William Wordsworth's long autobiographical poem *The Prelude; or, Growth of a Poet's Mind*.

76. See RS to DJ, [February 1949], in which Stern describes an essay he is writing on Ransom for Perry Miller's class.

77. *A Sentimental Journey through France and Italy* (1768), by Laurence Sterne (1713–68), a travel book that comically mixes autobiography with fictional accounts of European travel.

78. In an unpublished letter dated March 19, 1949 (RS to DJ, Stern Papers, Regenstein Library, 33:1), Stern predicted that the poet and editor William Abrahams (1919–98) would win the "prize contest" judged by poets Robert Penn Warren and Louise Bogan and publisher Alan Swallow (1915–66).

79. Poet Dunstan Thompson (1918–75) wrote his elegiac "Largo" for William Abrahams, his close friend and a fellow soldier. At the time of its publication in *Poems* (New York: Simon and Schuster, 1943) and later in Oscar Williams, *A Little Treasury of Modern Poetry* (New York: Scribner's, 1947), 702–7, "Largo" was widely admired for its technical skill.

80. Unidentified.

81. Unidentified.

82. Dr. Lyman Cotten: see "Correspondence of 1948," note 36.

83. William Shakespeare, *The Tempest* (1610–11).

84. American businessman Thomas Fortune Ryan (1851–1928).

85. Ford Madox Ford, *The Good Soldier* (London: John Lane, 1915).

86. Unidentified.

87. H. Mumford Jones (1892–1980) was a writer, critic, and professor of English at Harvard University beginning in 1936 and he served as dean of Harvard's

Graduate School of Arts and Sciences from 1943 to 1944. The professor to whom he is compared is unidentified.

88. Tate wrote a scathing review of H. Mumford Jones's volume *They Say the Forties*, reprinted in Tate's *Reason in Madness: Critical Essays* (New York: G. P. Putnam's Sons, 1941).

89. Unidentified.

90. Unidentified.

91. After meeting Gay Clark of Darien, Connecticut, Stern convinced her to join him in Germany. They were married in Paris on March 14, 1950. They divorced in 1972.

92. In Justice's unpublished story, a woman in the fictional town of Hope Springs invests in a perpetual motion machine. For the first page of "Hope Springs," see unpublished letter, DJ to RS, June 15, [1950], Stern Papers, Regenstein Library, 38:3.

93. Unidentified.

94. The Justices did not meet Stern abroad.

95. The square brackets are Stern's.

96. Unidentified.

97. Stern's mix of English and German means, roughly, "I must write to my aunts now."

98. "So my dear child—"

99. Editor and writer Henry Herschel Brickell (1889–1952) took over editorship of the *O. Henry Prize Stories* in 1940.

100. Justice's "The Lady" was chosen for the 1950 *O. Henry Prize Stories* collection.

101. William Perdue Halstead (1906-82), then professor and head of the English Department at the University of Miami.

102. Charlie Chaplin's 1931 silent film comedy.

103. Nathaniel Macon, Bill Thomas, and Sarah Tillet were friends of the Justices at Chapel Hill. Jean Ross Justice, e-mail to author, October 19, 2011.

104. An acquaintance from Chapel Hill.

105. Nathaniel Macon's cousin; not a close friend of the Justices.

106. Milton Abernathy, owner of the Chapel Hill bookstore known as The Intimate Bookshop, or The Intimate. Jean Ross Justice, e-mail to author, October 19, 2011.

107. Peter Taylor, *A Woman of Means* (New York: Harcourt, Brace, 1950).

108. As a child, Justice suffered from osteomyelitis, an infectious bone disease for which he underwent surgery.

109. Richard Martin Stern (1915–2001)—not Richard Gerald Stern—was an older writer of popular fiction.

110. The mystery stories in *Cosmopolitan* were written by Donald Kent Stanford (1918–92). Jean is thinking of the poet Donald Elwin Stanford (1913–98), who studied under Winters at Stanford University in the thirties and belonged to the literary group known as the "Winters Circle."

111. Eugene Rosenbloom met Justice in Miami. As an undergraduate at the University of Miami, Justice directed Rosenbloom's comic play *Beppo's Song*, in which the main character avoids the draft by faking mental illness. Harp, *For Us, What Music?*, 14–15. Rosenbloom volunteered for military service, but perhaps taking a cue from his own character, he was soon discharged because of mental instability. After changing his name to Eugene Rawls, Rosenbloom collaborated with the cartoonist for *Mad* magazine Don Martin.

112. Poet Karl Shapiro (1913–2000), then the editor of *Poetry*.

113. A professor and chair of the English Department at Carleton College, Arthur Mizener (1907–88) began the literary magazine *Furioso*, now published under the title *Carleton Miscellany*.

114. In 1941 the poet Paul Engle (1908–91) was appointed acting director of the Writers' Workshop, a position he held for the next twenty-four years. Justice here puns on the title of Engle's collection *Corn* (Doubleday, 1939), poems written in celebration of Engle's native Iowa.

115. A later version became the title poem of Justice's chapbook. *The Old Bachelor and Other Poems* was published in 1951 by Preston Dettman of Pandanus Press in Miami.

116. Perhaps written in response to Bowers's "Two Poems on the Catholic Bavarians."

117. Published as "A Certain Oriental on His Deathbead" in *The Old Bachelor and Other Poems*.

118. Paul Ramsey: see "Correspondence of 1946 to 1947," note 23.

119. The following appeared in Justice's chapbook, later to be published in his *Collected Poems* as "Two Sonnets"; the first is subtitled "On the Devil in Our Time" and the second "An Old Fashioned Devil," a much earlier draft of which can be found in an unpublished letter to Stern written in 1948, then titled "The Tourist."

120. Christopher Holmes Stern was born on January 20, 1951.

121. Unidentified.

122. Ernest Hemingway, *Across the River and into the Trees* (New York: Scribner's, 1950).

123. In an unpublished letter dated July 13, 1950 (DJ to RS, Stern Papers, Regenstein Library, 44:9), Justice joked, "With a PhD from Heidelberg you could wear stiff Victorian collars like Booker's." John Manning Booker (1881-1948) was a professor of English at Chapel Hill.

124. Unidentified.

125. Henry Luce (1898-1967), the influential publisher of *Time, Life, Fortune,* and *Sports Illustrated*.

126. Meaning John B. Ransom (see DJ to RS, March 4, 1949,), whose address in Paris Justice sent to Stern.

127. Vernon Louis Parrington (1871-1929), American literary historian and scholar.

128. William Dean Howells, *The Rise of Silas Lapham* (1884-85).

129. Rayford, otherwise unidentified, was a colleague of Stern's at the Department of the Army Message Control in Heidelberg, where they worked as clerks.

130. If Gay drafted a note, it was not found with this letter.

CORRESPONDENCE OF 1951 TO 1952

1. Justice was applying for a Eugene F. Saxton Fellowship.

2. See unpublished letter dated May 27 [1951] (DJ to RS, Stern Papers, Regenstein Library, 38:4), in which Justice wrote, "Paul says my poems reflect a 'facile despair'; you think me a nihilist."

3. Justice's poem "An Oriental on His Deathbed": see DJ to RS, September 1950.

4. Paul Ramsey.

5. Justice, *Old Bachelor*.

6. "I do not speak Dutch. I only speak French."

7. Unsure of job prospects, Justice again applied to Stanford for a writing fellowship.

8. Robie Macauley (1919-95) was a novelist and critic who, while studying under Ransom at Kenyon, met Taylor, Lowell, and Jarrell. He also attended the Writers' Workshop, and it was on his urging that Justice applied there for his PhD. Harp, *For Us, What Music?*, 15. Beginning in 1950, Macauley taught for three years at the University of North Carolina at Greensboro, and in 1958 he succeeded Ransom as editor of the *Kenyon Review*. His wife's name was Anne.

9. From 1949 to 1972 Robert Lowell was married to Elizabeth Hardwick (1916–2007), novelist, essayist, and cofounding editor of the *New York Review of Books*.

10. Warren's first wife, of six years, was Emma Cinina Brescia. In 1950 Cinina (as she was called) suffered a nervous breakdown, which led to her hospitalization. The following year her psychiatrist advised Warren to divorce her. Warren, *Selected Letters*, 186.

11. In 1951 Randall Jarrell left his wife, Mackie Langham Jarrell, for Mary von Schrader (1914–2007), a writer he met at a conference in Boulder, Colorado. He and von Schrader were married in November 1952. Burt, *Randall Jarrell and His Age*, 13–19.

12. Southern fiction writer Eudora Welty (1909–2001) was once, like her contemporary Taylor, a protégé of Fugitives Brooks and Warren. Welty never married. Beck, *Fugitive Legacy*, 191–95.

13. Unidentified.

14. Unidentified.

15. J. D. Salinger, *The Catcher in the Rye* (Boston: Little, Brown, 1951).

16. George Eliot, *The Mill on the Floss* (1860).

17. Unidentified.

18. V. S. Pritchett, *Mr. Beluncle* (New York: Harcourt, Brace, 1951).

19. In an unpublished postcard dated September 11, 1951 (RS to DJ, private MS), Stern wrote, "Dear Don & Jean, Just had a lunch on Thomas Mann & his wife (I mean they bought me lunch [. . .]) Will write the pleasant if prosy details next letter." His "next letter" was not found.

20. Wystan Hugh Auden: see Justice's Christmas card of the same year (DJ to RS, [December 1951]) for the full poem.

21. Auden's contemporaries Christopher Isherwood (1904–86) and Stephen Spender: Isherwood collaborated with Auden on several plays, including *The Dog beneath the Skin* (1936) and *The Ascent of F6* (1937); Spender printed Auden's first book, *Poems* (1928), which was dedicated to Isherwood.

22. The "successful" story is possibly Justice's 1950 O. Henry Prize Story, "The Lady." His "major work" must refer to one of his novels in progress.

23. After moving back to Miami from Stanford, Justice learned chess. He picked it up quickly and played competitively. "The Coming Thing" was his story about a middle-aged widower who is an amateur chess player and the author of a book titled "Chess without Tears." Walking in Washington Square Park one day, the widower encounters a young man who teaches him a game he believes

will be the next craze, or "the coming thing." The young man's character is based on "a fanatic in these parts who believes 'the Oriental game of Go' is even more complicated than chess." See unpublished letter, DJ to RS, November 13, 1950, Stern Papers, Regenstein Library, 56.

24. All parenthetical remarks in White's letter are the commentary inserted by Justice for Stern's amusement and clarification.

25. Katharine S. White (1892–1977) was a long-time editor of fiction and verse for the *New Yorker*.

26. "Vineland's Burning," published in the Spring 1953 issue of *Western Review*, was an O. Henry Prize Story in 1954.

27. Lewis Carroll, *Alice's Adventures in Wonderland* (1865); the following "motto" is excerpted from chapter 6, "Pig and Pepper."

28. For his application to the Saxton Fellowship, Justice proposed to write a novel based on "Vineland's Burning." In this letter he enclosed a synopsis describing the novel as "a sort of fable of what some people call 'the New South,' of the time when the South was still different from the rest of the country, not long ago." Stern Papers, Regenstein Library, J-R.

29. Justice found and enclosed Paul Ramsey's translation of "Les elephants" by Leconte de Lisle (1818–94).

30. Lisa Dyer was a managing editor at the *Hudson Review*.

31. Pandanus Press: see "Correspondence of 1949 to 1950," note 115.

32. The early novels of French writer Sidonie-Gabrielle Colette (1873–1954) were published under her husband's pen name.

33. Stendhal's unfinished novel, *Lucien Leuwen*, was published posthumously in 1894.

34. Paul Engle's wife, Mary Engle.

35. Paul Bowles (1910–99) was a novelist and composer for plays, films, and operas.

36. Unidentified.

37. In an unpublished letter, Stern wrote, "Am looking forward to 'Christopher Macomber in song.' Tho it is Christopher Holmes & will, I think, be Kate Macomber. However, Macomber is a dactyl in this pronunciation." RS to DJ, private MS. Stern's daughter Kate was born on August 19, 1952.

38. It is unclear whether Justice was aware of his own pun.

39. Straight Street, the Biblical site of St. Paul's conversion, runs east to west in the old Syrian city of Damascus. Stern's letter to follow describes eight photographs, including one of "the street called Straight."

40. Walter Van Tilburg Clark (1909-71), a writer of realist fiction about the American West, including "The Wind and Snow of Winter," in *The Watchful Gods, and Other Stories* (New York: Random House, 1950).

41. The painter Grant Wood (1891-1942) was known for his depictions of the American Midwest. A native of Iowa, he taught at the University of Iowa's School of Art.

42. After receiving this "preliminary report," Stern began to consider Iowa for his PhD. In an unpublished letter from Europe (dated, simply, "Saturday"), he wrote, "The second word from Iowa was so much nicer than anything we hear around here that we are aiming more and more for there, and sooner and sooner, say the Spring of '53, rather than the one after that." RS to DJ, private MS.

43. In "Primitivism and Decadence," Winters explained the effect of experimentation with traditional modes, as when, for example, a poem suggests earlier conventions of simplified meter and rhyme. He alludes to Richard Crashaw's "The Twenty-third Psalm," which evokes "earlier love poetry and drinking songs." Justice's couplet echoes Crashaw's: "How my head in ointment swims! / How my cup o'erlooks her brims!" Quoted in Winters, "Primitivism and Decadence," 132.

44. Eudora Welty, "Powerhouse," in *A Curtain of Green* (Garden City NY: Doubleday, 1941).

45. See Justice's Christmas card of 1951 (DJ to RS, [December 1951]).

46. The bassoonist John Lenox met Justice in middle school in Miami. Justice admired Lenox's dedication to music: see his poem "In Memory of My Friend, the Bassoonist, John Lenox," in Justice, *Collected Poems*.

47. Justice studied under composer Carl Ruggles (1876-1971) at the University of Miami. Like Justice, Ruggles was a meticulous reviser. His creative output was markedly slow and his oeuvre small.

48. American modernist composer Charles Ives (1874-1954) was a friend of Ruggles. Though his music was largely ignored during his lifetime, more recently his influence on experimental musical techniques has grown in appreciation.

49. Samuel Richardson, *Clarissa* (1747).

50. Walter Van Tilburg Clark, *The Track of the Cat* (New York: Random House, 1949).

51. An allusion to Faulkner's fictional Snopes family, from his trilogy *The Hamlet* (1940), *The Town* (1957), and *The Mansion* (1959).

52. The twenty-second prime minister of Yugoslavia, Josip Broz Tito (1892-1980), was elected as the country's first president in 1953, an office he held until

his death; Mustafa Kemal Ataturk (1881–1938) was the first president of Turkey, who held office from 1923 to 1938; Mohammed Ali Pasha of Egypt (1769–1849) ruled from 1805 to 1848; and Reza Shah (1878–1944), of the Imperial State of Iran, ruled from 1925 to 1941.

53. Stern is here poking fun at his self-portrait. He is the Macy's balloon, of course.

54. Unidentified.

55. Unidentified.

56. This excerpt is Justice's suggested revision of the first lines of Stern's story "Cooley's Version."

57. Justice's alternate beginning, which he crossed out in pen, reads, "Cooley put her novel down with care. He leaned his head back on the chair and shivered a little. 'Unbelievable,' he said softly. 'Unbelievable.'"

58. A draft of Justice's unpublished story "Caboose-Red," dated March 1952, can be found in Stern's papers, DJ to RS, Stern Papers, Regenstein Library, 56:9.

59. Unidentified.

60. "Ladies by Their Windows," SA.

CORRESPONDENCE OF 1954 TO 1955

1. In 1951 Thomas Rogers (1927–2007) began teaching at the University of Iowa and enrolled in the Writers' Workshop. After earning his PhD, he taught at the University of Chicago for six years and later at Penn State University.

2. Leaving Iowa City following graduation.

3. Ernest Jones, *The Life and Work of Sigmund Freud* (New York: Basic Books, 1953).

4. *Amos 'n' Andy* was a popular situation comedy that took place in the African American community in Chicago and featured the characters Amos, Andy, and George "The Kingfish" Stevens.

5. In his unpublished letter dated January 7, 1955 (RS to DJ, private MS), Stern wrote of that year's MLA conference and of possible job openings. Delora Cunningham, who knew Walter Blair, the dean at the University of Chicago, mentioned that Blair was looking for "a writing man who's a PhD."

6. Edgar Bogardus, *Various Jangling Keys* (New Haven CT: Yale University Press, 1953).

7. A later draft of "A Dream Sestina" was published in SA.

8. The poetry of Weldon Kees (1914–55?) attracted new attention after his mysterious disappearance in 1955, which many believe was his suicide. Justice

first encountered Kees's poetry in the early 1950s, in small literary journals. His interest gave rise to his edition *The Collected Poems of Weldon Kees*, published by Stone Wall Press in 1960.

9. A final version of Justice's poem, "Sestina on Six Words by Weldon Kees," was published in SA.

10. Published as "Thus," SA.

11. Puzzle contests sponsored by the *Miami Daily News* that offered cash prizes.

12. The play *Another Part of the Forest* (New York: Viking Press, 1947) by Lillian Hellman (1906–84); Stern developed a literary friendship with Hellman at the University of Chicago.

13. Ray West (1909–90), a professor of English at the University of Iowa from 1949 to 1959, played a key role in the development of the Writers' Workshop in its formative days. West was also founding editor of the *Western Review*, which Justice and Stern assisted in editing while students at Iowa.

14. Elder Olson (1909–92) taught at the University of Chicago from 1939 until the late seventies. In 1955 he won the Poetry Society of America Chapbook Award for *The Poetry of Dylan Thomas* (Chicago: University of Chicago Press, 1954).

15. Wallace Stevens won the Pulitzer Prize for his *Collected Poems* (New York: Knopf, 1954) in 1955.

16. At the time, Chicago's academic bent was toward the Aristotelian method, which, in keeping with New Criticism, promoted a kind of pluralist criticism.

17. Morton Dauwen Zabel (1901–64), critic and scholar at the University of Chicago and one-time editor of *Poetry*.

18. Unidentified.

19. George Williamson (1898–1968) was the editor of *Modern Philology*, published by University of Chicago Press.

20. Norman Fitzroy Maclean (1902–90) began as an instructor at the University of Chicago in 1930, earned his PhD there in 1940, and stayed on as a professor of English until 1973. Best known for his novel *A River Runs through It* (Chicago: University of Chicago Press, 1976), Maclean did not write seriously until his retirement, except for a longer piece on General Custer, a project that occupied him during his teaching career. See also Stern's essay "On a Writer's Endgame," which describes the trials of marking up Maclean's unfinished manuscript.

21. Unidentified.

22. The poet Emma Swan (1914–), author of *The Lion and the Lady* (New York: New Directions, 1950).

23. Justice met fellow poet Peter Everwine (1930–) as a student at the University of Iowa, where they later taught together.

24. Poet Donald Petersen (1928–2005) and his wife, Jeanine, met Justice and Stern at the Writers' Workshop. Petersen was assistant editor of *Western Review* from 1950 to 1955.

25. Jacqueline Ragner met Tom Rogers at Iowa, where she earned a PhD in French.

26. Gertrude Buckman was a writer and the first wife of poet and critic Delmore Schwartz (1913–66), a close friend and contemporary of Randall Jarrell.

27. Mackie Langham Jarrell, Randall Jarrell's first wife. See "Correspondence of 1951 to 1952," note 11.

28. In 1952 Paul Ramsey married fiber artist and quilter Bets Miller (1923–) and adopted her daughter Starr.

29. Summoned to Chicago, for the position Justice turned down.

30. A reference to Cold War anxiety about the atom bomb. Justice seemed particularly affected by such anxiety, expressing it frequently in his letters of this period.

31. William Belvin, a poetry student at the Writers' Workshop, and his wife, Anne.

32. Carol Blair, the wife of Walter Blair (1900–92), who taught American folklore and humor at the University of Chicago for more than thirty-five years. At the time this letter was written, Walter Blair was chair of the English Department.

33. For "A Hopeless Case," see DJ to RS, January 17, 1949.

34. Dorothy Sayers (1893–1957) was a popular English mystery writer and classicist. The following epigraph, credited to *The Londoner*, opens chapter eighteen of her novel *Unnatural Death* (New York: Dial, 1955).

35. Stern's story "After the Illuminations" appeared in the Spring 1955 issue of *Western Review*, as did "A Session of Summer," by Iowa writer James Byron Hall (1918–2008).

36. "The Sorrows of Captain Schreiber" (*Western Review* 17 [Summer 1953]) won the 1954 O. Henry Prize Story contest. *Prize Stories of 1954: The O. Henry Collection* (New York: Doubleday, 1955). The story was one of several that Stern developed into his novel *Europe; or, Up and Down with Schreiber and Baggish* (New York: McGraw-Hill, 1961).

37. Unidentified.

38. Richard Stern, "Arrangements at the Gulf," *Epoch* 8 (Fall 1957).

39. Poet Donald Drummond: see Donald Justice's review of the poetry of

Drummond and several others, "San Francisco and Palo Alto," *Western Review* 22, no. 3 (Spring 1958): 231–34.

40. Stern's children, Christopher and Kate, memorized Justice's then-unpublished verse "A Pleasant Red-Haired Man"; a later and much-changed version was published in *SA* as "Anniversaries." See DJ to RS, June 14, [1955], for a later draft.

41. Donald and Jeanine Petersen: see "Correspondence of 1954 to 1955," note 24.

42. Joseph Baker taught Victorian literature at the University of Iowa, where Stern audited his class.

43. Malcolm Cowley, *The Literary Situation* (New York: Viking Press, 1954).

44. Howard Nemerov, *The Salt Garden* (Boston: Little, Brown, 1955).

45. *The Letters of Hart Crane, 1916–1932*, ed. Brom Weber (New York: Hermitage House, 1952).

46. Poet John Berryman (1914–72) taught at the Writers' Workshop in the winter of 1954. Robert Lowell recommended him for the position. Mariani, *Dream Song*, 271–72.

47. George Murray Nauss studied poetry at the Iowa Writers' Workshop.

48. Poet Louis Simpson (1923–2012) taught English at Columbia University and the New School for Social Research from 1953 to 1959. In 1955, following the publication of his first book of poems, *The Arrivistes: Poems, 1940–1949* (New York: Fine Editions, 1949), Scribner's published his *Good News of Death and Other Poems*.

49. Paul Engle, not Ramsey.

50. Poet and novelist Marguerite Young (1909–95) taught at the University of Iowa from 1955 to 1957. In 1955 she co-taught with Berryman a course on the short story. A dispute between them arose—recounted as hearsay in Stern's unpublished letter dated October 18, 1954 (RS to DJ, private MS)—which triggered Berryman's rage and his heavy drinking. The next day he was dismissed from his teaching duties at the Writers' Workshop. Young later left to teach at the New School for Social Research. Mariani, *Dream Song*, 286.

51. Robert Lowell.

52. Catharine Carver (1921–97) was a highly esteemed editor at Harcourt, Brace and Company.

53. "On a Painting by Patient B of the Independence State Hospital for the Insane," *SA*.

54. "Song" and "Prayer," in the Autumn 1954 issue of *Accent*.

55. "Aboard! Aboard!" *Poetry* 81, no. 6 (March 1953): 354.

56. "A Pleasant Red-Haired Man;" see the previous letter, DJ to RS, April 27 [1955], for the stanza Stern's children memorized.

57. *Botteghe Oscure* was a small but influential literary magazine published in Rome by Princess Marguerite Caetani from 1948 to 1960. The magazine published poetry and prose in English, Italian, and French and was distributed in the United States by Farrar, Straus, and Young and Gotham Book Mart.

58. Bantron, no longer sold in stores, was an over-the-counter drug used to ease the symptoms of nicotine withdrawal.

59. Reed Whittemore (1919–2012) taught at Carleton College from 1939 to 1953 and was the editor for *Furioso*, known today as *Carleton Miscellany*.

60. Novelist and critic Marianne Hauser (1910–2006).

61. Early in her career, poet May Swenson (1919–89) was an editor at New Directions. Her first book of poems, *Another Animal*, was published by Scribner's in 1955.

62. Playwright and teacher Robert Hivnor (1916–2005) taught at Reed College in Portland, Oregon, for one year beginning in 1954.

63. Poet W. D. Snodgrass (1926–2009) met Justice and Stern at the University of Iowa, where he received his BA in 1949 and his MA in 1953. His first book, *Heart's Needle* (New York: Knopf, 1959), won the Pulitzer Prize in 1960.

64. Stern's poem "Eunuch, Spectator and Pupil" was published in the Winter 1956 issue of *Chicago Review*.

65. Justice's poems "Thus," "Sonnet" (here enclosed and later titled "Sonnet about P."), and "Sestina on Six Words by Weldon Kees" were printed in the Spring 1957 issue of the *Hudson Review*.

66. The following is a draft of "Anniversaries" (SA).

67. Draft of "A Winter Ode to the Old Men of Lummus Park, Miami, Florida," which appeared in the anthology *New World Writing 11* (New York: New American Library, 1957), edited by Louis Simpson. Justice included it in SA.

68. *Laura* (1944), film noir directed by Otto Preminger.

69. Racine's Cigar Store in downtown Iowa City sold Layman's Asperline, an over-the-counter drug similar to aspirin.

70. Lines of an early draft of Justice's "Here in Katmandu" (SA); the poem never appeared in the *New Yorker*.

71. Howard Moss (1922–87) was the poetry editor of the *New Yorker* from 1950 until his death.

72. "Sestina on Six Words by Weldon Kees," SA.

73. "To Satan in Heaven," SA.

74. "A Winter Ode to the Old Men of Lummus Park, Miami, Florida," *SA*.

75. "Bad Dreams": see "Correspondence of 1956 to 1958," note 27.

76. Edgar Bowers, *The Form of Loss* (Denver: Swallow, 1956).

77. Stern's friend Thomas Higgins was a pianist living and working as a bell-hop in Chicago. Justice's poem "Variations for Two Pianos" is dedicated to Higgins. *Collected Poems*, 78.

78. The Justices embarked on their first trip to Europe on October 3, 1954, aboard the *Maasdam*, a liner owned by Holland America. Traveling through heavy fog, the liner hit another ship and had to return to New York, where it boarded. For the Justices, the accident was a startling introduction to sea travel. A few days later they boarded the *Ile de France*.

79. Lewis "Ace" Dwight and Helen Levang (1929–2003) were close friends of the Justices in Iowa.

80. Justice and Stern did collaborate on a play that summer, which Stern completed. *The Gamesman's Island* is included in his *Teeth, Dying and Other Matters* (New York: Harper and Row, 1964). See "Correspondence of 1956 to 1958, note 4.

81. Elder Olson, *The Scarecrow Christ, and Other Poems* (New York: Noonday, 1954).

82. John Berryman, *Stephen Crane* (New York: Sloane, 1950).

83. *Berryman's Shakespeare* was edited posthumously by John Haffenden (New York: Farrar, Straus, and Giroux, 1999).

84. Berryman's *Homage to Mistress Bradstreet* (New York: Farrar, Straus, and Giroux, 1956) was illustrated by Ben Shahn (1898–1969), a Lithuanian-born artist and author-illustrator.

85. Unidentified.

86. Hardin Craig: see "Correspondence of 1948," note 38.

87. Stern lived in Steele Dormitory, on the Chapel Hill campus.

88. "Ladies by Their Windows" and "Sonnet," in *Borestone Mountain Poetry Awards 1955*, ed. Robert Thomas Moore (Stanford CA: Stanford University Press, 1955), 65–67.

89. William Harwood Peden (1913–99) taught at the University of Missouri from 1946 to 1979. In 1958 he founded the University of Missouri Press, and in 1978 he cofounded the *Missouri Review*.

90. K. S. White: see "Correspondence of 1951 to 1952," note 25.

91. Unidentified.

92. Novelist and short story writer J. F. Powers (1917–99), whose story "The Green Banana" appeared in the November 10, 1956, issue of the *New Yorker*.

His collections include *Prince of Darkness and Other Stories* (1947), featuring his O. Henry Prize Story "The Valiant Woman," and *The Presence of Grace* (Garden City NY: Doubleday, 1956).

93. T. S. Eliot, *The Confidential Clerk* (New York: Harcourt, Brace, 1954).

94. T. S. Eliot, *Four Quartets* (New York: Harcourt, Brace, 1943).

95. W. B. Yeats, *Purgatory*, in *The Collected Plays of W. B. Yeats* (New York: Macmillan, 1952).

96. W. H. Auden with Christopher Isherwood, *The Dog beneath the Skin* (New York: Random House, 1935): the first collaboration between Auden and Isherwood.

97. W. H. Auden, *The Orators: An English Study* (London: Faber, 1934).

98. Christopher Fry (1907-2005), English playwright known for his verse dramas, most notably *The Lady's Not for Burning* (1948).

99. *Anthology of the One-Act Play Magazine 1937-38*, ed. Alfred Kreymbourg (New York: Contemporary Play Publications, 1938).

100. T. S. Eliot, *Sweeney Agonistes: The Complete Poems and Plays, 1909-1950* (New York: Harcourt, Brace, 1952).

101. W. H. Auden, *Paid on Both Sides: A Charade, The Collected Poetry of W. H. Auden* (New York: Random House, 1945).

102. W. H. Auden with Christopher Isherwood, *The Ascent of F6* (New York: Random House, 1936).

103. W. B. Yeats, *The Herne's Egg and Other Plays* (New York: Macmillan, 1938).

104. Christopher Fry, *A Phoenix Too Frequent* (New York: Oxford University Press, 1949).

105. E. E. Cummings, *Him* (London: Boni and Liveright, 1927).

106. Dylan Thomas, *Under Milkwood* (New York: New Directions, 1954).

107. W. B. Yeats, *The Words upon the Windowpane* (1934).

108. William Inge, *Come Back, Little Sheba: Four Plays* (New York: Random House, 1958).

109. Clifford Odets's *The Country Girl* (1950) was adapted into a film in 1954, starring Grace Kelly (1929-82) and Bing Crosby (1903-77).

110. Lillian Hellman.

111. Tennessee Williams, *A Streetcar Named Desire* (New York: New Directions, 1947).

112. Arthur Miller, *Death of a Salesman* (New York: Viking Press, 1949).

113. Unidentified.

114. A draft of "Southern Gothic," which was included in SA.

115. Writer Herbert Wilner (1925–77) and his wife met Justice and Stern at Iowa. Wilner later taught at San Francisco State University when Ray West was there.

116. Princess Marguerite Caetani, founding editor of *Botteghe Oscure*: see "Correspondence of 1954 to 1955," note 57.

117. Donald Hall (1928–), *Exiles and Marriages* (New York: Viking Press, 1955) winner of the 1956 Lamont Poetry Prize.

118. Una Ellis-Fermor (1894–1958) was a scholar of English literature and drama and a translator of the plays of Henrik Ibsen (1828–1906).

119. Elizabeth Bishop, *A Cold Spring* (Boston: Houghton Mifflin, 1955).

120. James Joyce, *Portrait of an Artist as a Young Man* (New York: B. W. Huebsch, 1916).

CORRESPONDENCE OF 1956 TO 1958

1. "Sonnet about P.," *SA*.

2. These stipulations applied to the feature issue "American Poetry of the Fifties," edited by Stern, *Western Review* 21 (Spring 1957).

3. "Sonnet to My Father," *SA*: Justice's father, Vascoe J. Justice, was born in 1892 and died in April 1956.

4. In his essay "A Very Few Memories of Don Justice," Stern describes the argument that brought to an end their first attempt at collaborative creative work. Their two families stayed for parts of the summer at a house belonging to Gay Stern in Twin Lakes, Connecticut. They worked from the porch and each day traded off the more comfortable chair. One day they disagreed over whose turn it was to use the chair, and that dispute ended their collaboration. Stern finished writing the play, titled *The Gamesman's Island*, which is included in his *Teeth, Dying and Other Matters* (New York: Harper and Row, 1964).

5. Unidentified.

6. In 1956 John Berryman divorced his first wife, Eileen Patricia Mulligan (1918–2002), and married Elizabeth Ann Levine. Haffenden, *Life of John Berryman*, 255.

7. An excerpt from *Don't Go Near the Water*, William Brinkley's farce of World War II naval duty, was published in the July 2, 1956, issue of *Life*.

8. Unidentified.

9. Robert Penn Warren was known to his friends as "Red."

10. Unidentified.

11. American modern composer Ernst Kreneck (1900–91) taught at Hamline University from 1942 to 1947.

12. Medievalist and fiction writer Arthur Heiserman (1929–75) was a professor of English at the University of Chicago from 1952 to 1963 and a close friend of Stern's.

13. Stern's son, Christopher.

14. Unidentified.

15. *Europe; or, Up and Down with Schreiber and Baggish*: see "Correspondence of 1954 to 1955," note 36.

16. "A Birthday Candle," was published in the March 16, 1957, issue of the *New Yorker*. This short poem became the last stanza of "Anniversaries."

17. Unidentified.

18. Chicago-born novelist Saul Bellow (1915–2005) won his first of three National Book Awards for *The Adventures of Augie March* (New York: Viking, 1953). Bellow and Stern became good friends during their long-term tenure at the University of Chicago.

19. The March 18, 1957, issue of *Life* featured a photo of Hardwick and Lowell with their newborn child, Harriet.

20. George Williamson (see RS to DJ, April 15, 1955) and seventeenth-century scholar Ernest Sirluck (1918–2013), were colleagues of Stern's at the University of Chicago.

21. Kingsley Amis, *That Uncertain Feeling* (New York: Harcourt, Brace, 1956).

22. Scholar of American literature and drama Napier Wilt (1899–1975) taught on the faculty of the University of Chicago and was dean of the humanities from 1951 to 1962.

23. Referring to their annual Christmas visit, which took place that year in Chicago.

24. Eugene Lichtenstein (1929–92), writer, editor, and journalist.

25. In "San Francisco and Palo Alto," written for *Western Review* 22, no. 3 (Spring 1958), Justice reviewed Allen Ginsberg's *Howl and Other Poems* (San Francisco: City Lights Books, 1956), Kenneth Patchen's *When We Were Here Together* (New York: New Directions, 1957) and *Selected Poems* (New York: New Directions, 1957), Donald Drummond's *The Battlement* (New York: Swallow, 1958), Edgar Bowers's *The Form of Loss* (New York: Swallow, 1956), and Donald Hall's *Exiles and Marriages* (New York: Viking, 1955).

26. "Bad Dreams."

27. "Bad Dreams" was based in part on Peter Taylor's story of the same title,

which appeared in the May 19, 1951, *New Yorker*, though the poem began as a blank verse narrative of Justice's story "Vineland's Burning."

28. The novelist Vance Bourjaily (1922-2010) began teaching at the Writers' Workshop in 1957, where he met Justice. He taught there for just over twenty years, and in 1980 he left to launch the creative writing program at Louisiana State University. Bourjaily's third novel, *The Violated* (New York: Dial, 1958), was preceded by *The End of My Life* (New York: Scribner's, 1947) and *The Hound of Earth* (New York: Scribner's, 1955).

29. In 1958 poet and editor Jerome Rothenberg (1931-) founded Hudson River Press (later known as Hawk's Well Press), a small outfit in New York City that published paperbacks in multiple genres. Rothenberg, who was to become a leading anthologist, admired Justice's writing and encouraged him to send plays, stories, and poetry. After problems with the printing of SA, Rothenberg released Justice from his contract. Wesleyan University Press soon picked up the volume, and Rothenberg nominated Justice for the Lamont Poetry Prize, which he was awarded in 1959.

30. The following, with a slight variation in the final line, is the epigraph Justice published in dedication to Jean.

31. Jarrell was consultant in poetry at the Library of Congress from 1956 to 1958.

32. Bettina Bourjaily, Vance Bourjaily's first wife.

33. The poems were not found with the letter.

34. The section of the long poem following the letter is a draft of "Bad Dreams," Justice's verse play, published as an excerpt (with slight adjustments) in *Poetry* 95, no. 3 (December 1959): 149-52. He later refers to it as his "chorus poem," which Stern, who had reservations about the choral mode, likened to Eliot's *Murder in the Cathedral*.

35. "On a Painting by Patient B of the Independence State Hospital for the Insane," SA.

36. Unidentified.

37. Broadway and film producer Michael Todd (1909-58) died in the crash of his private jet on March 22, 1958.

38. Professional boxer Sugar Ray Robinson (1921-29) made a comeback in 1955; Stern saw his 1958 fight against Carmen Basilio, in which he reclaimed the middleweight championship.

39. Michael Zwerin: see "Correspondence of 1948," note 50.

40. Robert D. Mack was the chair of the Philosophy Department at Connecticut College for Women, where Stern taught from 1954 to 1955.

41. Sam Gelfman, otherwise unidentified.

42. Actually, one-quarter of nine hundred dollars—though this does not answer Justice's question.

43. Unidentified.

44. Auden's "For the Time Being" was his most overtly religious work. "The Sea and the Mirror" was its secular companion piece and a commentary on Shakespeare's *The Tempest*. They were published together in *For the Time Being* (New York: Random House, 1944).

45. Justice's sonnet "Speaking of Islands" appeared without revisions in *SA*.

46. Jean Ross Justice's "An Old Man's Winter Night" was published in *Esquire*, March 1959, the first of several of her stories they would publish.

47. Unidentified.

48. Delmore Schwartz was poetry editor for the *Partisan Review* from 1943 to 1954. Around this time, his addiction to alcohol and prescription drugs began affecting his physical and mental health. In 1959 Schwartz won the Bollingen Prize and the Shelley Memorial Prize for *Summer Knowledge* (New York: Doubleday, 1959). Despite his continued success, Schwartz found himself unable to fulfill his obligations as a poet and editor and relied on friends for financial support. Atlas, *Delmore Schwartz*, 350-63.

49. James Hall: see "Correspondence of 1954 to 1955," note 35.

50. Stern met the young, already-controversial Norman Mailer (1923-2007) at Chicago when Mailer was a visiting lecturer. Intrigued, Stern asked to interview him. The interview "Hip, Hell, and the Navigator," was printed in *Western Review* 23, no. 1 (1959) and reprinted in Mailer's *Advertisements for Myself* (New York: Putnam, 1959).

51. Leonard Bernstein (1918-90), American conductor and composer.

52. When this letter was written, William Averill Harriman (1891-1986) was the governor of New York. In 1956 Harriman was endorsed by President Harry S. Truman for the Democratic presidential nomination but lost to Adlai Stevenson (1900-65), whom Schwartz and Berryman, along with other writers of their generation, strongly supported in that year's presidential bid.

53. Jesus Christ.

54. R. V. Cassill (1919-2002) taught at the Writers' Workshop from 1948 to 1952 and again in the sixties. Between stints of teaching, Cassill was editor for the magazines *Dude* and *Gent*. The story rewritten by Cassill without Stern's

permission was published in the September 1958 issue of *Gent* as "Toujours l'audace."

55. Allen Funt (1914–99) was the creator and host of the radio show *Candid Microphone*, which was later broadcast on television as *Candid Camera* and ran from the 1940s through the 1980s. *Golk*'s antagonistic title character is based on the Funt persona, hence Funt's interest in seeing the manuscript.

56. Napier Wilt: see "Correspondence of 1956 to 1958," note 22.

57. Edward Shils (1910–95), then married to Irene Shils, was a famous sociologist on the University of Chicago's Committee on Social Thought. According to Stern, Shils dropped in esteem among a number of his colleagues, including Stern and Bellow. The latter lampooned Shils with the character of Rakhmiel Kogon in his novel *Ravelstein* (New York: Viking, 2000).

58. "Angry Young Men," a catchphrase referring to certain young British writers in the postwar period, coined by a theater critic in response to a play by John Osborne (1929–94), *Look Back in Anger* (1956).

59. John Wain, *The Contenders* (1958).

60. John Osborne, *The Entertainer* (New York: Criterion, 1958).

61. Osborne's play *Look Back in Anger* (1956) was made into a 1958 film. Both productions were directed by Tony Richardson.

62. Kingsley Amis, *I Like It Here* (London: Victor Gollancz, 1958).

63. American actor Alvin Epstein (1925–) starred in Samuel Beckett's *Endgame* at New York's Cherry Lane Theater in 1958.

64. American playwright Eugene O'Neill (1888–1953).

65. Ralph Freedman was acting editor of *Western Review* in 1958.

66. Anthony Hecht (1923–2004) studied under Ransom at Kenyon and later, though less formally, under Tate.

67. Poet James Wright (1927–80) also studied with Ransom at Kenyon College in 1952 and as a graduate student with Stanley Kunitz (1905–2006) and Theodore Roethke (1908–63). His first book of poems, *The Green Wall* (New Haven: Yale University Press, 1957), was selected by Auden for the Yale Younger Poets Series.

68. Stern's story "Nine Letters, Twenty Days" appeared in the *Western Review* (Fall 1958), and "Arrangements at the Gulf" in *Epoch* 8 (Fall 1957).

69. "The Unhappy Fate of the 'Poetic,'" Justice's review of Williams's *Orpheus Descending, with Battle of Angels* (New York: New Directions, 1958) and *Suddenly, Last Summer* (New York: New Directions, 1958) was published in *Poetry* 93, no. 6 (March 1959): 402–3.

70. Jean Ross Justice's "The Maid of Scarborough," about a folklorist looking for a lost ballad, was published in *Esquire*, November 1959.

71. In December 1958 Justice gave a reading at the YMHA Poetry Center in New York City, also known as the 92nd Street Y.

72. Justice's *SA* was chosen for the Lamont Poetry Prize that year.

73. Stern's second novel, *Europe; or, Up and Down with Schreiber and Baggish*.

74. The first poem enclosed, "Love's Map," was published in *Poetry* 95, no. 3 (December 1959): 152. Later titled "A Map of Love," it appeared with slight changes alongside the second, "Love's Stratagems," in *SA*.

CORRESPONDENCE OF 1959 TO 1961

1. Justice's *Collected Poems of Weldon Kees* was published by Stone Wall Press in 1960 and reprinted by the University of Nebraska Press in 2003.

2. Hondorp, Stern's main character, is cajoled into collaborating with Golk and his team of pranksters, after having himself fallen victim to a "golk," a joke set up for the purpose of being captured on film.

3. Poppa Hondorp, the protagonist's meddling father.

4. Hendricks, Hondorp's love interest and a member of the Golk crew.

5. Gladys Culley is the colleague of one of *Europe*'s principal characters, Schreiber. Her "insult" was to serve fish on a Friday.

6. Robert Ward, the foil character for Baggish.

7. Stern's review of Boris Pasternak's *Dr. Zhivago*, "Dr. Zhivago as a Novel," *Kenyon Review* 21, no. 1 (Winter 1959): 154–60.

8. Robert Silvers (1929–) was associate editor of *Harper's Magazine* from 1959 to 1963, when he cofounded the *New York Review of Books*.

9. The *Western Review* moved with Ray West to San Francisco, where it merged with the newer magazine *Contact*.

10. James Gould Cozzens (1903–78) wrote the controversial *By Love Possessed* (New York: Harcourt, Brace, 1957), which Stern reviewed in *Kenyon Review* 20, no. 1 (Winter 1958): 140–44.

11. Unidentified.

12. Polish harpsichordist Wanda Landowska (1879–1959).

13. Unidentified.

14. An Iowa City bar and a popular hangout for students at the Writers' Workshop.

15. Marvin Mudrick (1921–86) was on the English faculty at the University

of California, Santa Barbara, where in 1967 he founded the College of Creative Studies.

16. Novelist, poet, and essayist George P. Elliott (1918–80) met Justice while teaching at the University of Iowa. In 1962, following the mixed reception of *SA*, Elliot wrote a detailed and favorable review: "Donald Justice," *Perspective* 12, no. 4 (Spring 1962): 173–79, reprinted in *CS*, 214–15.

17. Justice's review of A. E. Housman's *Complete Poems* (New York: Henry Holt, 1959) was published in *Poetry* 96, no. 1 (1960): 44–47.

18. Unidentified.

19. Hyung Woong Pak (1932–) took over as editor of the *Western Review* in 1958, following the controversy that erupted when student-editor Irving Rosenthal (1930–) and his staff published selected chapters of *Naked Lunch* (Paris: Olympia Press, 1959). Rosenthal resigned when the university's administration and its financial backers stepped in to censor the magazine's content.

20. Joan Didion, "Seventeen Interns, One Golk," *National Review* 8, no. 19 (May 7, 1960).

21. David Boroff, "A New Kind of TV Novel," *New York Post Weekend Magazine*, April 24, 1960.

22. *Golk* was reviewed for the *New Yorker* (May 14, 1960: 44) by Whitney Balliett, who enjoyed the first chapter but felt that in the later chapters Stern got "winded."

23. Charles Poore, "Books of the Times," *New York Times*, April 23, 1960, 21.

24. Stern's "A Valentine for Chicago" was published in *Harper's Magazine*, February 1962.

25. Chicago's improv comedy club Second City began as a cabaret revue show in 1959. In 1961 it sent its show *From the Second City* to Broadway.

26. Henri Coulette (1927–88) studied alongside Justice in Berryman's poetry workshop at Iowa. Coulette's long poem, *The War of the Secret Agents*, included in the 1962 anthology *New Poets of England and America*, edited by Donald Hall (1928–), Robert Pack (1929–), and Louis Simpson, was based on Jean Overton Fuller's *Double Agent?* (London: Pan Books, 1961). It became the title poem of his first collection, which won the 1966 Lamont Poetry Prize. In 1990 Justice and Robert Mezey (1935–) edited *The Collected Poems of Henri Coulette* (Fayetteville: University of Arkansas Press, 1990).

27. Poet David Galler (1929–) reviewed *SA* quite unfavorably (*Sewanee Review* 69, no. 1 [1961]: 169–70) and dismissed Justice's poetry as merely derivative. In an unpublished letter dated January 27, 1961 (Stern Papers, Regenstein Library,

76:2), Justice wrote, "Reading the Galler review I felt as if a perfect stranger had slapped me in the face without provocation." The review was reprinted in *CS* (212–13) with a note describing Galler's eventual retraction of his criticisms.

28. The final paragraph in a review by poet and critic Dudley Fitts (1903–68) read, "There is little to be said, at least by me, of *Summer Anniversaries.*" "Separate Voices," *New York Times Book Review*, February 19, 1961. With regard to "Love's Map," Fitts wrote of Justice's "diction deaf to latent absurdities."

29. Kenneth Rexroth (1905–82), "Bearded Barbarians or Real Bards?" the front-page article in the *New York Times Book Review*, February 12, 1961, evaluated the "new minor renaissance in American verse" fostered by the San Francisco poets of that period.

30. Poet Thom Gunn (1929–2004) reviewed *SA* for the *Yale Review* (June 1960).

31. The following letter to Fitts was not published, and based on Stern's advice in a later letter, it likely was never sent.

32. National Book Awards, for which Justice was a finalist that year.

33. Greek American poet, editor, and translator Kimon Friar (1911–93), best known by his generation for his translations of modern Greek literature into English.

34. A famous downtown Chicago hotel, now known as the Palmer House Hilton.

35. The Justices' son Nathaniel was born in August 1961.

BIBLIOGRAPHY

Alighieri, Dante. "Canto XXXIV." In *The Divine Comedy of Dante Alighieri*, trans. Carlyle Wiksteed, 180-84. New York: Random House, 1948.

Atlas, James. *Delmore Schwartz: The Life of an American Poet*. New York: Farrar, Straus, and Giroux, 1977.

Auden, W. H. "The Dyer's Hand." In *The Complete Works of W. H. Auden: Prose*, vol. 2, ed. Edward Mendelson, 29-31. Princeton NJ: Princeton University Press, 2002.

———. "Petition." In *The Collected Poetry of W. H. Auden*, 110-11. New York: Random House, 1945.

———. "The Rake's Progress." In *The Complete Works of W. H. Auden: Libretti and Other Dramatic Writings, 1939-1973*, vol. 2, ed. Edward Mendelson, 47-93. Princeton NJ: Princeton University Press, 1993.

———. *W. H. Auden: Lectures on Shakespeare*. Edited by Arthur Kirsch. Princeton NJ: Princeton University Press, 2000.

Beck, Charlotte. *The Fugitive Legacy*. Baton Rouge: Louisiana State University Press, 2001.

Bishop, John Peale. "Perspectives Are Precipices." In *The Collected Poems of John Peale Bishop*, ed. Allen Tate. New York: Scribner's, 1948.

Blake, William. "London." In *Songs of Experience*, 37. New York: Dover, 1984.

Bowers, Edgar. "With Don and Jean Justice at Chapel Hill." In Gioia and Logan, *Certain Solitudes*, 127-28.

Burt, Stephen. *Randall Jarrell and His Age*. New York: Columbia University Press, 2005.

Callan, Edward. "The Development of Auden's Poetic Theory since 1940." *Twentieth Century Literature* 1, no. 3 (October 1958): 77–79.

Cowan, Louise. *The Fugitive Group: A Literary History*. Baton Rouge: Louisiana State University Press, 1959.

Donovan, Laurence. "Donald Justice's Miami." In Gioia and Logan, *Certain Solitudes*, 103–10.

Eberhardt, Richard. "Empson's Poetry." In *Accent Anthology: Selections of Accent, a Quarterly of New Literature, 1940–1945*, ed. Kerker Quinn and Charles Shattuck, 571–88. New York: Harcourt, Brace, 1946.

Eliot, T. S. "Before Morning." In *Poems Written in Early Youth*, ed. John Hayward, 25. London: Faber, 1967.

———. "The Love Song of J. Alfred Prufrock." In *The Collected Poems, 1909–1962*, 3–6. New York: Harcourt, 1963.

———. "The Metaphysical Poets." In *Selected Prose of T.S. Eliot*, ed. Frank Kermode, 59–67. New York: Harcourt, 1975.

———. "Ode." In *Poems Written in Early Youth*, ed. John Hayward, 25. London: Faber, 1967.

Elliott, George P. "Donald Justice." In Gioia and Logan, *Certain Solitudes*, 214–15.

Ellmann, Richard. "The First *Waste Land* I." *New York Review of Books*, November 18, 1971.

Empson, William. "Honest in Othello." In *The Structure of Complex Words*, 218–49. Ann Arbor: University of Michigan Press, 1967.

———. "Invitation to Juno." In *Collected Poems*, 5. London: Hogarth Press, 1984.

———. "This Last Pain." In *Collected Poems*, 32. London: Hogarth Press, 1984.

Frank, Elizabeth. *Louise Bogan: A Portrait*. New York: Columbia University Press, 1986.

Galler, David. "From 'Four Poets.'" In Gioia and Logan, *Certain Solitudes*, 212–13.

Gioia, Dana. "A Poet's Poet." Review of *A Donald Justice Reader: Selected Poetry and Prose*. *New Criterion* 10, no. 9 (1992): 68.

Gioia, Dana, and William Logan, eds. *Certain Solitudes: On the Poetry of Donald Justice*. Fayetteville: University of Arkansas Press, 1997.

Haffenden, John. *Among the Mandarins*. New York: Oxford University Press, 2005.

———. *The Life of John Berryman*. Boston: Routledge, 1983.

Harp, Jerry. *For Us, What Music?: The Life and Poetry of Donald Justice*. Iowa City: University of Iowa Press, 2010.

Herbert, George. "The Pilgrimage." In *The Complete English Poems*, ed. John Tobin, 133. New York: Penguin, 2004.

Izzo, David Garrett. *The Writings of Richard Stern: The Education of an Intellectual Everyman*. Jefferson NC: McFarland, 1996.

Joseph, Charles. *Stravinsky Inside Out*. New Haven CT: Yale University Press, 2001.

Justice, Donald. *Collected Poems*. New York: Knopf, 2004.

———. *A Donald Justice Reader: Selected Poetry and Prose*. Hanover NH: Middlebury College Press/University Press of New England, 1991.

———. Papers. University of Delaware Special Collections Library, Newark. F386.

———. "The Fugitive-Agrarian 'Myth.'" MA thesis, University of North Carolina, 1947. Donald Justice Papers. University of Delaware Special Collections Library, Newark, MS 191, box 6, F259.

———. *The Old Bachelor and Other Poems*. Miami: Pandanus Press, 1951.

———. *The Summer Anniversaries*. Middletown CT: Wesleyan University Press, 1960.

Justice, Donald, and Philip Hoy. *Donald Justice in Conversation with Philip Hoy*. London: Between the Lines, 2001.

Keats, John. "Ode to a Nightingale." In *The Complete Poems*, 3rd ed., ed. John Barnard, 346–47. New York: Penguin, 1988.

Kees, Weldon. *The Collected Poems of Weldon Kees*. Edited by Donald Justice. Iowa City: Stone Wall Press, 1960. Reprint, Lincoln: University of Nebraska Press, 2003.

Lowell, Robert. "Four Quartets." In *Robert Lowell: Collected Prose*, ed. Robert Giroux, 45–48. New York: Farrar, Straus, and Giroux, 1987.

Mariani, Paul. *Dream Song*. New York: W. Morrow, 1989.

Marvell, Andrew. "To His Coy Mistress." In *The Complete Poems*, ed. Elizabeth Story Donno, 50–51. New York: Penguin, 2005.

McQuade, Molly, ed. *An Unsentimental Education*. Chicago: University of Chicago Press, 1995.

Morgan, Frederick. "*Hudson Review*'s Early Years: An Interview with Frederick Morgan." Conducted by Michael Peich. *Hudson Review* 57, no. 3 (2004): 363–76.

Schiffer, James. *Richard Stern*. New York: Twayne, 1993.

Searle, Leroy. "New Criticism." *The Johns Hopkins Guide to Literary Theory*, 2nd ed., ed. Michael Groden, Martin Kreiswirth, and Imre Szeman, 528–34. Baltimore: Johns Hopkins University Press, 2005.

Shakespeare, William. "Sonnet 87." In *Complete Sonnets and Poems*, ed. Colin Burrow, 555. New York: Oxford University Press, 2002.

———. "Sonnet 104." In *Complete Sonnets and Poems*, ed. Colin Burrow, 589. New York: Oxford University Press, 2002.

Snodgrass, W. D. "Justice as Classmate." In Gioia and Logan, *Certain Solitudes*, 129–32.

Sperling, Cass Warner, Cork Millner, and Jack Warner Jr. *Hollywood Be Thy Name: The Warner Brothers Story*. Lexington: University Press of Kentucky, 1998.

Stallman, Robert Wooster, ed. *Critiques and Essays in Criticism, 1920–1948*. New York: Ronald Press, 1949.

Stern, Richard. "Bellow in Five Hundred Words Or Less." In *What Is What Was*, 25–26.

———. "Bellow's Moving Day." In *What Is What Was*, 13–24.

———. "Cooley's Version." In *Almonds to Zhoof: Collected Stories*, 257–66. Evanston IL: Northwestern University Press, 2005.

———. *Europe; or, Up and Down with Schreiber and Baggish*. New York: McGraw-Hill, 1961.

———. *Golk*. New York: Criterion Books, 1960.

———. "The Illegibility of This World." In *Almonds to Zhoof: Collected Stories*, 3–22. Evanston IL: Northwestern University Press, 2005.

———. "Mailer." In *What Is What Was*, 46–49.

———. "On a Writer's Endgame." *Daedalus* 133, no. 1 (2004): 98–102.

———. *Stitch*. New York: Harper and Row, 1965.

———. *Teeth, Dying and Other Matters*. New York: Harper and Row, 1964.

———. "Two Iowan Baudelaires Sweating Out Tetrameters." In *The Invention of the Real*, 135–37. Athens: University of Georgia Press, 1982.

———. "A Very Few Memories of Don Justice." In *What Is What Was*, 42–46.

———. *What Is What Was: Essays, Stories, Poems*. Chicago: University of Chicago Press, 2002.

———. "With Auden." In *What Is What Was*, 3–12.

St. John, David. "Memory and Melody." In *Where the Angels Come toward Us: Selected Essays, Reviews, and Interviews*, 119–28. Buffalo NY: White Pine Press, 1995.

Strand, Mark. "Mark Strand on Donald Justice." Poetry Society of America. Accessed January 28, 2012. http://www.poetrysociety.org/psa/poetry/crossroads/tributes/mark_strand_on_donald_justice/.

Tate, Allen. "The Oath." In *Collected Poems, 1919–1976*, 43. New York: Farrar, Straus, and Giroux, 1977.

Warren, Robert Penn. *The Selected Letters of Robert Penn Warren*. Vol. 4. Baton Rouge: Louisiana State University Press, 2008.

Wilson, Edmund. "The Ambiguity of Henry James." *Hound and Horn* 8 (1934): 385–406.

Winters, Yvor. *Edwin Arlington Robinson*. New York: New Directions, 1946.

———. *In Defense of Reason*. New York: Swallow, 1947.

———, ed. *Poets of the Pacific: Second Series*. Palo Alto CA: Stanford University Press, 1949.

———. "Primitivism and Decadence." In *In Defense of Reason*, 15–150.

Wordsworth, William. "In London, September, 1802." In *Selected Poetry of William Wordsworth*, ed. Mark Van Doren, 460. New York: Modern Library, 2002.

———. "It is a beauteous evening, calm and free." In *Selected Poetry of William Wordsworth*, ed. Mark Van Doren, 457–58. New York: Modern Library, 2002.

Wright, Charles. "Jump Hog or Die." In Gioia and Logan, *Certain Solitudes*, 137–40.

INDEX